SARANAC

By the same author
In Red Weather
(novel)

ROBERT TAYLOR

SARANAC

America's Magic Mountain

PARAGON HOUSE PUBLISHERS
New York

First paperback edition, 1988

Published in the United States by

Paragon House Publishers
90 Fifth Avenue
New York, NY 10011

The Adelaide Crapsey poem "To the Dead in the Graveyard
Under My Window" is reprinted from *The Complete Poems
and Collected Letters of Adelaide Crapsey* by Susan
Sutton Smith by permission of the State University of New York Press.
© 1977 State University of New York

Library of Congress Cataloging-in-Publication Data

Taylor, Robert, 1925-
Saranac : America's magic mountain.

Reprint. Originally published: Boston : Houghton
Mifflin, 1986.
Bibliography: p.
Includes index.
1. Tuberculosis—Hospitals—New York (State)—
Saranac Lake—History. 2. Sanatoriums—New York
(State)—Saranac Lake—History. 3. Saranac Lake
(N.Y.)—History. I. Title.
[RC309.N7T39 1988]   362.1′96995   87-29104
ISBN 1-55778-069-2

To Brenda

He rowed alone and slowly over the quiet waters, gazing to right and left at a scene fantastic as any dream. In the west it was still broad day with a fixed and glassy air; but in the east he looked into a moonlit landscape, wreathed in the magic of rising mists and equally convincing to his bewildered sense.

The Magic Mountain

❧ CONTENTS ❧

(Following page 148)

W. J. Stillman's painting *The Philosophers' Camp. Courtesy the Concord (Massachusetts) Free Public Library*

Jeffries Wyman. *Courtesy Anne Wyman*

Magazine spoof aimed at "Adirondack" Murray's famous book

The Reverend William Henry Harrison Murray

Dr. Edward Livingston Trudeau. *Courtesy the Adirondack Collection, Saranac Lake (New York) Free Public Library*

Robert Louis Stevenson and his family at Saranac Lake during the hard winter of 1887–88. *Courtesy Lady Stair Collection, Lochnich Castle, Stranaer, Scotland*

Adelaide Crapsey a few days before her death in 1914. *Courtesy State University of New York Press*

Christy Mathewson with his son, about 1920. *Courtesy Mel Sokolow Associates*

Norman Bethune. *Photo by Charles Comfort in* The Mind of Norman Bethune *by Roderick Stewart. Courtesy Fitzhenry and Whiteside*

Chinese lithograph of Bethune's encounter with Mao Tse-tung

Sara and Gerald Murphy at Camp Adelaide. *Courtesy Honoria M. Donnelly*

Baoth, Sara, Patrick, and Honoria Murphy. *Family portrait by Man Ray. Courtesy Honoria M. Donnelly*

Albert Einstein with physicist Leo Szilard at Saranac Lake, 1945. *Courtesy Gertrud W. Szilard, American Institute of Physics, Niels Bohr Library*

Béla Bartók at Saranac in 1945. *Courtesy Collection of G. D. Hackett*

Larry Doyle leaving Trudeau Sanatorium in 1954. *Courtesy Fritz Goro,* Life *magazine, © Time Inc.*

SARANAC

Emerson's Deer
1858

DEATH IN THESE WOODS was shadowy and discreet, and even Emerson had promised to kill a deer. "Is it true that Emerson is going to take a gun?" Longfellow asked. "Then someone will be shot." He declined to join the party.

William J. Stillman's 1858 painting, *The Philosophers' Camp in the Adirondacks*, depicts their outing on Follansbee Pond, which is in fact a lake near the Saranacs. Some thirty years later the crisp Adirondack watercolors of Winslow Homer, the sparkle of white paper defining birches, cascades, and braided ferns, will proclaim the artist's conquest of his medium; Stillman's picture records an event. His holiday keepsake has a place in American art history because of its intellectual overtones — nineteenth-century nature worship, the wilderness as sylvan playground, arcadia despoiled. Homer's watercolors evoke the epiphanies of hunters and fishermen; Stillman's communal gathering suggests a tableau of eminent figures on public display. Alone beneath a sun-dappled pine, Emerson marks the center of the friezelike composition; behind him, at far left arrayed around a stump, a science-minded group — Dr. Jeffries Wyman, John Holmes, Dr. Estes Howe — absorb zoological lore from shirt-sleeved Louis Agassiz dissecting a fish; on the right, the artist, Judge Ebenezer

Rockwood Hoar, James Russell Lowell, and four guides intently watch Horatio Woodman aiming his rifle at a target. With one exception, the campers are members of Boston's Saturday Club, and indeed Woodman, in 1855, inspired by Emerson's long-standing proposal of a literary dining society, had formed the group.

> The great achievement of his life, not only in his own estimation but in that of his friends, was the organizing of the Saturday Club [states Alfred Donaldson, the Adirondack historian], and the proudest badge he wore was that of membership in it, which, it is said, could only have come about through his being its founder.

Stillman was the expedition's official host. He had chosen the head of the lake site; it had a beach and spring and two massive maples, and he instantly set to work constructing a shelter. To his task he brought the manual dexterity of a hunter-trapper and artist. Years before he had been accepted as the first student of Frederick Church, the painter of eerie icebergs and panoramic landscapes, and at Church's studio met Edgar Allan Poe, "a slender, nervous, vivacious, and extremely refined personage." But Church disappointed Stillman; he found no schools of art in the United States, so in December 1849 he boarded a packet for Liverpool. The leading painters of London already had more students than they needed; Stillman spent his days seeking out pictures by his idol, J. M. W. Turner. The search led to Griffiths' gallery, where the proprietor, Turner's special agent, was delighted by the unexpected provincial connoisseur.

One morning, while Stillman was eulogizing Turner to Griffiths, Ruskin entered (the motifs of art gallery and forest, society and solitude, punctuate Stillman's career), and after a brief exchange invited the American to dinner. That evening in Grosvenor Street there was repartee with buoyant Effie Ruskin and theological talk with her husband, whose opinions about art were subordinated to his views on religion. Subsequently, Stillman and Ruskin held as many conversations about religion as about art, "the two being then to me almost identical and to him closely related."

More than a half century later, the details remained limpid in Stillman's recollection:

> I remember his saying once, in speaking of the doctrine of fore-ordination (to me a dreadful bugbear), as I was drinking a glass of sherry, that he "believed that it had been ordained from all eternity whether I should set that glass down empty or without finishing the wine." This was to me the most perplexing problem of all that Ruskin put before me, for it was the first time that the doctrine of Calvin had come before me in concrete form.

England also gave Stillman the opportunity to discover the contemporary medievalism of the pre-Raphaelite painters. The chivalric legends of Millais and Rossetti, however, dimmed before the actuality of a meeting with Turner. The diminutive old man with an eagle's beak of a nose and bright restive eye confused his admirer by first refusing to grasp his hand and then accepting it, but the occasion otherwise passed cordially. Turner, Ruskin, and the pre-Raphaelites now dominated Stillman's thoughts. When he returned to New York his paintings attracted the attention of critics who hailed him as the American pre-Raphaelite, but he was a restless intellectual with interests too encyclopedic for any label. Stillman had come to painting late, after his graduation from Union College, and his work suffered technically from his haphazard formal training. Possibly that accounted for his on-again, off-again flirtation with his muse. Captivated by the rhetoric of Louis Kossuth, the Hungarian nationalist, Stillman volunteered his services to the cause. Revolution was imminent; meanwhile, he posed as a tourist during a cloak-and-dagger mission to Vienna and Budapest that involved the Austrian crown jewels and a cipher dispatch in the hollowed-out heel of a boot. The mission misfired, the revolution failed, he did not stay a secret agent long. Once more he took up the brush, though he had developed a rueful appreciation of his talents: "I influenced some of my contemporaries and gave a jog to the landscape painting of the day, and there it ended, through a diversion of my ambition to another sphere, but there it must have ended; even if I had never been so diverted." Stillman was a jack-of-all-trades — a writer, though hardly a prose stylist; a debater of abstract aesthetic theories; a pioneer photographer; an investigator of psychic phenomena; a skillful outdoorsman. In brief, he possessed the salient qualities of the journalist he was soon to become: curiosity about the world, and the capacity to cast his net wide.

For a time he settled in Paris and resumed his painting. His talent for singling out talent had not deserted him. Soon he had visited the studios of Delacroix, Gérôme, Théodore Rousseau, Ingres, and, at Barbizon, Millet. Would Delacroix accept him as a pupil? Delacroix declined, but this did not prevent the insatiably curious Stillman from cross-examining the master and soliciting his opinion about the principal defect of modern art compared with ancient models. "The execution," Delacroix answered, and to demonstrate what he meant, produced his own portfolios of copies of classical images.

Presently, cash running out, Stillman again sailed home and found New York enraptured by spiritualism. Table-tippings and spirit-rapping flourished; mediums crooned; séances brought the sexes together in the dark. Stillman maintained a genial open-mindedness about the phenomenon he called spiritism; the subject attracted him as intensely as painting. To a medium he gave a letter of Ruskin's without disclosing the source, and in the course of her ruminations "she said that the writer was not married, to which I replied that in this she was mistaken, and she rejoined, 'Then he ought *not* to be.' At that time Mr. and Mrs. Ruskin were living together, and no rumor of their incompatibility had come about." A robust exchange of gossip across the shadow line had its charms; nevertheless Stillman preferred to pursue the metaphysical in nature. Perhaps the Adirondacks — "I hoped here to find new subjects for art, spiritual freedom, and a closer contact with the spirit world" — would satisfy his numinous yearnings.

Before dawn, when mist drifted on the water, he heard spectral flocks of loons, marsh frogs, the splash of a trout fading into threadlike vibrations. The Adirondacks in the early 1850s seemed to the American imagination as strange as the interior of Africa or Tartary — unbroken northern forest, dark, primal, a place of deceptive and tangled shadows. Sportsmen seldom penetrated the terrain with its gut-wrenching portages around waterfalls and ravines. Roads were rudimentary; a labyrinth of deer runways coiled reflexively through the undergrowth. There were wolves, panthers, bears. Winters were protracted and harsh; summers merely interrupted the brief splendors of autumn and spring. At intervals of ten to twenty miles or so, log houses served as impromptu inns catering to lumberers; here and there a cluster of guides' cottages promised to bunch into a community; but the Adirondacks combined the lure of natural beauty with the panic of a maze. In the blind alleys of that solitude one might never find the way back.

Sanford Gifford, a fellow landscapist, had visited the Saranac Lakes the year before and "gave me the clue to the labyrinth" — a log cabin where Stillman lodged with a farmer and his small household for two dollars a week and painted in the open air. Carrying easel and brushes, he roamed the woods and cultivated transcendental sensations. He did not take a gun and went bareheaded in the hope he might somehow be more receptive to spiritual messages; but he was such an ardent fisherman he could not bear to dispense with his rod and fly book. When he did not paint, he was either in his boat on the lake or strolling beneath the trees.

Spiritual illumination proved refractory; as a matter of fact, Stillman's devotion to the transcendent went hand in hand with the fallacy that by painting a "different" kind of subject, the unknown Adirondacks, he would improve his perceptions. Before the summer was over he realized the Adirondacks were not the romantic riddle he wished to decipher. Sometimes he encountered an isolato who heard voices and had intimations of immortality; but for the most part the settlers were louts. They wallowed in frontier debauchery; the old farmer, his landlord, abandoned the cabin at intervals on sullen sprees. "The humanity of the backwoods was on a lower level than that of a New England village — more material if less worldly; the men got intoxicated, and some of the women — nothing less like an apostle could I have found in the streets of New York."

Deeper in the woods, Stillman escaped rural disillusionment, but the skein of shadows disturbed his sense of direction. One day he rowed along a trout stream of considerable size, which appeared to empty into a lake. The site was new to him; maybe there was a subject for a painting. After a half mile, however, the stream became so clogged by fallen trees that Stillman secured his boat and scouted the bank to see if there might be clear water ahead. All at once he came upon the stream running back on its previous course and parallel to it.

Instantly, in the twinkling of an eye, the entire landscape seemed to have changed its bearings — the sun, which was clear in the sky, it being about three o'clock, shone to me out of the north, and it was impossible to convince myself that my senses deceived me, or accept the fact that the sun must be in the southwest, the general direction from which the stream was flowing, and that, to get home again, I must turn my back to it, if I had lost my boat, as seemed certain . . . I had one terrible moment of clear consciousness that if I went astray at that juncture no human being would ever know where I was, and the absolute necessity of recovering my sense of the points of the compass was clear to me. By a strong effort of the will, I repressed the growing panic, sat down on a log and covered my face with my hands, and waited, I had no idea how long, but until I felt quite calm; and when I looked out on the landscape again I found the sun in his proper place and the landscape as I had known it. I walked back to my boat without difficulty and went home, and I never lost my head again while I frequented the wilderness.

Sitting on a log, hands over his face, Stillman struggled against the vertigo of personal annihilation. He *had* summoned spirits, not, alas, the spirits he bargained for. The Saranacs inspired artists and attracted venturesome homesteaders, but the region was illusive, and its clouds and mountains and conifer-bordered lakes glimmered like the substance of a waking dream.

The problem of earning a livelihood once more confronted Stillman, and back in Manhattan he plunged into journalism. His first job, as fine arts editor of the *Evening Post,* then edited by William Cullen Bryant, did not interfere with studio hours; but the paper was not an ideal forum for a zealous disciple of Ruskin. Stillman resolved to create his own journal, a weekly called *The Crayon,* from which he might receive an income while he pursued his painting. With characteristic ebullience, he enlisted a partner, John Durand, the son of the president of the National Academy of Design, then sought backers. *The Crayon* was the first art magazine published in this country, and the support of the New England literary establishment was essential. Stillman journeyed to Boston, where, in the late 1850s, he transferred his studio.

The first literary grandee he approached, a card of introduction in hand from the realist painter William Page, was James Russell Lowell. The fervor of the visitor's Ruskinian views disarmed Lowell, who was in a state of depression following the death of his wife, and their first meeting launched a permanent friendship. Eventually, Stillman persuaded Lowell to inspect the north woods: in August 1857, Charles Eliot Norton wrote to the poet Arthur Hugh Clough,

> I found Lowell very well and in capital spirits, having just returned from a wild, camping-out journey to the Adirondack Mountains. He had been cutting paths through woods in which

no paths have ever been made before, he had shot a bear that was swimming a lake, he had seen herds of wild deer, and measured pine trees whose trunks three men could not clasp around.

Through Lowell and Norton, another eager Ruskinian, he met the New England pantheon: Emerson, Agassiz, Charles Sumner, Thomas Bailey Aldrich, Richard Henry Dana, Longfellow, Oliver Wendell Holmes, Motley, Whittier, and Longfellow's brother-in-law, Thomas Gold Appleton. The Saturday Club — potential contributors all — welcomed him, but their liking for Stillman transcended professional ties and he responded in kind. Volume one, number one, of *The Crayon* appeared. It was a *succès d'estime;* Lowell, Bryant, Aldrich, Henry James Sr., and Bayard Taylor contributed, and within a month the subscription list numbered above 1200. Unfortunately, Stillman was not by temperament an editor and had only a hazy understanding of the business side of the enterprise. Exhausted by an urgent day-and-night schedule, he was relieved to turn over his share to Durand and go off to the mountains and paint.

His Adirondacks stories continued to intrigue members of the Saturday Club, particularly after Stillman heard that a tract including island-studded Ampersand Pond would be offered at a sheriff's sale because of nonpayment of taxes. The price, Lowell agreed, was attractive, so he and Stillman chartered the Adirondack Club, an offshoot of The Saturday, and the club purchased Ampersand's 22,500 acres — pond, mountains, and lofty Norway pines — for $600. The members, intending to build a clubhouse, made a tentative start toward using the property, but the Civil War intervened and time took care of the rest. While the Ampersand purchase was under negotiation, however, Stillman, elected captain of the hunt and chief guide, preceded the band of ten campers and eight guides to Follansbee Pond. More accessible than Ampersand, the lake's situation permitted the guests to arrive by boat from Lower Saranac, which they would reach after a long jolting wagon ride from Keeseville, on the Ausable River near Lake Champlain.

At Keeseville the populace turned out to greet Agassiz, in August 1858 the most famous of the campers. Emerson and Lowell had their devotees, but Keeseville wanted a glimpse of Agassiz, who had not long before refused a lucrative offer from Napoleon. The directorship of the Jardin des Plantes carried senatorial privileges if Agassiz would settle in Paris, and his decision to devote himself instead to his natural history collections in Cambridge was widely publicized and approved. A deputation of selectmen awaited, a bustling knot of bumpkins out of a genre painting by Woodville or Bingham. Was this the real Agassiz or not? they wondered. No one was going to outfox them. When Agassiz appeared, the head of the delegation stepped forward with the scientist's engraved portrait, and after a pause for comparisons, turned to the others and announced, "Yes, it's him." Then, with the gravity of high priests, each selectman shook hands in order with Agassiz, ignoring Emerson, Holmes, Lowell, and their companions.

Stillman hoped to witness Emerson's pristine initial reactions to "absolute nature," but because of repairs to a guide boat, joined the others amid a downpour the first night. The next day they glided along the Raquette River, each camper and a guide to a boat, except for Agassiz and Stillman, who rowed together. Majestic and tranquil, the stream coiled through unbroken forest where sweeps of dark water broadened into small lagoons covered by pond lilies and sagittaria. Deer paced along the banks and butterflies flickered in the gloom beyond crumpled shallows where minnows darted and turtles lay in terra-cotta lassitude. No longer did Stillman regard the woods as nightmarish, and it was many years since Emerson in his address to Harvard's Phi Beta Kappa Society had spoken of nature as a "dumb abyss" in which the self must awake echoes. As they approached the expanse of lake and, at its head, the rectangle of Stillman's spruce bark shelter, open wide in front beneath the huge maples and the surrounding hills, the landscape must have seemed without a history, which they as men of letters were prepared to write.

That landscape had remained unaltered since it came into existence according to divine plan. Never again would it be experienced in the same manner, for the following year Darwin's *Origin of Species* transformed nature. "The tempered light of the woods is like a perpetual morning and is stimulating and heroic," Emerson had observed, and Stillman listened for the pantheistic cadences of the essayist in his presence. Within a few years, Harvard's esteemed comparative anatomist and Agassiz's associate, Dr. Jeffries Wyman, would accept Darwin's evolutionary hypothesis, and Agassiz's status as science's apologist for religion would dwindle. Stillman would regret the decline of the Swiss-American's reputation. "Even the little dogs of physical science bark at his name; but his greater contemporaries knew and esteemed him better." Agassiz's position was similar to Emerson's: the universe disclosed a conscious mind in the process of creation. In *Nature* (1836) Emerson had defined the world as the projection of a mind corresponding to the human mind yet infinitely more powerful. Emerson's capacity for intellectual paradox, however, had anticipated Darwin in the 1850 lectures collected and published two years after the Adirondacks expedition under the title *The Conduct of Life*, in which human existence is predicated upon struggle, the survival of the fittest.

Both aspects of Emerson — the nature mystic and the forerunner of Social Darwinism — were manifested at the Follansbee campsite. The mystic was at first evident, and Stillman revered him: "The rest of us were always at the surface of things — even the naturalists were only engaged with their anatomy; but Emerson in the forest, or looking at the sunset from the lake, seemed to be looking through the phenomena, studying them by their reflections on an inner speculum."

Stillman's painting and its title *The Philosophers' Camp* — they themselves called it Camp Maple — pay homage to Emerson, the seer. Committed to neither party, he stands apart, pilgrim's staff in hand, opposing metaphysical consciousness to Agassiz's analytical discourse and Woodman's gregarious diversion. Already, however, Emerson was making preliminary sketches for his blank-verse narrative poem "The Adirondacs," which would celebrate their August idyll. In the poem he suggests escape from civilization is impossible, that the savants of the Saturday Club are playing at primitive life, but the guides, who are loggers in winter, are "the doctors of the wilderness."

> *Ten scholars, wonted to lie warm and soft*
> *In well-hung chambers daintily bestowed,*
> *Lie here on hemlock-boughs, like Sacs and Sioux,*
> *And greet unanimous the joyful change.*

Once settled in the shelter, they enjoyed a uniform routine — up at dawn, breakfast, and after breakfast, firing at a mark. Lowell with the hunters followed their dogs into the hills; the fishermen rowed out to haul in the lines baited the previous evening for lake trout; Agassiz and Wyman led naturalists to dredge for specimens. There were explorations of lake and shore:

> *All day we swept the lake, searched every cove,*
> *North from Camp Maple, south to Osprey Bay,*
> *Watching when the loud dogs should drive in deer,*
> *Or whipping its rough surface for a trout;*
> *Or, bathers, diving from the rock at noon;*
> *Challenging Echo by our guns and cries.*

On the surface there was a pronounced lack of incident. Yet none of the participants ever forgot the vacation that Stillman cherished as the supreme memory of his life. A later commentator, William Chapman White, complains with a certain justification that nothing happened at Camp Maple. Nothing did. The events documented are mundane. History, nonetheless, often consists of things not happening — of matters that conceal immediate recognition of the relationships between men and landscape. The undemanding regimen at Camp Maple anticipated the lack of surface incident among patients who someday would undertake their own pilgrimages to the region.

There is no reason to regard *The Philosophers' Camp* from a medical standpoint, yet considered from that standpoint, the scene acquires unusual perspective. The death rate from consumption, as tuberculosis was then called, hovered between 300 and 400 per 100,000 from 1830 to 1880 in cities of the Eastern seaboard, Boston, New York, and Philadelphia; and New England, in particular, was afflicted. That statistical ratio was maintained by the Saturday Club. Two members of Stillman's party were consumptives: Dr. Jeffries Wyman, the Hersey Professor of Anatomy at Harvard Medical School, and Ralph Waldo Emerson.

Thanks to Wyman we call one of the highest of the anthropoid apes a gorilla. The name existed in the chronicles of Hanno, the fifth century B.C. Carthaginian explorer of Africa, having passed into New Latin from the Greek *Gorillai,* a tribe of hairy women. Until Wyman's restyling, however, apes were "pongoes," an African tribal denomination. Andrew Battell, an English seaman, in *Purchas His Pilgrims,* published in 1625, mentions "two kinds of monsters which are common in these woods and very dangerous. The greater of these two monsters is called Pongo in their language and the lesser is called Engenco." The probability is that the Engenco was the chimpanzee, while the gorilla was the Pongo. A genus comprising the orangutans of Southeast Asia is still thus described (and, in The Drones Club of P. G. Wodehouse, that eminent anthropoid Pongo Twistleton).

In 1847, the Episcopalian missionary Thomas S. Savage, visiting a Presbyterian colleague, John Leighton Wilson, at the latter's house on the Gaboon River, had seen the skull of a large ape. Savage recognized it as differing from the chimpanzee's and began investigating. From chiefs of the Mpongwe tribe he obtained four skulls and other bones, and sent these to Wyman, a collaborator on an 1843 paper about the chimpanzee, "Observations on the External Characters and Habits of *Troglodytes niger*," in the *Boston Journal of Natural History*, which made the first step toward a scientific understanding of chimpanzee behavior, ultimately to become a psychological cottage industry. Wyman, no doubt, was seeking a more precise nomenclature for the chimpanzee's relative, the mighty ape of the forests of equatorial west Africa, and came up with the binomial *Troglodytes gorilla* for their collaborative paper on a "New Species of Orang from the Gaboon River." The paper was another pioneer study; it was noteworthy for the accuracy and clarity of its observations; and the name lasted.

A photograph of Jeffries Wyman on his fifty-fifth birthday, taken by Oliver Wendell Holmes in 1865, shows Wyman in a lawn chair under a small canvas canopy, probably in the back yard of his Cambridge home. The trunk of a giant elm repeats nearby the sylvan motif of *The Philosophers' Camp*. Quietly facing the camera, Wyman sits with his hands folded in his lap at some distance from the lens, among the dappled shadows at the base of the elm, yet his features are visible above his frock coat, dark cravat, and high collar — broad forehead and receding hairline, emphatic intelligent nose, determined mouth, and mildly skeptical expression behind steel-rimmed spectacles. His face is somewhat gaunt and his figure tall and spare. He is both neat, displaying the careful tailoring of a tidy scientist, and shy, blending into the protective coloration of his surroundings. Wyman, who abhorred celebrity, was the introverted opposite of the bluff, exuberant Agassiz, though each admired the other. One might attend Agassiz's lectures and catch his robust enthusiasm for the vast surge of creation, but Wyman's classes were an acquired taste. When he delivered the Lowell Lectures in the series newly established by John Amory Lowell in 1840, he was regarded by his critical lay audience as diffident; those who knew comparative anatomy or physiology, however, recognized the skill of his organization and the pertinent charm of his illustrations. "Symmetry and Homology in Animal Structure," his Harvard course, did not sound exciting, but he brought it alive through surprising associations and a capacity to dramatize observations, such as "the ciliary motion, like waving rye, of the microscopic epithelium of a frog's windpipe." Agassiz was the classic undergraduate teacher; Wyman's most effective moments occurred in intimate surroundings where the subtlety of his observations flew to the mark. Holmes's photograph portrays a private but assured man. Upright in his chair, Wyman gains attention despite his frailty and obvious reserve. The space brims with foreground lawn, weighty elm, and shade, but the unassertive figure is neither vulnerable, lonely, nor pathetic. The angular structures of the canopy protect him like the fabric of an order imposed upon nature. He emanates cordiality combined with unyielding will.

Pulmonary tuberculosis appeared before Wyman's graduation from Harvard at nineteen, continuously hampered him throughout his life, and finally ended his career in 1874. Thirty-three years after his death, an authority would name him "the ablest anatomist this country has yet produced," though Wyman's influence was out of proportion to his meager output of scientific papers. A medical doctor before he turned twenty-three, he found the first years of his practice difficult. The botanist Asa Gray, a lifelong friend, declared, "His means were very slender, and his life abstemious to the verge of privation." So few were Wyman's patients, indeed, that he applied for and received a job as a Boston fireman. Then an appointment as demonstrator of anatomy at Harvard Medical School, followed by the curatorship of the Lowell Institute, delivered him from penury.

Teaching and research took Wyman to a professorship in Hampden-Sydney College in Richmond, Virginia, and back to Harvard; but he had an adventurous streak and the instincts of a collector. In the summer of 1849 he joined an expedition to Labrador aboard a fishing schooner. Subsequent winters in Florida provided him with zoological specimens, and his health improved. Shortly after his marriage, in 1850, he envisioned a Harvard museum of comparative anatomy and zoology. From his student days he had evidenced a talent for preparing and arranging natural history exhibitions, and he also showed promise as a pencil and pen-and-ink draftsman. (His tender letters to his only son, Jeffie, born in 1864, are embellished by perky sketches. "These letters," says George E. Gifford Jr., their editor, "are the works of a great scientist trying to instill in his son the concepts of acute observation and wonder. Wyman's papers on biology and anthropology are profound and significant; his letters to Jeffie are like the little piano pieces for children by Bach and Beethoven — charming, simple and elegant — but displaying the hand of a master.") During the early 1850s, he visited prototype museums in Europe, then, shattered by the death of his first wife, Wyman took up travel as an anodyne.

The pietistic and high-minded Henry I. Bowditch records meeting him "in the Saranac wilds":

> He is now at a pretty camp, where he passed, three years since, one of the happiest weeks of his life with his wife, who recently died. . . . He has counted no less than forty species of birds. He is quietly studying the sand waves as they roll upon his little beach, and argues back from them to the ripple-marks of ancient sandstone. He has measured the largest, or among the largest of boulders in the known world, now resting on the shores of the lake. . . . Finally and naturally, we turned from nature to the God of nature, and we discoursed on the tendency of modern materialistic philosophy to refer all force to the sun.

His journeyings assumed the emotional, escapist character of the globetrotting in the 1880s of Henry Adams and John La-Farge. In 1856, Wyman, with two of his students, traveled by canoe into the interior of Surinam. Notwithstanding tropical fever and a slow recuperation, he was anxious to visit the jungle again, and the year in which he camped with the Saturday Club on Follansbee he traveled across South America with his friend George Augustus Peabody. On both occasions, vast quantities of material were collected for the special museum established in Boylston Hall, the nucleus of the present-day collections of the Peabody Museum. "Failing strength demanded a respite from oral teaching" in 1866, when George Peabody — a distant relative of George Augustus Peabody — endowed the Museum of American Archeology that bears his name, and Wyman became its first director.

The post enabled him to winter in Florida. Every year his Cambridge friends could only hope that he might return. In spite of his health he persisted in research — investigations confirming Pasteur's rejection of spontaneous generation in liquids, investigations of the shell mounds of Florida and Maine, resulted in a classic paper, published posthumously, *Fresh-Water Shell Mounds of the St. Johns River, Florida.* John Murray Forbes told Edward Emerson that one day he and Wyman were walking along the banks of the St. Johns River and came suddenly upon a huge alligator. Forbes raised his rifle and fired at close range.

> The monster, though badly wounded, started for his native element, but a few feet away, below the steep bank. In an instant Wyman was astride of him, probably behind the forelegs, and just as he was reaching the edge, drove his hunting-knife between the scales, and with anatomist's security, between the base of the skull and the first vertebra, instantly severing the *medulla oblongata*, the vital nexus. Exact knowledge was safety and power. He knew just how far the sweep of the tail could reach.

Characteristically, Wyman preserved the skeleton and suspended it from the ceiling of his lecture hall, but the tempestuous impulse of his struggle with the alligator was atypical. Self-effacement, fairness, and probity are the traits cited by contemporary after contemporary. "His word would be accepted on a miracle," said Oliver Wendell Holmes. Less than a month before Wyman's fatal hemorrhage, he wrote Jeffie, the young son whose mother had died in childbirth. Wyman had scooped a brilliant Polyphemus moth from a Brattle Street fence. "I have saved it for you," he said, and no doubt, had he been able to present the moth, would have expressed delight at the conformation and color of the markings on the wings. It was the remembrance of a consummate observer. Once, accompanied by Elliot Cabot and a group of students, Wyman explored a bluff in Concord where layers of charcoal and calcined mussel shells indicated an Algonquin encampment. Evidence of freshwater mussels in the mound proved interesting; the Indians usually considered these unpalatable. The students moved across the edge of the bluff, turning the soil carefully with hoes and spoons, and all at once Wyman bent and picked up a brown triangular object resembling a decayed knot of wood. "Ulna of a deer," he exclaimed, and then looked upset, parading his erudition. "They seem to have been a tid-bit," he added. "I often find them in shell-heaps."

Wyman's health improved at Saranac; ailing tourists made similar discoveries. Joel T. Headley, a New York journalist, twice visited the north country to cure "an attack on the brain," and then, in 1849, wrote *The Adirondacks; or, Life in the Woods,* which sold briskly for nearly three decades. Beyond the bustling spas of Saratoga stretched the wilderness; by 1886, the publishing firm of G. P. Putnam's advertised Joseph W. Stickler's *The Adirondacks as a Health Resort.*

Emerson went to the woods for recreation rather than therapy, although he must have been keenly conscious of the beneficial air. His medical history was gloomy. Thomas Emerson, who sailed from England and settled in Ipswich in 1638, did not suffer from tuberculosis, nor did his descendants for a century and a half. They were long-lived, save for those struck down by the deadly diseases of childhood. The first Emerson to die of tuberculosis was Ralph's older brother John, who succumbed in his sixth year, having been sent to relatives in Maine after displaying symptoms of lethargy. Exposed to this case in his household, the Reverend William Emerson himself experienced severe hemorrhages of the lungs and endured declining health until his death in 1811 at the age of forty-two.

The doctors in Portland, Maine, where William Emerson died, did not think the hemorrhages of the lungs were related to his subsequent death; but four of his five surviving sons developed tuberculosis, and the disease harassed the family through the tenth generation of Thomas Emerson's descendants, until the advent of antibiotics.

Edward Bliss Emerson, prior to his diagnosis in 1825, seemed the most gifted of the brothers, and he had begun the study of law in Daniel Webster's office. Increasing mental instability, however, aggravated by his physical condition, resulted in a complete breakdown. Among his delusions, perhaps psychologically significant, was that at the time he stopped reading law he was cured of tuberculosis. Presently he regained sanity and tried to recover his health in Puerto Rico. There, drenched by a sudden rain that intensified a chronic cough, he sought medical advice. The doctor found Edward's lungs terminally affected. He was twenty-nine.

Charles Chauncey Emerson, the youngest, graduated second in his class at Harvard (Ralph Waldo had an undistinguished undergraduate record), where he was also awarded the Bowdoin essay prize. The most eloquent orator of the family, he too studied for the bar and demonstrated legal promise. Pulmonary complaints caused him to visit Puerto Rico, preceding Edward, but Charles later pleaded cases in Boston and opened an office in Concord. He became engaged to Elizabeth Hoar, sister of the prominent lawyer and judge, Ebenezer, who was then making his mark at the Middlesex Bar. During the winter of 1836 Charles seemed unable to throw off a cold that had settled in his chest. In April, his perturbed older brothers sent him to New

York en route to the South, but he died of galloping consumption within the fortnight. He was twenty-seven.

Waldo's older brother William graduated from Harvard, studied theology in Germany, and succeeded in obtaining an audience with Goethe. To the poet William confided theological doubts; Goethe, adopting a pragmatic view, advised him not to dwell on his misgivings, and instead to concentrate on running a parish. This, William's conscience would not permit. When he returned to America, he switched careers and studied for the law with a Wall Street firm. Ultimately, he became a New York State district judge.

Like his brothers, William in early adulthood exhibited signs of pulmonary distress. Nevertheless, despite an annual winter "bronchitis," he survived till the age of sixty-seven, succumbing to pneumonia. A singular irony occurred in 1843 when he needed a tutor for his seven-year-old son, and at Ralph Waldo's recommendation hired Henry Thoreau. As a schoolteacher, Thoreau was well qualified, but his family history displayed an alarming incidence of consumption. His grandfather and sister died of tuberculosis; his father probably did, and a brother, who died of lockjaw, exhibited pronounced tubercular symptoms. Of course, Thoreau was almost twenty years away from the final stages of phthisis; still, he would be in close contact at William's Staten Island house with a child who also came from an equally vulnerable background. In any event, the new tutor was uncomfortable with the starchy William Emersons, hated New York, and returned to Concord within six months.

Gay Wilson Allen, a recent Ralph Waldo Emerson biographer, speculates that the illness which beset Emerson in Divinity School when he sensed "a mouse was gnawing" at his chest was psychosomatic. All other biographers have assumed that what went wrong with Emerson's lungs was tuberculosis. Given his medical context, the assumptions do not seem unwarranted, yet it is possible both elements were present. Selman A. Waksman, prominent among the pioneers of antibiotics in the treatment of tuberculosis, believes Emerson managed to overcome the acute stage of the disease, which thereafter remained latent. What is known, however, is that in September 1826, Ralph Waldo wrote William and confessed to lung complaints. It is a curiously phrased letter that leaves matters ambiguous.

> You must know that in my vehement desire to preach I have recently taken into my bosom certain terrors not for my hip which does valiantly, nor my eyes which deserve commendation, but for my lungs without whose aid I cannot speak, and which scare me & thro me scare our poor mother's sympathies with strictures [chest plasters] & jenesaisquoisities.

What were those terrors? Doctors agreed a New England winter was inadmissible and recommended Charleston, South Carolina, to the newly approbated minister, but Emerson's health did not improve there — "My chest is a prey to certain oppressions & pangs, chiefly by night, which are very tolerable in themselves, but not very tolerable in their auspices to such an alarmist as I" — and in January 1827 he took passage for St. Augustine, where he had been "promised the most balmy air in the world."

The air proved invigorating. Emerson regained his customary vigor and found stimulation in the return trip to Charleston that spring, when he shared a cabin with Napoleon Buonoparte's philosophic nephew, Napoleon Achille Murat.

That same year Emerson was introduced to the young woman he would marry: Ellen Tucker, whose shy, muslin beauty fulfilled the ethereal standards of the period's feminine ideal. The consumptive heroine was in vogue. Rouge had been abandoned in favor of whitening powders, while mixtures of lemon juice and vinegar were popular as appetite suppressants. Anorexic languor accorded with the vital statistics of tuberculosis; it is moot which encouraged which. The denial of the flesh symbolized the brevity of existence, indicated that a lover had transcended grosser appetites, and often concluded in harrowing and clinical deathbed scenes. René and Jean Dubos state: "It seems not unlikely that many of those who regarded a consumptive appearance as the utmost in refinement and distinction eventually became victims of the real disease out of their efforts to play the part." Ellen, however, did not play at invalidism. Already gripped by consumption, she was a mere sixteen when Emerson came to her father's home in Concord, New Hampshire. Her age reflected another period ideal, the child-woman. Adolescence was less a stage from childhood to maturity than a state of being in which one dared not look beyond.

The depth of Emerson's feeling for Ellen, the halcyon years of their marriage and the intensity of his eventual bereavement, constitute the major emotional event of his life. His remarriage to Lydia (Lydian) Jackson was serene and relatively staid. The years with Ellen were touched by a lyricism that could never bear repetition.

Owing to his own apparent conquest of the disease, Emerson had reason for hope of Ellen's recovery, but she was suffering from active pulmonary tuberculosis at the time of their marriage in 1829. Her immediate family's mortality rate from the disease was as multiple as the Emersons' — her mother; possibly her father; a stepbrother, George; and a sister, Margaret. Consumption spared few early nineteenth-century New England households; it reappeared in Emerson's second marriage as well, for Lydian Emerson's mother suffered from tuberculosis for ten years, and Lydian herself was not strong, preferring to sleep year round with the windows flung open, four hours a night, supposing this would strengthen her as it had evidently strengthened Napoleon.

During his first marriage of slightly more than a year, Emerson's happiness was tempered by dismay at Ellen's condition. The course of her illness followed a familiar inexorable pattern, and when she died, grief demolished his accepted pieties. There is, for instance, a terrible weight of anguish in the macabre journal entry for March 29, 1832: "I visited Ellen's tomb & opened the coffin." Did this morbid event literally take place, or was it a dream? Scholars disagree, but the psychic toll is evident, and the picture, whether literal or figurative, is of an Emerson at variance with the public image of the mild-mannered sage of Concord.

By 1858, however, the passionate and controversial young iconoclast had long since become the more conventional sage. Emerson accepted the transition calmly; the accelerating crisis over slavery demanded a different mood; the spokesman for the spirit must address society. At Camp Maple the Emerson of the essay "Self-Reliance" is most apparent in his attitudes toward the guides. He studied them avidly; they embodied his notion of the authentic individual "who has ventured to trust himself." Emerson, given to cigar smoking and conviviality, was on easy terms with these generally illiterate woodsmen: the Social Darwinian emerged in a thoroughly unexpected guise. The enthusiasm of Lowell for hunting, the talk around the campfire about firearms — discussions of make, calibre, and quality — kindled an atavistic urge: "The strong return to our heredity of human primeval occupation gradually involved [Emerson] and made him desire to enter into this experience as well as the rest of the forest emotions. He must understand this passion to kill."

The impulse had flared on a Sunday morning after Stillman rowed Emerson across the lake to a secluded cove. Going into the woods where Emerson intended to meditate, they suddenly heard the baying of Lowell's hound. Emerson listened with excitement as the hound pursued the quarry over the hills and around the lake. "Let us go after the deer," he said, and they jumped into the boat and flew down the lake, but before they arrived the reverberant crack of a rifle announced Lowell had arrived first.

So insistent was Emerson on killing a deer that Stillman arranged a "jack hunt," which even then was condemned by conservationists. The deer are stalked by night; the hunter waits for them to come to the water to feed, and shines a jacklight, which illumines the space immediately ahead of the boat. Blinded by the light, the deer is a point-blank target, though standing absolutely still in the darkness provides a minimal protection. The hunt began with the guide spotting a buck and paddling within twenty yards of it before throwing the light and giving Emerson the signal to shoot, but Emerson was also dazzled by the glare.

> Finally the creature took fright and ran, and all we got of him was the sound of galloping hooves as he sped away, stopping a moment, when at a safe distance, to snort at the intruders, and then off again [Stillman relates]. We kept on, and presently came upon another, toward which we drifted even nearer than the first one, and still Emerson could see nothing to distinguish the deer from the boulders among which he stood; and we were scarcely the boat's length from him, when, Emerson still unable to see him, and not caring to run the risk of losing him, for we had no venison in camp and the luck of the morning drive was always uncertain, I shot him.

Emerson returned home bilked of his deer, yet this, as Stillman said, was probably a relief. It had been an impulse; the view from Concord was not the same. In the autumn Stillman came back alone to survey the lodge site on Ampersand Pond for the Saturday Club. A northwest wind filled the air with a chill fog that crystallized, glittering on every branch and twig. Four feet of snow covered the ground. He had a cold that had settled in his chest, and a racking cough, and without leaving his inn, drew with the assistance of guides a map of the site. A few days later he arrived with the plan in Boston, called the executive committee of the club to dinner, made his report, drank a glass of champagne to the future lodge, and went to bed in the early stages of pneumonia. The New York wilderness would never again assume such a paramount role in his life. Meanwhile, Emerson's

forest notebook hymned the stirring headline event of that
August:

The lightning has run masterless too long;
He must to school and learn his verb and noun
And teach his nimbleness to earn his wage.

The Atlantic Cable — "Thought's new-found path" — had
been completed. They heard about it by chance from a traveler
with a newspaper who happened by the camp where Emerson,
Stillman, Agassiz, and the others had escaped from society in
their sequestered grove.

CHAPTER TWO

Ministers and Medicine Men
1869

THE HEROIC STAGE of exploration resounds with the eager accents of public relations — Eric the Red and his greening of polar Greenland; threadbare though gem-laden Marco Polo returning to Venice; John Smith delivered from the headsman's axe by Pocahontas. In the development of the New York wilderness that mythifying role might well have fallen to Edward Judson, "Ned Buntline," the rowdy dime novelist and Buffalo Bill's press agent, who before the Civil War sought refuge on the shores of Raquette Lake from his slipshod marital alliances. Equipped with a plentiful supply of alcohol, Buntline was in an ideal position to invent fables. Instead he devoted his literary hours to pulp fiction and doggerel verse, and when not hunting or fishing he indulged in a noisy quarrel with a churlish and celebrated guide, a descendant of self-exiled Tories, Alvah Dunning. The fabulist's role was assumed ten years later by an unlikely figure, a flamboyant sporting parson from Boston, the Reverend William Henry Harrison ("Adirondack") Murray. He nurtured the instincts of a conservationist, but his best-seller, *Adventures in the Wilderness; or, Camp-Life in the Adirondacks*, published early in April 1869, had the ironic effect of starting a stampede into the region and threatening the wild landscape he so prized.

Murray, an eloquent, charismatic, muscular Christian and staunch democrat, exemplified Emerson's doctrine of self-reliance. Arriving at Yale College in 1858 with $4.68 and two small carpetbags, he distinguished himself by resolutely and successfully opposing the freshman hazing system. Upon receiving his degree, he married the remarkable Isadora Hull, a woman of notable independence herself: when their marriage ended in divorce some fifteen years later, she studied medicine in New York and Vienna, where she became the first American woman to earn a European diploma for the practice of surgery. But in the 1860s, Isadora and Murray seemed well matched; they shared an enthusiasm for the outdoor life, and she helped support him by teaching school during his theological studies and early Congregational pastorates.

The efforts of a Meriden, Connecticut, lawyer and later United States senator, Orville Platt, assured Murray's call to a Meriden pulpit. He and Platt began taking periodic Adirondack excursions in the immediate postwar period, and Murray's accounts of their camping trips appeared in the *Meriden Weekly Recorder* during the fall and winter of 1867. The following year he was invited to become the minister of Boston's prestigious Park Street Church.

Still under thirty, Murray had passed from professional success to success. The church, celebrated for its graceful spire after Wren, its site, "Brimstone Corner," across from the Common, its history intertwined with William Lloyd Garrison's first abolition address and the patriotic song "America," was a Boston institution. The minister was a Boston institution, too. Among clergymen — and nineteenth-century American clergymen enjoyed a celebrity many a twentieth-century film star might envy — Murray's status rivaled that of the country's best-known divine, Henry Ward Beecher. The handsome Dr. Murray doubtless fluttered feminine pulses; he knew his theology and Scripture, and he was beyond all demur a galvanic preacher whose volumes of edifying sermons, published in the early 1870s, testified to his piety. His tenure at the Park Street Church ought to have been a flawless triumph, but three issues marred it: his populist ideals, his fast horses, and his Adirondacks book.

"The real controversy concerned the proper role of a large metropolitan church," Warder H. Cadbury has declared. Right away, Murray proposed a broader ministry to meet the needs of the poor in a changing urban society. To the finical members of a congregation that had not long before feared for its survival, he seemed innovatory, reckless. "This plea for a more relevant church program was greeted by the [congregation's] more aristocratic and sedate elements with stiffening resistance."

Moreover, the new preacher exhibited a zest for horseflesh unseemly in a man of the cloth. He had been reared on a farm and loved horses, recognized their fine points, didn't mind racing, and lavished on his stable the same pride of possession a present-day adolescent might demonstrate toward his first car. Again the conservative elements of the Park Street congregation bristled.

If the Adirondacks volume hadn't achieved overnight nationwide notoriety, the parishioners might have accommodated themselves to their minister's progressive views and his high-stepping trotters. Respectability, by ironic coincidence, was one of Murray's motives in publishing his hunting and fishing tales. Moving to Boston, he had been told that publishing a book with Ticknor & Fields ought to lend him the cachet necessary for proper Bostonian recognition. The minister at Park Street should fraternize with Holmes, Longfellow, and Parkman. Although the prospect from the slopes of the New England Parnassus was agreeable, Murray lacked literary ambitions; for all his idiosyncrasies, his pretensions were few. The office of James T. Fields was opposite the church, though, and, recalling the newspaper pieces from Meriden, Murray gathered a sheaf of clippings from a desk drawer and strolled across Tremont Street.

Fields tried to let Murray down gently. The spring list was already closed, the publisher said, but he would take home the clippings and look them over. Two days later Murray received a hasty summons to Fields's office and heard a prophecy: "This little book, I am confident, is destined to a great career. We have decided to reopen our list this spring and illustrate it in the best manner that time will permit."

Never was publisher more prescient: *Adventures in the Wilderness,* which reached the stores two months later, attained a giddy success. The book sold at the rate of five hundred copies a week; printing after printing poured off the presses. In early July, a Tourist's Edition appeared with a waterproof cover, twelve pages of timetables, and a map tucked inside the end pocket. The railroads gave it as a premium to customers buying round-trip tickets to the Adirondacks. Charles Dickens endorsed Murray's chapter titled "The Ball." "Write eleven more chapters as good and stop, for while the English-speaking people love to laugh you will never be forgotten." The minister of the Park Street Church became famous within weeks not for his exemplary devotions but for his waggish woodsmanship.

What prompted the success of Murray's account? Of the many preceding books on the Adirondacks, some were successful but none had touched his popular chord. According to its introduction, *Adventures* was intended as "a series of descriptive pieces, unencumbered with the ordinary reflections and jottings of a tourist's book, free from the slang of guides, and questionable jokes, and 'bear stories,' with which works of a similar character have to a great extent been filled." He would avoid the excesses of his predecessors, then, and to a great extent he succeeded. Murray's diction is vigorous and unembellished, and notwithstanding its period flourishes, still retains the vital tang of spoken English. Obviously he is an adroit practitioner of the art of the storyteller, introducing suspense, building up to climaxes, keeping the audience wondering what will happen next. The

voice is intimate; Murray puts himself into the text, and his readers identify with him as though he spoke from the flickering
shadows of a campfire. Nor does he sound boastful, because he
gives the lion's share of the credit for doughty angling and hunting feats to his guide, "Honest John" Plumley.

Joel T. Headley had attempted the same relaxed tone, but
Headley's droning, discursive narrative told his reader what one
ought to feel and didn't stir the imagination with dramatic
scenes featuring thunderstorms and loon cries, churning rapids,
and remote lakes stocked with jumbo spotted trout. Headley
could only inform you that he had gone to the woods for mental
refreshment; Murray supplied exact information about outfiting
yourself, what sections to visit, where to stay, how to get there
and select a guide, what to expect from weather, insects, wild
animals — the total experience. Although he felt obliged to gar-
nish fact with entertainment, his guidebook was an innovation.
He had written the first how-to book on the region.

The author of the how-to book is in trouble, alas, when his
formula doesn't produce the desired result. Hitherto, the woods
had seemed uncouth; Murray made them seem domestic, a setting as amenable to civilized pleasures as the croquet green. In
the spring of 1869 he was the sorcerer who had changed a waste-
land into a vacationland; by fall, he was the sorcerer's apprentice. The spring and early summer stampede of "Murray's
Fools" into the Adirondacks swelled into an August retreat like
a shattered army's. The backwoods lacked mass accommodations, hotels were primitive; fees reported in good faith by Murray multiplied; the fish didn't bite, the game scampered away,
guides proved venal, torrential rains lashed the mountains, and
roughing it brought out the worst, as it always has, in tourists
with unreasonable expectations.

Their stories of their experiences took perverse pleasure in
horrific detail. Alfred Donaldson relates a typical anecdote — of
the New Yorker who arrives late one night at an overcrowded

hotel and is told there is only one place in the house to sleep: on a decrepit pool table. The next morning he rises painfully and meets the landlord.

> "How much do I owe you?" the New Yorker asks.
> "Lemme see," says the landlord. "What room was you in?"
> "Room!" The guest describes his comfortless night.
> "Five dollars," says the landlord.
> "Five dollars!"
> "Sure thing," says the landlord. "Dollar an hour is the regular charge for the pool table after midnight."

Disillusionment was so widespread and bitter that Murray felt obliged to defend himself. He had not been captivated by his fools any more than they had been captivated by each other. "Early in July, a swarm of people rushed into the Adirondacks," he wrote in a letter to Horace Greeley's *New York Tribune* that autumn. "It was a motley crowd, indeed." Among them he discerned city swells carrying kid gloves and rattan canes, workmen from the Troy iron foundries, toffs with English suits and monocles, rowdies galore.

> Several hundred people of this character rushed to the woods in the first half of July. They took Martin by storm [of Martin's inn on Lower Saranac, at the terminus of the stagecoach route from Keeseville, Murray had written, "At his house you can easily and cheaply obtain your entire outfit for a trip of any length. Here it is that the celebrated Long Lake guides with their unrivalled boats, principally resort. Here, too, many of the Saranac guides, some of them surpassed by none, make their headquarters"]; and introduced the habits of Newport and Whitehall, Broadway and the Bowery, to the hitherto retired and peaceful region of Lower Saranac. The character and breeding of these classes are best ascertained from their inscriptions on the hotel register. Coarse expressions, vulgar quotations, some of them in a feminine hand, and not a little profanity testify to their character and position at home.

The Reverend Mr. Murray felt offended; the sportsman in him was dismayed by the outcries of hunters and fishermen, veterans of the Adirondacks for over a quarter century, whose wilderness was violated. Worse still, indignant letters to the editor accused Murray of misrepresenting the region's therapeutic qualities and luring chronic invalids to their doom. Unquestionably Murray's claims were sweeping: "The amount of venison steak a consumptive will consume after a week's residence in that appetizing atmosphere is a subject of daily and increasing wonder," or "Acquainted as I am with many ladies, some of them accustomed to every luxury, and of delicate health, who have 'camped out' in this wilderness, I have yet to meet with a single one who ever 'caught cold,' or experienced any other inconvenience to the bodily health in the woods." It was bad enough to be called a liar, a cleric given to the exaggerations of the tall tale; it was profoundly disturbing to read letters that charged him with murder, however inadvertent. A peremptory voice raised in Murray's defense was that of the author and traveler Kate Fields, who went to Raquette Lake and addressed the *Tribune*, "If consumptives with both legs in the grave visit the Adirondacks, and after a few days or weeks leave the woods somewhat less alive than when they entered, surely their friends display the most extraordinary absence of reason in attributing their decease to Mr. Murray's book." The tone may have been acerb, but the lady was angry.

A host of similar guidebooks soon streamed onto the market, along with parodies and near-imitations. *Adventures* expressed the edgy confidence of a new spirit of middle-class play; in the postwar boom there was opulence, yet people also felt the increasing pressures of industrialism; they needed refuges from nervous tension. In terms of Murray's career, however, the impact of his Adirondacks book was unhappy; he embarked on lecture tours, the schism with his conservative parishioners widened, while his marriage tottered. During the 1870s he devoted his energies to his stock farm; in 1873, he published *The Perfect*

Horse with a prudent introduction by the Reverend Henry Ward Beecher. The following year Murray resigned from Park Street and organized his own independent Congregational assembly. The move was successful, as was *The Golden Rule,* the weekly newspaper in which he published his sermons and his tales of Trapper John Norton, a fictional replica of "Honest John" Plumley. Then, taking a leave of absence from preaching, he designed "The Murray Buckboard," overextended his capital to finance his vehicle, and, hounded by creditors, left Boston. This coincided with the collapse of his marriage. Emotionally drained, he tried travel, ranching in Texas, the lumber business — an odd choice for a man vehement about the destructive effects of lumbering on the Adirondacks — and ultimately settled in a dogleg street of Montreal as the proprietor of an oyster bar.

> A large man with a mane of iron-gray hair and a drooping iron-gray mustache [his presence impressed many a former parishioner]. His massive frame denoted great physical strength but also carried the suggestion of waning vitality — a weariness that appeared also in his voice, which was like the soft deep tones of an organ floating out at dusk from the shadowy depths of an old cathedral.

Ultimately he remarried and came home to Connecticut, and the final years of his life were spent in writing and in performing on the lyceum circuit, where his specialty was his elocutionary rendition of the tale, "The Dear Old Trapper, John Norton, and How He Kept His Christmas," which had originally appeared in a special illustrated Christmas supplement to *Harper's Weekly.* The paperback edition of the story, issued by the Murray Lyceum Bureau, was peddled in the lobby or foyer of the theaters, churches, and halls on his lyceum circuit.

Murray maintained his interest in outdoor life. Indian lore became a hobby of his Canadian period, and when Buffalo Bill's Wild West Show played Montreal, Adirondack Murray was featured as a guest star with Sitting Bull. They were photographed together, the minister and the medicine man, and each signed autographs for a public to whom they represented a vanished past, the idyllic Adirondacks of Murray's heyday and the plains belonging to the Sioux. Later, after Sitting Bull's death at the hands of American troops, Murray wrote a stinging letter of condemnation to the *New York World*. He had always upheld humane principles, and the tragedies of history did not invalidate them. Dickens was right: Murray introduced a magnanimous spirit into the wilds, a stately innocence larger than any claims he might advance. Barnstorming the circuit of theaters, opera houses, and lyceums of small-town New England, where he recited "Dear Old John Norton," did his thoughts ever stray to his former wife in her Viennese surgery? Probably not. As he repeated his rhetorical gestures for the five hundredth time, however, he may well have recalled the festive Adirondack days in which his program originated: "We were seven in all — as jolly a set of fellows as ever rollicked under the pines, or startled the owls with laughter, that summer of '67, when camping on the Raquette."

A less companionable clergyman spent the winter of 1877–78 trying to mend his health in the village of Saranac Lake. The Reverend John Patterson Lundy of Philadelphia was an Episcopalian who, during his diaconate, had been the chaplain of the state prison at Sing Sing. The prison experience was merely a prelude to his Saranac winter. Dr. Lundy unquestionably preferred Sing Sing.

As a result of his Saranac ordeal, however, he issued in 1880 a privately printed volume titled *The Saranac Exiles, A Winter's Tale of the Adirondacks*, "not by W. Shakespeare." The book, dedicated to Lundy's wife, carries the epigraph, "Pray that your flight be not in winter," and while it is in many respects a bizarre performance, it supplies the only eyewitness account of the village before it became an internationally known sanatorium.

Lundy felt himself superior to his provincial environment,

and his book, offered as a corrective to Murray, overflows with the spleen of a cultivated man obliged to endure the company of yokels. Because of his combative nature, Lundy is not infrequently ill-humored, but when he isn't heavy-handed he often displays a mordant facetiousness. There wasn't much choice between Saranac Lake, as he saw it, and the prehistoric forests out of which it sprang. A bird's-eye view of the territory (it is difficult not to imagine Dr. Lundy suspended above Saranac like a mousing owl) would have disclosed before the 1850s only the pine tops bent by the prevailing easterlies, and afterward a cluster of huts, houses, and two diminutive schools. The outlines of a community had emerged by Lundy's time.

"The miserable hamlet of Saranac Lake — its present name twice changed from that of Baker's and Harrietstown, as if the people were ashamed of having it long known under one appellation — consists of about fifty or sixty log and frame-houses," he complained. (In fact, the name of the village was never changed once the post office was established in 1854. The name Saranac was said to have been applied to the Saranac River by the Banaka or St. Francis tribe of Indians, whose hunting grounds were south of Montreal and who are recorded as making annual pilgrimages to the Saranac for a necessary ingredient of their war paint, the red sumac berries along the river's banks. The Indians supposedly gave the word — which meant sumac — a liquid pronunciation; but linguists also speculate that Saranac might be a corruption of the French, Saint Armand's.)

It is in a little deep basin of hills on every side of it, on the main branch of the Saranac River, a few miles from its leaving the lower lake of that name, and one mile below Martin's. It is nearly forty miles distant from the terminus of the branch railroad from Plattsburg to Ausable, and is reached by daily stage. The Montreal Telegraph Company has a station here from which dispatches can be sent anywhere. It is this sheltered position of the place in winter, this daily stage and the telegraph that have given

Saranac Lake its main attraction to invalids, aside from the pure invigorating mountain air.

It has two country stores of the usual heterogeneous assortment of coarse dry-goods, boots and shoes, groceries, hardware, and quack medicines, but no books or magazines. An old rickety saw-mill supplies the place and neighborhood with building materials; and a steam-mill occasionally makes shingles and clapboards. There is also a small gristmill; one shoemaker but no tailor. The barber of the place is a peripatetic on crutches, going from house to house or from room to room on call, to discharge his tonsorial duties and do the main headwork of the community at the rate of twenty-five cents for each clipping and manipulation. . .

To the everlasting honor of Saranac Lake, it must be said that it has no lawyers or newspaper editors to do the mischievous and harassing headwork of keeping the community in an uproar of needless excitement and agitation. No newsboys din your ears to deafness or startle your nervous sensibilities by their loud shrill cries and startling announcements; no lawyers plot for fat fees or manufacture bogus cases; all is peace and quietness. Far distant Malone, the county-town of Franklin and the residence of lawyer, Vice-President Wheeler, is rather the place of these tumultuous cries and harassing trials. . .

Saranac Lake has one flourishing tavern, whose landlord, it is needless to say, is the richest man in the place; and who, publican and sinner as he is, gave us the choice of a half-acre lot on which to erect our church. A traditional blacksmith shop and two large boarding houses, of which "The Berkeley," our home, was one, complete the list of attractions in our immediate environment.

Patently the Reverend Dr. Lundy was not W. Shakespeare, even though he addressed "all Saranac Exiles, past, present, and future, whose winter experience is sure to be, Reader, not As You Like It." The words *liars, drunkards, thieves,* and *rascals* pepper his recollections, and he returned to Saranac only once, briefly in July for the consecration of the Church of St. Luke the Beloved Physician, shortly before the Philadelphia publication of his book. During his winter's stay, Dr. Lundy held services in the parlor of The Berkeley, which, with its lazy porches, tall chimneys, and mansard roof, remained a landmark of downtown Saranac until it was destroyed by fire more than a century later. At Lundy's suggestion, the proprietors named it for Bishop George Berkeley, the Irish philosopher, who proposed that nothing exists unless it is perceived.

Among the satires following upon Murray's volume, a *Harper's New Monthly Magazine* cartoon captioned "Before and after going into the Adirondacks" shows a consumptive, knock-kneed fop carrying a carpetbag (before) and a stalwart and tanned stripling carrying a fisherman's rod and his catch (after). The cartoon might well have been used as a straightforward illustration for Murray's most controversial pages — early on, where no one could miss the incident — describing a consumptive young man cured by the mountain air and the aromas of the forest. About to meet his guide, he is too enfeebled to walk. Another guide, "feeling that one so near death as he was should be gratified even in his whims," arranges a boat "half-filled with cedar, pine, and balsam boughs," and the young man is placed at full length upon them. Then, with the guide in the stern, the little boat, like some mysterious bark plying between two worlds, vanishes among the islands of a dark lake.

> The first week the guide carried the young man on his back over all the portages, lifting him in and out of the boat as he might a child. But the healing properties of the balsam and pine, which were his bed by day and night, began to exert their power. Awake or asleep, he inhaled their fragrance. Their pungent and healing odors penetrated his diseased and irritated lungs. The second day out his cough was less sharp and painful. At the end of the first week he could walk by leaning on his paddle. The second week he needed no support. The third week the cough ceased entirely. From that time he improved with wonderful rapidity. He "went in" the first of June, carried in the arms of his guide. The second

week of November he "came out" bronzed as an Indian, and as hearty. In five months he had gained sixty-five pounds. . . . The wilderness received him almost a corpse. It returned him to his home and the world as happy and healthy a man as ever bivouacked under its pines.

No passage in Murray excited warmer dispute: he insisted every detail was true, and pointed to his wife as corroboration, "the color of whose cheek, and the clear brightness of whose eye, cause my heart to go out in ceaseless gratitude to the woods, amid which she found that health and strength of which they are the proof and sign." After the summer of the "Murray Rush," however, readers placed the young man's miraculous cure in the same yarning category as the supernatural Indian maid who appeared at twilight and beckoned to fishermen, or the "Butternut Falls" Murray claimed he shot in a guide boat. Curiously enough, like the cartoon in *Harper's,* he was relating a literal event. The story proved clairvoyant. Four years after the publication of *Adventures,* the incident took place, and it followed Murray in every particular: the young man who had come to the woods to die, the boat heaped with balsam branches, the extraordinary return from the dark shore.

CHAPTER THREE

Return from the Dark Shore
1873

FOR GENERATIONS, as many as could be traced, doctors of medicine had embellished his mother's family tree. Playfulness, elegance, and aestheticism had distinguished his father's forebears from easygoing New Orleans. Dr. Edward Livingston Trudeau remembered his maternal grandfather, Dr. François Eloi Berger, a French physician, deploring the flair for caricature demonstrated by his son-in-law, Dr. James Trudeau. Studying medicine in New York, "he made a set of statuette caricatures of the medical faculty, which were so well done and such telling caricatures that many of the gentlemen never forgave him." The talent remained in the Trudeau family: Dr. James's great-great-grandson, Garry, is known to a national audience of present-day newspaper readers as the creator of the popular "Doonesbury" comic strip. Edward Livingston Trudeau — though he scarcely had time for either — preferred collecting art to inventing it, and for years kept on his desk a photograph (eventually replaced by an edition of the bronze) of *Gloria victis* by the French artist Marius Jean Antonin Mercié. A typical late-Victorian salon piece combining a didactic lesson, pseudohistorical allusion, and muffled erotic undertones, the statuette may at any moment be resurrected as an example of eclectic postmodernist taste: Dr. Trudeau prized it for its allegory. Mercié had designed the intimate bronze in 1871 as commentary on the outcome of the Franco-Prussian War, but the figures were generalized enough to serve as archetypes. A young half-clothed Roman gladiator has just received a fatal blow. As he falls, broken sword in hand, an angry winged female figure of Victory swoops down and, draperies aswirl, bears him aloft. The message is unmistakable; we may endure material defeat, yet the authentic triumphs of life reside in the spirit. Trudeau, grappling with the invincible powers of tuberculosis, heard a sympathetic echo.

Like intrepid Victory, he was subject to passionate emotional extremes. His contemporaries, who wrote numerous accounts of his personal charm and tonic effect on people, sometimes allude to his darker moments. He could support the spirit of a dying man or woman as valiantly as the winged Victory, and then, completing his task, lapse into unshakable depression. You might see him in one of these moods, ask how he was, and receive a litany of complaint; the next day you might confide how miserable you were, whereupon his compassion would emerge like a sun, and you would find yourself basking in his solicitude, humor, and assurance. Friends learned to assess his emotional swings. The nature of the situation affected these: when all was lost Trudeau was at his best; when he confronted or assumed the catastrophes of others, he was indomitable; but when the fight seemed half-won or when he brooded over his desperate endeavor, then the hopelessness of the odds seized him and he faltered. He had no miracle cure. He knew the causes of tuberculosis, but could not end its sway of suffering. To conquer the disease he had only his conviction that someday he would prevail.

His great-grandfather Zenon Trudeau, lieutenant governor of upper Louisiana under the Spanish flag from 1792 to 1799, had played an important role in the European exploration of the North American continent. Interested in the expansion of the fur trade, he organized, in 1794, an expedition led by Jean-Baptiste Truteau, a schoolteacher from St. Louis described by the governor as a kinsman, although he spelled his name differently. Truteau was charged with exploiting the fur trade, investigating the sources of the upper Missouri, and penetrating "beyond to the Southern Ocean," as the Pacific was then called; and the governor's instructions also directed Truteau to keep a journal. The venture, divided by jealousies and desertions, showed no profit, but for a year and a half Truteau faithfully maintained the journal, which provided an accurate account of the Indian tribes and conditions along the route; this ultimately came to the attention of Thomas Jefferson in the White House. Jefferson sent extracts from it to Captain Meriwether Lewis in 1803, and a translation of the entire account in 1804, and thus the Trudeau undertaking became the direct precursor of the Lewis and Clark expedition.

The Trudeau men reveled in the outdoor life and the lore and traditions of the hunt. When, in 1873, Edward Livingston Trudeau came to the Adirondacks to die, he was bidding farewell to memories of hunting and fishing at the Saranac Lakes; his father, James deBertz Trudeau, had been an equally fervent sportsman. With his close friend John James Audubon, he completed many scientific and fine arts projects, and he accompanied Audubon on the expedition to the Rockies led by John C. Frémont in 1842. Audubon named the White-winged Dove for Trudeau, but the name has been dropped for this bird. It survives, however, in Trudeau's Tern, the type specimen of which Trudeau secured for Audubon. In his *Ornithological Biography* (1839) Audubon remarks,

> This beautiful tern, which has not hitherto been described, was procured at Great Egg Harbour in New Jersey, by my much esteemed and talented friend, J. Trudeau Esq. of Louisiana, to whom I have great pleasure in dedicating it. Nothing is known of its range, or even the particular habits in which it may differ from other species. The individual obtained was in the company of a few others of the same kind. I have received from Mr. Trudeau an intimation of the occurrence of several individuals [also] on Long Island.

"The love of wild nature and of hunting was a real passion with my father," Edward observed in his *Autobiography*, "— a passion which ruined his professional career in New Orleans, for he was constantly absent on hunting expeditions."

James Trudeau assisted Audubon by drawing detailed and dexterous illustrations of birds and eggs and, as anatomist, by preparing ornithological specimens. During Frémont's return journey, James left the expedition and lived for two years with the Osage Indians. Surprisingly, he was an invited guest. Years before, Zenon Trudeau, sailing the Mississippi aboard his governor's barge, had rescued an Osage chief found wounded on the riverbank after a tribal skirmish. Brought to the Trudeau plantation in New Orleans and restored to health, the chief proved equal to such romantic circumstances and vowed perpetual gratitude. The delegation of Osage braves who parlayed with Frémont immediately recognized James Trudeau's name (or perhaps even retained memories of Truteau) and he accepted their hospitality. "He always mentioned that his stay with the tribe had been most agreeable and enjoyable, affording him an opportunity to study their customs and manners, learn their language (which he spoke quite fluently) and an ability to ride and use their arms as they did."

Upon his departure, the squaws of the tribe presented him with an embroidered Osage ceremonial costume, and he soon posed in it for a portrait by Audubon. The psychological picture of James that also emerges from his roving, however, does not inspire confidence: domesticity was not his forte. Shortly after Edward Livingston Trudeau's birth, in October 1848, James separated from his wife, Céphise, the only daughter of Dr. Berger. She fetched her young boys to Paris, where in time she obtained a divorce and remarried. (Edward's older sister stayed in New Orleans.) James also remarried, continued to hunt and fish, served as a Confederate officer briefly, commanding Island No. 10 of New Orleans's defenses, and in the postwar era practiced medicine for a few years before his death.

Edward and his brother Francis, now reared by their grand-parents, attended the Lycée Bonaparte. Their English grew rusty, yet they sympathized with the Union cause, and Edward's finest childhood hour struck when Mason and Slidell, the Con-federate envoys of *Trent* case fame, arrived in Paris. As Slidell proceeded through the Champs-Élysées, Edward whipped out a slingshot and bounced a chunk of putty off the diplomat's broad back. Slidell, a stout, florid man with a large white mustache, uttered a roar and gave pell-mell pursuit. The boy was fright-ened enough to have fled, but the violence of the unexpected response took him by surprise. Slidell grabbed him by the coat collar and began thrashing him with an umbrella; Edward des-perately wriggled out of the coat and dashed home. Within days the story had circulated, and Edward was taken to the U.S. Em-bassy, where he received a cordial greeting, "So you are the young man who shot at Mr. Slidell on neutral territory."

It is tempting but perhaps overwrought to interpret Trudeau's slingshot in terms of parental revenge, the reflexive defiance of a deserted son toward a father-figure soldiering for the South. Whether or not the chase in the Champs-Élysées signified more than a backfiring prank, Edward's Parisian days were numbered. His grandfather's health was failing, so the family left France and settled among New York relatives. The war was over, and at seventeen Edward had to relearn English and adjust to Ameri-can manners. Moreover, he must decide on a career; his older brother was already employed in a business office. An influential uncle promised to secure him an appointment to the U.S. Naval Academy, and accordingly, Edward was packed off to a naval preparatory school in Newport, Rhode Island, where midship-men were then trained aboard the historic frigate *Constitution.*

He never settled down to his nautical studies, for almost im-mediately, in September 1865, Francis Berger Trudeau, the brother whose health had always been impaired by a heart con-dition and who more and more had come to depend on Edward, developed unmistakable symptoms of tuberculosis. Before the institutionalization of medicine this meant round-the-clock home nursing: Edward immediately threw up his appointment and devoted himself to his brother's care.

Each day and night of that harrowing fall, Edward Trudeau watched Francis fight for breath. The literature of tuberculosis abounds in images of air; and tuberculosis symptoms, as Susan Sontag observes in her book on the mythology of TB and cancer, *Illness as Metaphor,* were regarded by the nineteenth century as testimony of the spiritualized consciousness. Tuberculosis was a disease of febrile passions that consumed the body and the body's burden of original sin. The struggle for breath took place at the border of the corporeal and the otherworldly. The lesions of the disease might appear in any organ, but consumption primarily remained localized in the lungs and, notwithstanding its clinical manifestations, seemed to lend its victims a mystical aura. Legend is a by-product, it would appear, of incurable illness; controllable disease rapidly loses its mystery. The long vigils affected Edward like Dickens's funereal cadences in *Nicholas Nickleby:*

> There is a dread disease which so prepares its victim, as it were, for death; which so refines it of its grosser aspect, and throws around familiar looks, unearthly indications of the coming change — a dread disease, in which the struggle between soul and body is so gradual, quiet and solemn, and the result so sure, that day by day, and grain by grain, the mortal part wastes and withers away, so that the spirit grows light and sanguine with its lightening load, and feeling immortality at hand, deems it but a new term of mortal life.

Victorian sentimentality drew the line at documentary realism, the stench, the squalor, and the agony of the sickroom. The situation of the Trudeau brothers that fall reiterated the situation of the Keats brothers forty-seven years before: John Keats, devotedly nursing his dying brother, had followed accepted medical wisdom in keeping the windows of the sickroom tightly shut, and, like the poet, Edward Trudeau probably became infected in the same airless confinement.

> We occupied the same room and sometimes the same bed. I bathed him and brought his meals to him, and when he felt well enough to go downstairs I carried him up and down on my back, and I tried to amuse and cheer him through the long days of fever and sickness. My sister and grandmother often sat with him in the daytime and allowed me to go out for exercise and change, but he soon become very dependent upon me and I had to be with him day and night. The doctor called once a week to see him and usually left some new cough medicine, but the cough grew steadily worse. Not only did the doctor never advise any precautions to protect me against infection, but he told me repeatedly never to open the windows, as it would aggravate the cough; and I never did, until toward the end my brother was so short of breath that he asked for fresh air.

Sustained by cups of green tea, Edward watched his brother around the clock while the waning light of autumn washed into darkness. Francis died two days before Christmas. Edward's immediate response was one of relief. Later he would witness countless deathbed scenes, but none would affect him so profoundly. It was "the first great sorrow" of a life destined to be spent "in the midst of a perpetual epidemic of tuberculosis," and he never forgot his vigils or his brother's pleas. So painful was the memory that, describing Francis's death in the *Autobiography,* Edward could not bring himself to set down his brother's name. The formal and abstract "my brother" distances those nights punctuated by coughing and pleas for air, when Edward no doubt wished for — and probably paid the price of personal guilt — the end of the ordeal.

He resolved to make his future role a fraternal commemoration, but how? From time to time he halfheartedly launched a career, three months in the School of Mines of Columbia College, a stint in a broker's office. It was a relief not to remember the strain of Francis's last months. Time passed quickly; Trudeau was too well connected for the vulgarities of trade or the vanities of public life. Although his trust fund was insufficient for more than clothes and spending money, he frequented the circles of his prosperous, socially prominent cousins, the Livingstons, maintained membership in the Union Club, and cut a figure — a man about town indistinguishable from dozens of other polished hedonists constitutionally incapable of earning a livelihood. Tall and spare, with aquiline features, muttonchop whiskers, and a somewhat prominent forehead, he took pains with creases and buttons and might have stepped out of a novel of manners by Henry James or William Dean Howells, a young man of intelligence and breeding, unable to commit himself to an orthodox future. Yet there was a commitment, for, through a cousin, Trudeau had met and fallen in love with Charlotte ("Lottie") Beare, the slender, blonde daughter of an Episcopalian clergyman from Douglaston, Long Island. To Lottie he would always ascribe his later renown, and it was she who set him thinking about medicine in the early fall of 1868. His announcement that he was about to enroll as a medical student at the College of Physicians and Surgeons (now a part of Columbia) was greeted with gleeful incredulity at his club. One member proposed a bet, five hundred dollars that Trudeau would never graduate, but found no takers.

The College of Physicians and Surgeons, on the corner of Twenty-third Street and Fourth Avenue, was a shabby brick building with a drugstore and an ice cream parlor tucked in the basement. Matriculation at the college was effortless. Upon payment of five dollars the prospective doctor was registered; he would then attend two or more courses of lectures and undergo the brief oral examinations that each professor gave the members of the graduating class in his own subject. Then the graduate would serve a three-year apprenticeship with a practicing physician and go forth on his own.

Having enrolled, Trudeau returned to his rooms carrying a crisp copy of *Gray's Anatomy* and a brown-paper parcel containing two polished human bones given him to study. The first he identified on sight as an arm bone; the other, which resembled the flange of a propeller, was baffling. A search through *Gray* led him to the conclusion it must be a shoulder blade, and he began to memorize the musculature. The erstwhile playboy was acceding to the man of science.

Trudeau's medical education was sound enough by late nineteenth-century American standards, but he always felt conscious of its shortcomings. The curriculum relied heavily on descriptive techniques, doctors and students analyzed theories of the causation of disease, and the lecturer stood in front of a wall chart and flourished a wooden pointer. The charts in particular impressed Trudeau. They were hung just before the entry of the speaker by a teacher's pet, executing his humble task beneath a fusillade of cigarette butts, erasers, and spitballs. "I can see some of the [images] distinctly now, so strong an impression did their exaggerated characteristics make on my mind." The operative word is *see*: he retained an ancestral sensitivity to the visual. The crudeness of the charts, however, duplicated the evident limitations of medicine at a time when personal observation took the place of laboratory technology. The lecturer on tuberculosis, for example, Dr. Alonzo Clark, taught that it was a

> non-contagious, generally incurable and inherited disease, due to inherited constitutional peculiarities, perverted humors and various types of inflammation, and dwelt at length on the different pathological characteristics of tubercle, scrofula, caseation, and pulmonary phthsis, and their classification and relation to each other.

With students the aged but Olympian Dr. Clark, cross-grained, erudite, remorselessly ironic, was unsparing. He became a bugbear of Trudeau's. When a member of the class developed unmistakable symptoms of tuberculosis, Trudeau, keenly sympathetic, plucked up his courage and consulted the resident authority on the disease. Listening intently to the description of the case, Clark rose from his armchair and said, "Tell your friend to go to the mountains and become a stage driver for a few years. Good evening." In other words, there was no hope: Trudeau's classmate might as well drive a stagecoach; but Clark, the dispenser of standard clinical misconceptions, had inadvertently prescribed a course most likely to prove beneficial — open air, nontaxing work, and a favorable climate — though it seems unlikely his advice was followed.

As his medical school career drew toward a close, Trudeau, facing the brief but all-important final oral examination, was unlucky enough to fall again into the inquisitorial hands of Dr. Clark. Misgivings assailed the candidate en route to the old man's Spartan office. Much depended on the outcome. The previous year Miss Beare had permitted Trudeau to announce their engagement. Clark waited in the dusty office, his fur coat flung over his knees.

"My name is Trudeau, sir," Trudeau said.

"I know it."

Trudeau sat down.

"Mr. Trudeau," Dr. Clark began, "what is pain a symptom of?"

Trudeau was taken aback; his imaginary rehearsals of possible exchanges did not include an examination couched in the diction of a Socratic dialogue. Nevertheless, he gathered his wits and began to specify inflammations, neuralgias, and contagions.

Clark said, "You have omitted one long pain."

"Sciatica."

Clark nodded.

"Well, Mr. Trudeau, what is fever a symptom of?"

At length the interview concluded, and Trudeau fled. Upon learning he had passed the test, however, he recovered mightily. The future opened, bright and beckoning. Should he try for a position at the New York Hospital or Bellevue? Lately he had been tiring easily. He had never been quite the same since his walking exploit the year before, but he had allowed himself to be talked into that ridiculous contest out of sheer pride. . .

His cousins, the Livingstons, were at the nub of it, and a bet, the wager of a dinner that he couldn't walk from Central Park to the Battery inside an hour. While no one at the club had been willing to back him as a medical student, his athletic finesse was another matter. The Livingstons knew he could do it; they held golden opinions of Trudeau's ability to walk against time. Granted, he seldom exercised and the long hours of study in medical school had exacted a physical toll, but he had amazing endurance and his storklike legs covered ground with matchless ease.

At midnight they rode in carriages to Fifty-ninth Street. From the carriages floated laughter and chattering voices; the glow of cigars dilated in the darkness, jewelry twinkled against the dull sheen of leather, and as the carriages passed beneath the frosted globes of streetlamps, the gaslight swayed upon brasses, satins, the flanks of horses, and then skimmed away, brief as breath. The processional reached the starting line and Trudeau clambered out. Watches were adjusted; he waited at the curb, lean and bantering, and gradually the chattering died away and the starter began his countdown.

Striding into the night, Trudeau received amiable cheers. The city spread around him, each dark cornice and keystone arch looming beneath the stars, and almost instantly he realized he had made a mistake. He pressed on, his pace forced, and the air tore through his lungs. Near Twenty-third Street he glanced at the façade of the Fifth Avenue Hotel, where the lights burned in a watery red haze. The lights of the hotel, he remembered, were white; he wanted to stop, yet it was impossible to stop, and he paced the final blocks in a muddle of exhaustion and pain until the harbor glimmered ahead, out of plumb. He had covered the distance to the Battery in less than forty-eight minutes and the bets were settled. Was he all right? Fine, fine.

His fatigue did not pass; for several days afterward he felt ill and then consulted a doctor. The examination disclosed a cold abscess beginning to form, but the doctor attributed the abscess to the demands of the walk. In any event the condition was temporary . . .

Miss Beare's father had greeted the news of her engagement without enthusiasm; she was squandering herself on a prodigal; Edward Trudeau's newfound earnestness failed to compensate for his uncertain future. About to graduate, Trudeau decided to become a candidate for the staff of the Strangers' Hospital, a small institution accommodating one hundred twenty patients on Tenth Street, and to his considerable elation qualified as house physician. He was without practical experience. Placed in charge of the wards, forced to improvise when emergencies arose, he acquired valuable experience. Meanwhile he carried on his courtship, and evenings when the pace slackened at the hospital, he rushed to Long Island to spend the time with Lottie.

An evening on Long Island meant a five-mile midnight buggy ride back to Flushing and the one o'clock New York train. Sometimes there might be an emergency when he arrived, an operation or a fracture, and Trudeau would not reach his bed before dawn. Although the lack of sleep and the constant pressure began to wear him down, still his health proved adequate, and he felt overworked but fit. At the end of his six months' tour of duty, in June 1871, his wedding to Miss Beare took place.

It was a large-scale affair, even by late-Victorian upper-class standards. Trudeau's friends arrived from the city on a chartered train. His friend Willie Douglas's yacht *Sappho*, which had successfully defended the America's Cup, stood on the Sound, decked in bunting. After the wedding breakfast, held at Douglas Manor, which was also festooned with signal flags, the reception line shuffled past for some two hours. Amid showers of rice, the newlyweds eventually left through a side door, where Dr. Trudeau's two small mares, white rosettes decorating their harness,

were hitched to a gleaming coupé, with a liveried stableman occupying the driver's seat. Then they were trotting at a smart
pace on the New York turnpike.

The White Mountains, London, and the Continent: in Paris,
Edward showed Lottie his grandfather's Rue Matignon apartment. The porte-cochère and the courtyard remained the same;
the superannuated concierge remembered Edward and his
brother and their playmates, and, introduced to Lottie, exclaimed: *"Ils étaient tout mauvais — mais celui-là!"* Switzerland delighted them, Germany disappointed them, and the climate
bothered Edward in England, where he experienced a mild
swelling of the lymphatic glands in his neck. Before sailing
home, he saw a well-known Liverpool physician. The swollen
glands indicated a run-down condition and tendency to scrofula,
declared the doctor; he prescribed swabbing the patient's throat
with iodine, eating another helping of bacon at breakfast, and
taking a patent medicine containing iron.

Upon their return, they settled into the gatekeeper's cottage
on the Douglas estate. The modest inheritance from Edward's
grandfather and Lottie's family money allowed them to live comfortably, and Edward established a Long Island practice. Their
daughter Charlotte ("Chatte") was born at the Douglas cottage.
Despite his domestic felicity, Edward grew restive: bucolic, or-
chard-studded Long Island, within earshot of the Atlantic surf,
was, after the hurly-burly of the Strangers' Hospital, a kind of
exile. Moreover, this climate was no better for him than London's, for on three occasions he suffered attacks diagnosed as
malarial fever. Everyone came down with it, he was told; the
pastoral beauties of Long Island overshadowed its still extensive
swampland. Trudeau took quinine, which had scant effect.
When, in 1872, he received a partnership offer from his colleague Dr. Fessenden Nott Otis (destined for medical distinction
as the first person to cure urethral stricture), the opportunity
seemed a godsend.

Lottie found and began furnishing a house on West Forty-sixth Street. She was pregnant again, this time with their son, Ned. A hectic routine soon engulfed Trudeau; he was making up to six calls a day for Dr. Nott, attending hospital clinics, and, with his friend Dr. Luis P. Walton, conducting a biweekly Demilt Dispensary class in diseases of the chest. Following the class they also examined patients and prescribed for them, and before long Dr. Walton noticed his associate's haggard appearance. Trudeau assured him it was the result of his indoor rounds; nevertheless Walton insisted on taking a temperature. The 101-degree reading shocked Trudeau, and Walton immediately sat him down and delivered a stern lecture on having a complete physical examination at once. This Trudeau dismissed; he shrugged and smiled at the idea; he was really too busy.

The next day, though, on passing the office of Dr. Edward Gamaliel Janeway on West Fourteenth Street, Trudeau recalled the urgency in Walton's voice. Dr. Janeway was a redoubtable clinician and pathologist who, though he lacked the benefits of a European postgraduate education (then deemed necessary for a progressive physician), still had built up a reputation through observation and study in the wards of Bellevue and the city morgues. Almost on impulse, Dr. Trudeau rang the bell. At least this would stop Walton's scolding.

Janeway greeted him cordially and Trudeau explained he was there as a patient. They already knew each other: Trudeau belonged to the class on physical diagnosis that Janeway conducted at Bellevue. The examination began at once, and Dr. Janeway proceeded through the techniques of mediate auscultation and percussion. When he finished he said nothing.

"Well, Doctor Janeway, you can find nothing the matter?" Trudeau ventured.

Janeway said, "The upper two-thirds of the left lung is involved in an active tuberculous process."

Trudeau, hearing the death sentence, thought of his brother.

I pulled myself together, put as good a face on the matter as I could, and escaped from the office after thanking the doctor for his examination. When I got outside, as I stood on Dr. Janeway's stoop, I felt stunned. It seemed to me the world had suddenly grown dark. The sun was shining, it is true, and the street was filled with the rush and noise of traffic, but to me the world had lost every vestige of brightness.

He slowly proceeded in the direction of West Forty-sixth Street to bring the news to Lottie.

Dr. Janeway advised a winter in the South, an outdoor existence, and horseback riding, but when Edward and Lottie returned from South Carolina in the spring of 1873, he was feverish every day. He resigned his practice; illness left him unnerved and bitter. Lou Livingston, the cousin who had helped arrange the walking match, did his best to amuse Edward and scoured New York in search of diversion. One halcyon day they went out to Long Island, where a trap-shooting match had been arranged between Paul Smith, the Adirondack hotelier, and a stockbroker named Harry Park. Paul Smith was already an Adirondack legend, a brawny middle-aged entrepreneur of charismatic vitality. Born Appolos Smith in Vermont, he had — in the manner of many northern Vermonters — crossed into upper New York State and worked for a time on a canal boat between Lake Champlain and the Hudson River. Though he knew the woods as well as any guide, he preferred the less nomadic pleasures of innkeeping, where his prosperity stemmed from his wife's excellent cookery and his talents as a raconteur. Moreover, he filled and enjoyed a hoary role as the servant superior to his masters, a court jester to city millionaires whom he never tired of chaffing.

On Lower St. Regis Lake, some fifteen miles northwest of the Saranacs, Paul Smith's would grow from a tiny commissary (board and lodging $1.25 a day, no provision for ladies) into a forerunner of the contemporary resort hotel. The other hotels of the region — Baker's, or Martin's in Saranac Lake, where provisions still had to be shipped in from Ausable — were countrified, but Paul Smith's ultimately suggested the palm-court opulence of Saratoga. Only the three-hundred-room Prospect House overlooking Blue Mountain Lake boasted as many conveniences. At the Prospect House each bedroom had electric lights, while a two-story outhouse could be reached from a second-floor, twenty-foot-wide piazza, so that guests on the upper floors would not have to descend to ground level; but for civilized touches like lawn tennis and croquet you couldn't beat Paul Smith's. Opened in 1859, the original seventeen-room building became the nucleus of a five-hundred-room compound. There was a telegraph to keep visitors in touch with their investments, spacious piazzas, ample lawns, billiard tables, pianos, a guide house for sixty or more guides and their boats. (The Adirondack Guide Boat, ideally adapted to glacial ponds and streams, weighed from sixty to eighty pounds, carried two or three persons, and drew only three inches of water. The design would later be refined by William A. Martin of Saranac Lake and T. Edmund Krumholz, a consumptive curing there, but the basic lightness and durability of the craft were already established, and flotillas of guide boats swarmed around Paul Smith's like gondolas plying the Venetian lagoon.)

Trudeau and Livingston had met Paul Smith at his hotel two years before and, like most of his guests, took to him right away. Then a male hunter's stamping ground, the hotel and its facilities were primitive; the inn would soon expand and change character drastically. Charles Hallock, founder of the magazine *Forest and Stream,* visited Paul Smith's during the 1870s and described a social extravaganza different from the rustic simplicity of a few years before:

> ribbons fluttering on the piazzas; silks rustling in dress promenade; ladies in short mountain suits, fresh from an afternoon

picnic; embryo sportsmen in velveteen and corduroys of approved cut, descanting learnedly of backwoods experience; excursion parties returning, laden with trophies of trout and pond lilies; stages arriving top-heavy with trunks, rifle-cases, and hampers, guides intermingling, proffering services, or arranging trips for the morrow.

Although the metamorphosis of Paul Smith's may have been imminent, meantime the lodge remained roughhewn, and the proprietor and his rival, Park, neither of whom had ever shot a bird on the wing before, agreed on a match for one thousand potatoes, followed by a dinner and a general sweepstakes. Each contestant was entered for five dollars. Trudeau gulped a glass of champagne, which immediately went to his head, and he allowed himself to chance the sweepstakes, though he was unfamiliar with shotguns. The match was a handicap: he stood sixteen yards from the traps, while Lou Livingston, a crack shot, stood thirty-two yards away, with other sureshots stretching into the distance. The pigeons were released. Once a contestant missed he went out, with last man collecting the stakes. Trudeau was so weak he could scarcely support the stock of the gun; nevertheless he blazed away and to his amazement won the first two sweepstakes, and, restored by further toasts of champagne, a third. Moved back, he took a fourth round. Never had he shot so well. He proclaimed food and drinks for everyone, retired in triumph, went home, and sank into bed.

The stimulus of the disease allowed him this final gesture, an achievement of the will, but the next day, exhausted, he realized he had used himself up. Doctors urged him to leave for the mountains immediately; he waited until the baby was born in mid-May, and several days later departed despairingly from Lottie, who was still in bed, the infant at her side, while a nurse cradled their daughter in her arms. In the hansom cab, Lou Livingston babbled about the sport they would have at Paul's.

They traveled to Saratoga by train, stayed overnight, and the next day made connections with the Champlain boat at White-hall, reaching Plattsburg by evening. Trudeau felt so feverish he skipped supper at the Fouquet House and went directly to bed. The following morning he was worse, too feeble to attempt the taxing journey into the Adirondacks. The manager of Fouquet's tried to persuade Livingston to take Trudeau back to New York, but when the subject was broached Trudeau responded so vehemently that Livingston decided to push ahead as planned.

Forty-two miles over punishing corduroy roads lay beyond the iron mines of Ausable Forks. Livingston hired a double-hitch wagon, placed a board between the seats, and arranged the wagon so that Trudeau could rest on a mattress. They left the town and followed the rutted road beside the sunlit bends and boulders of the Ausable River, wagon wheels jolting on half-buried logs. Livingston swayed against the driver, smoked a pipe, and occasionally accepted a nip from the driver's flask; Trudeau endured the teeth-jarring bumps as best he could. The trip seemed to lurch from one redoubtable slope after another, and the wagon shook as it labored upward.

Toward sunset they caught sight of the tapering shadows of the tall pines around Paul Smith's. Guides who had been yarning on the front steps rose and greeted the wagon. Livingston jumped down from his seat, but Trudeau was unable to do more than extend a hand to stalwart Fred Martin in the vanguard. "I'm sick," he said in a husky whisper. The subsequent moments belong to Adirondack lore: Martin scooped up the invalid and, carrying him in his arms, bounded up two flights of stairs, two steps at a time, flung open the door of Trudeau's room, and lowered him onto the bed. "Why, doctor," he said, "you don't weigh no more than a dried lamb-skin," and they both broke into laughter.

Warren Flanders, the guide assigned Dr. Trudeau, came into the room after breakfast and said he had fixed up a guide boat real comfortable. The boat was filled with balsam boughs and blankets and Flanders put Trudeau's rifle on the boughs. If the doctor felt up to it, they would row "kind of slow" to Keese's Mill.

It was a soft June day: Trudeau lay on the heaped balsam while the misery of the past weeks subsided in the sky and the glinting lake. Suddenly Flanders dragged his oar and the boat swung sideways. About two hundred yards ahead, onshore, browsed a buck and a doe. Unable to sit erect, Trudeau rested his rifle on the gunwale. He squeezed the trigger and the shot fluttered the leaves. "Let us go after the deer," Emerson had exclaimed. On the point of submitting to death, the hunted Trudeau became the hunter.

The boat was moored and Warren Flanders jumped ashore to load the dead buck.

From that moment Trudeau's health improved. The fever ceased and he began to eat and sleep. Later he would ascribe his recovery to the essential value of rest, for he often spent the entire day fishing or watching for deer from his balsam-laden guide boat. Recumbent in the stern, he drifted over the lake half in reverie until a tug on his fishing line roused him. Lottie's letters gave assurances that all on Long Island was tranquil; at the end of July, however, Livingston had to return to the city. They parted, unaware they would meet afterward only sporadically, and Livingston's place as companion and male nurse was assumed by E. H. Harriman, then a clerk but dreaming of railroads and empire, and in September by another Livingston cousin, James. At the end of September, Trudeau decided he was well enough to rejoin his family. Fifteen pounds heavier, thanks to Mrs. Smith's culinary prowess, sunburnt and ebullient, he embraced Lottie.

Of course he was not cured, he would never be cured; during his remaining forty-two years Trudeau would live with the disease and suffer demoralizing setbacks. Always in danger, he was never sure when tuberculosis would flare up again and whether or not he would survive.

> Of late years on several occasions I have been taken to Paul Smith's from Saranac Lake in the spring so ill that my life was despaired of; and yet little by little while lying out under the great trees, looking out on the lake all day, my fever has stopped and my strength slowly begun to return [he wrote in his *Autobiography* during his final year. This pattern was recurrent]. Last spring — 1914 — at Saranac Lake I was so ill and weak that I had ceased, for the first time in my life, even to care to live any longer. I arrived at Paul Smith's at the end of June on a mattress which had been placed in the automobile of a good friend, and the same feeling of hope and courage came back when I was carried up to my airy porch in the little cottage with the stillness of the great forest all about me, the lake shimmering in the sunlight, and a host of recollections of many happy days and many good friends crowding in on me from every side. Again imperceptibly the fever began to fall, and strength — and with it the desire to live — to return. During the previous two months in the spring at Saranac Lake I did not want to live from day to day; much less did I ever dream I should be willing to live over again in retrospect the long years of the past and write about them.

When, however, the disease reasserted itself in the autumn of 1873, after the idyllic summer at Paul Smith's, doctors prescribed wintering in St. Paul, Minnesota. The climate would prove therapeutic and the city, despite its frigidity, enjoyed an unusually large proportion of sunny days. Trudeau went, but did not improve; spring found him almost as enfeebled as he had been the previous year. Once more he sought out the Adirondacks and took his family with him to Paul Smith's — a move regarded morosely by guests opposed to changing the tone of the establishment. That summer, though, the miracle was not repeated. He was re-examined with discouraging results and decided on a desperate course — to stay through the winter. Tired of moving from place to place, he preferred to take his chances and, if he worsened, to die in congenial surroundings.

Lottie said she and the children would winter with him. It was a decision of considerable boldness, since they would be almost as isolated as polar explorers. The hotel normally closed in October. Paul, his wife, their three small boys, and a hired man and woman staffed the otherwise empty building, but no outsider had ever passed a winter at St. Regis Lake. The nearest doctor was at Plattsburg, sixty miles distant over primitive forest roads. A telegraph wire connected them with the outside world, though the summer operator had gone. Mail was carried in a stage sleigh to Saranac Lake and the Bloomingdale branch post office ten miles away and collected once a week by a guide on snowshoes. And Paul Smith himself, survivor of the cruel Adirondack winter, strongly opposed the idea.

In the end he relented, and at that point, when plans seemed settled, the Trudeaus, like many a young couple before them, had to reschedule everything around a mother-in-law's visit. Céphise Berger Trudeau Chuffart and her husband lived in a Fontainebleau cottage; she was, not surprisingly, distressed by reports of her son's health and wrote to announce that she was boarding the next steamer for a visit of a month or six weeks. This required rearrangements: Lottie and the children would go to Long Island, where they would visit her father, while Edward's mother spent the time at Paul Smith's; then they would rendezvous at Malone, which had rail connections for Madame Chuffart on her return journey.

The Trudeaus, mother and son, spent an uneventful, pleasant holiday from the end of November to the middle of January, when Edward hitched his mare to a cutter and they skimmed across the forty miles to Malone. The silence of the landscape, their shadows upon the sparkling snow, the ice-fringed streams, the bluish tint of distant peaks, the fox's bark ringing through the firs, proved so compelling they could almost forget they were in uninhabited country, bundled in furs, and dependent on the horse's stamina. The element of nonthreatening danger, how-ever, heightened their pleasure in their undeniably picturesque surroundings. Had the mare stumbled or the temperature turned, the raw circumstances of survival would have inter-vened; but it was delightful to pass through this space with its trembling slivers of pine-screened light, as though they were spectators inside a composition of Cole or Bierstadt, paying trib-ute to virgin nature.

They reached Malone before dusk. The next day Lottie ar-rived and Madame Chuffart greeted her grandchildren for the first and last time. The weather did not cooperate: the sky was grim and the wind rising, and when her train pulled into the depot and they said good-bye, flakes swarmed in the locomo-tive's headlight. All night the snow fell and the next morning lay in deep blowing drifts throughout the town. Fortunately Paul Smith and a teamster by the name of Brink had driven to Ma-lone earlier; the logistics of transporting a Victorian family from one place to another required close coordination. The children and their nurses rode in Paul Smith's sleigh, Brink drove a lum-ber sled on which the trunks were lashed, while Edward and Lottie followed in the cutter.

Because of the snow and a delay in starting they decided to halt overnight at the Duane Farm, a country hotel fourteen miles from Malone. As the small procession set out that after-noon and the houses of the town dropped behind the ever-greens, Edward noticed it was growing colder. The temperature failed to worry him, everyone was in high spirits, the horses fresh. Their progress, however, impeded by drifts, was slow. The straining horses soon glistened with lather; more often than not the Trudeaus trudged alongside the mare.

By four o'clock, darkness was closing in and the snow was fall-ing once more. Edward wondered how far they had to walk, then saw the teams ahead had halted. Paul and Brink were tram-pling the snow on a steep hill ahead of the horses. Strenuous as these efforts proved, the path blurred almost as quickly as they could stamp, but Paul and Brink urged the horses up the indistinct track. The teams wallowed among drifts. A glittering wind swept off the ridge, bleaching the horses. Half-blinded, Edward and Lottie groped through the icy haze. The children began to cry, and the nurses, catching their panic, wailed. Paul Smith fought his way to the cutter and, with the wind snatching away his words, said the hill was solid with snow, they must get the children to shelter right away. He and Brink would shovel a cave in the drift and put the family inside, unhitch the horses and lead them over the hill. "We can leave the trunks where they are," Paul shouted and, imperturbable as always, gave the doctor a wink. "I don't think anyone will steal them trunks before morning."

The ice-sheathed horses were blanketed. From the baggage sled the two men took shovels and hollowed out a cavern in the drift away from the wind. Lined with robes the refuge was snug enough, and there the family huddled like Eskimos while Paul and Brink stumbled back and forth through the bitter twilight. Each led a horse to the top, returning for another trip, and together they managed to haul the sleigh over the ridge. On the final trip each carried a child, the nurses following as best they could. Edward decided to chance it with the cutter, and he and Lottie were pulled through by the floundering mare. The snow fell thicker, night was on them, and they made the children and nurses as comfortable as possible in the sleigh. Astride one of the horses, Brink led the other. The visibility was so poor that the sleigh upset twice. No one was hurt, for the drifts cushioned them; nevertheless, Edward was relieved when they sighted the lights of Duane Farm among the trees.

The next morning dawned clear, temperatures rising to twenty degrees below zero. After the experience of the previous afternoon Paul cautioned them against setting out without scouting the road, so he spent the day with Brink exploring the route. Despite deep snow and a few drifts, which they shoveled out, they found the trails passable, and the following day the sleigh, the baggage sled, and the cutter started forth again.

The first ten miles took them through woods where thickets had stopped the drifting, but the snow became progressively deeper in the level country beyond. All the same, they were able to reach a farm where they had lunch and rested the horses before departing on the final seven-mile stretch. Covering recently burned-out ground, this was the worst section they had yet encountered. The sleigh upset constantly, and at each tumble the children yelled with delight. Finally, the file of vehicles crawled so slowly it approached a standstill; snow resumed; they had only reached Barnum's Pond by dusk, three miles away from Paul Smith's. The larger horses appeared spent. Brink and Paul, in the hope of forcing them through, switched places. Standing on the luggage in a shaggy buffalo robe with a red woolen sash about his waist, Paul, an epic figure, roared at the horses and cracked his whip; but the panting team simply sank on their sides in the snow.

Trudeau got out of the cutter to see what he could do. Before he reached Paul, one of the animals on the sleigh had collapsed as well. Paul regarded his horses and declared, "Doctor, don't you know Napoleon said, 'The dark regions of Russia is only fit for Russians to inhabit,'" then laughed and lit the stump of an old cigar.

Beyond Barnum's Pond lived a guide who owned a team and Paul left on foot to find him. Nurses, children, and parents tried not to fret among the angling flakes, and after a while a lantern gleamed — Paul returning with fresh horses harnessed to the front bobs of a lumber sleigh. The family finished the journey in the sleigh, Lottie and Edward followed with the mare and cutter, and the exhausted horses, eventually regaining their strength and sensing the nearness of familiar territory, straggled hours behind. Three days after starting from Malone, the Trudeaus were home.

Winter's isolation was offset by Edward's relatively stable health. Although he did not get better, neither did he get worse, and the children were not bothered by the colds they had suffered in the steam-heated rooms of St. Paul. The doctor resumed his hunting and fishing that spring, but after another summer Paul Smith announced that he was closing for the winter; he had just purchased the Fouquet House at Plattsburg, and the Trudeaus needed to winter elsewhere.

Eventually Edward located and leased a clapboard house owned by an old guide, "Lute" Evans, in Saranac Lake village. Saranac Lake remained the same rude settlement of Dr. Lundy's harangues. The sawmill and small hotel and straggle of guide's houses lent scant definition to a community that might have been flung down at random in the woods. There was no running water. Behind the Trudeau kitchen stove stood a water barrel that was refilled by "Lute," who would amble to the Saranac River with two pails suspended from a neck-yoke. Despite its lack of amenities, the place sufficed, and every day Edward hunted foxes and rabbits, the baying of his hounds reverberating among the snow-laden evergreens. He had few opportunities to practice medicine; the seasonal cycle, Saranac Lake in winter, Paul Smith's in summer, prevailed.

> I neither read medical literature nor practised my profession, except on the rare occasions when some of the guides were injured or sick or could get no other medical aid. I was so imbued with the idea that life for me was to be a short experience that I had apparently lost all interest in perfecting myself in a profession I should never live to practise.

Yet he had not entirely ceased to think about tuberculosis nor the pledge he had made to himself beside Francis's deathbed. Clearly Dr. Trudeau was not going to die as he had once assumed. Furthermore, provincial Saranac Lake was growing; a few more years, perhaps, and the railroad might connect the village with the outer world. Edward resumed his subscriptions to medical journals, and around 1880 began seeing patients referred to him by an eminent New York physician, Alfred Loomis, who had treated Trudeau and was interested in the effects of a cold climate on consumptive patients. What caused tuberculosis? How could it be diagnosed? Was there a cure? The answer to the cause emerged dramatically in 1882 when Robert Koch presented before the Physiological Society of Berlin his epochal paper announcing the discovery of tubercle bacilli and demonstrating that tuberculosis is an infectious disease. Once Edward, familiar with the pioneering work of Pasteur and Tyndall, learned of Koch's discovery through the English translation, *The Etiology of Tuberculosis,* he immediately arranged in his home a rudimentary laboratory and set about training himself in the infant science of bacteriology; but in 1882 he was inspired to take a different direction by an article on Herman Brehmer and his Silesian sanatorium.

Brehmer believed that pulmonary tuberculosis was curable and that high altitudes had a salubrious effect on it. Encouraged by his teacher, J. L. Schonlein, who had introduced the word *tuberculosis,* and by the explorer Alexander von Humboldt, who insisted the disease did not exist in mountainous countries, Brehmer in 1854 established a sanatorium among the Silesian mountains. His pupil Peter Dettweiler carried on Brehmer's program at his own sanatorium, opened in 1876 in the Taurus Mountains, where patients rested for months on open-air balconies. Before long the concept that tuberculosis could be healed by total rest in the open air was accepted throughout Europe. Physicians stressed the importance of walks in pine forests with "their health-giving resinous aroma" and Davos in the Swiss Alps became recognized as the best place to inhale "pure air." A puritanical aspect commended Davos; unlike more languorous sites, it tested character.

Consumption has always been too timorously, too leniently, too indulgently dealt with [asserts a Davos guidebook of 1880]. Davos demands qualities the very opposite of resigned sentimentalism in which too frequently the phthisical youth or maiden was encouraged. Here is no place for weak and despairing resignation; here you are not pusillanimously helped to die, but are required to enter into a hard struggle for life.

To Davos flocked prominent men and women, including Arthur Conan Doyle and his consumptive wife, John Addington Symonds, and Robert Louis Stevenson.

Trudeau pondered the article about Brehmer. Why not build a sanatorium of small cottages where ordinary men and women could cure? The rich could easily afford suitable accommodations, but the sanatorium system could be democratized. The idea remained within the tantalizing realm of possibility. Later, while hunting foxes on the side of Pisgah Mountain, he thought of the possibility again. On the fox runway, sheltered from the prevailing west and south winds, he faced a panorama of unbroken forest rising from the river several hundred feet below, toward the mountains that loomed against the clear sky. The air in Davos could not be more lambent. Yes, he reflected, gazing at the mountains that he had often admired under transformations of light and shadow, the Adirondack air held an elusive magic.

CHAPTER FOUR

"A House in the Eye of Many Winds"
1887–1888

ON MONDAY, September 26, 1887, a two-horse buggy with its waterproof leather flap buttoned around the hood jounced through the rain along the puddled road from Loon Lake to Saranac. The buggy was specially constructed for invalids and cushioned against the poor state of the road. Inside sat Margaret Balfour Stevenson, the fifty-eight-year-old widow of Thomas Stevenson, an Edinburgh lighthouse and harbor engineer who had died that May; Valentine Roch, a French Swiss retainer; and Robert Louis Stevenson, Margaret's thirty-seven-year-old son, a man of letters at the height of his genius and at the end of his physical tether.

The Strange Case of Dr. Jekyll and Mr. Hyde published the year before had made Stevenson a transatlantic celebrity. Queen Victoria shuddered over the fable, the English language gained a pungent idiom, and from St. Paul's Cathedral to country vicarages the tale supplied copious sermon fodder. Within six months forty thousand copies were sold. In the United States, where literary piracy flourished, owing to the absence of international copyright, an authorized edition and numerous illicit editions followed swiftly, and it has been estimated that during the novelist's lifetime *Jekyll and Hyde* sold a quarter of a million copies, legitimate and illegitimate.

Stevenson and his family, sailing to New York aboard the tramp freighter *Ludgate Hill* the last week of August, received a bon voyage case of champagne from Henry James. Louis used the champagne to dose seasick passengers while the reeking ship (with a cargo of apes for American zoos, stallions, cows, and matches) rolled and pitched along the Atlantic swells. En route, a baboon named Jacko, given the run of the deck, took a fancy to Louis, almost ruining his coat by embracing him extravagantly at every opportunity. After an eleven-day passage, the *Ludgate Hill* sighted Manhattan and discovered Jekyll-and-Hyde mania running rife: the boarding pilot went by the nickname "Mr. Hyde" while his sunnier partner was "Dr. Jekyll." Ashore, the Boston tryout-hit of T. R. Sullivan's stage adaptation starring Richard Mansfield — one of three dramatizations — was about to open. Without warning, Stevenson, accustomed to years of meager and erratic income, confronted financial offers that astounded him. First up the gangway rushed E. L. Burlingame, editor of *Scribner's,* with an offer of $3500 for a year's batch of monthly essays on any subject whatsoever. The *Scribner's* proposal countered a $10,000 bid by the enterprising S. S. McClure, who had tried to intercept Stevenson by mail in England (Stevenson had mislaid the letter) with a request to do a weekly column for the *New York World.* Journalists milled on the wharf; outside customs a carriage and a telegram awaited, both sent by Mr. and Mrs. Charles Fairchild of Boston. Wealthy patrons of John Singer Sargent, they had commissioned two portraits of Louis painted by Sargent at Bournemouth. The Fairchilds took cultural patronage earnestly, and their telegram announced a suite had been arranged at the Victoria Hotel, where the Stevensons were to stay as the Fairchilds' guests until joining them in Newport.

The journalists on the pier trailed the carriage to the Victoria. "Louis, who was very tired and far from well [he had caught a

cold off the Grand Banks] had gone to bed immediately to have
a rest, so they had to be dismissed and told to come back later
when they must take their chance of finding him," his mother
wrote a friend, "but it was hard to persuade them to go away,
and they kept sending up their cards even after Louis had finally
settled down for the night." At length, an impromptu press conference took place. Stevenson, inexperienced in such matters,
did not conduct a collective interview; rather, he submitted to
separate sequential interviews, but after four he called a halt,
having endorsed New York City, Grover Cleveland, the novels
of Henry James, and international copyright. The press was
ushered out, although one reporter managed to steal back after
Louis was finally asleep. Nevertheless, he preserved his equa-
nimity: "My reception here was idiotic to the last degree," he
wrote Sidney Colvin. "It was very silly and not pleasant, except
where humour enters; and I confess the poor interviewer lads
pleased me. They are too good for their trade; avoided anything
I asked them to avoid, and were no more vulgar in their reports
than they could help. I liked the lads." Fanny Osbourne Stevenson, Louis's Indianapolis-born wife and the keeper of his shrine,
deplored the press shenanigans, but his mother took the com-
motion in stride. "She was pleased with everything," wrote
Louis's friend Will Low, "with our icewater and our 'lifts,' with
the attention lavished on her son."

Stevenson, hottest of hot literary properties, had not landed
in America to publicize himself, of course; the fuss coincided
with the latest phase of his perpetual quest for health. As his
buggy splashed toward Saranac, he had reason to hope he might
find relief from lifelong respiratory illness near the Adirondack
Cottage Sanatorium founded by Dr. E. L. Trudeau.

Colorado had been the original destination of the Stevensons.
Before embarking for America they had spent a dismal thirty
months in Skerryvore, a secluded seaside villa at Bournemouth,
where Louis was constantly hemorrhaging and where his physical problems were compounded by the psychological burden of

a dying father. At Skerryvore, the slightest exertion — a stroll through the garden, a cliffside excursion — brought on a relapse and the dismaying reappearance of what Stevenson with his gift for mordant personification called "Johnnie Bright." The Bournemouth period, nevertheless, had been productive. In spite of seaside damps and perpetual relapses, Stevenson wrote *Jekyll*, the ghost story "Markheim," the finished version of *A Child's Garden of Verses*, the novel *Kidnapped*, "The Body Snatchers," a tale of the supernatural commenced earlier, *The Memoir of Fleeming Jenkin*, and a substantial sheaf of essays. His extreme industry, ignoring invalidism and the psychological repercussions of his father's terminal condition, exacted a price. Louis's behavior that winter proved jittery, for he immersed himself in music as though tugging shut a curtain between himself and the world while he reiterated tunes by the hour on the piano or his stepson's penny whistle. There was the matter, too, of the alarming Irish venture. Influenced by Tolstoy's doctrines of militant Christianity, Louis proposed in the name of human rights to rent a farm in Ireland, where continuing violent attacks had been mounted on those who leased farms from tenants evicted by the British. Above the fray, he intended to embody a moral principle, not a political stance. His assassination (and in all probability the murders of Fanny and her son Lloyd) would "throw a bull's eye light on this cowardly business . . . populations should not be taught to gain public ends by private crime."

The death of Thomas Stevenson released the pent-up tensions of Bournemouth. The Irish scheme was shelved. Having been away from America for seven years, Fanny wanted to visit her sister in Danville, Indiana. She and Louis persuaded his bereaved mother (Aunt Maggie, within the family circle) to accompany them. Doctors recommended that Louis seek out a Colorado resort, with its dry, pine-scented air; his volatile imagination kindled, and soon he was writing to Lloyd about mustangs and silver spurs and log cabins adorned by bearskin rugs.

Several factors canceled the Colorado plan, however. Foremost was Fanny's health: the mile-high altitude of Davos, the Swiss alpine village where they had spent two long stays during a prior convalescence, had affected her heart. Often she felt too depleted to go out, and from time to time left for the lower slopes. She feared Colorado might duplicate the hothouse environment of their Davos hotel, its social life characterized by the desperate efforts of the dying guests to feign gaiety and gusto. America's furor over Stevenson introduced yet another element: "I am getting spoiled," he wrote Burlingame. "I do not want wealth, and I feel these big sums demoralize me," yet for the first time he had a public. In spite of the vulgar hubbub it was folly to dismiss opportunity, and Louis sensibly passed up McClure's offer and came to terms with *Scribner's*. Colorado suddenly looked irrelevant to the New York publishing scene, while the expense of traveling in the American West prior to publication of the *Scribner's* articles could be exorbitant. What the Stevensons needed, therefore, was a medical refuge within striking distance of New York and situated at an altitude agreeable to Fanny.

Who suggested the Adirondacks and Saranac Lake is uncertain. Saranac may have been proposed by one of the New York lung specialists who examined Louis; the climate was said to resemble Davos's. Dr. Alfred Loomis had begun referring patients to Dr. Trudeau; other physicians were following suit. Possibly the Stevensons heard about Saranac as the guests of the generous Fairchilds at their Newport mansion. The suggestion in any case sounded feasible, so in the last week of September Fanny and Lloyd set out to explore the territory, boarding the Hudson riverboat and transferring to the train, which then ran as far as Loon Lake, twenty-five miles from Saranac.

The narrow-gauge railroad, spreading westward toward Saranac village, would not reach the village until December; Fanny and Lloyd hired a buggy to cover the last stretch of their journey. Instantly, they succumbed to the allure of the autumnal landscape. Enchanted by the foliage, the limpid skies, the changing mountainous prospects, they sped across the wilds and in the village decided to rent quarters. Upon inquiry they found Baker's available, a white wooden cottage with green shutters owned by trapper-guide Andrew Baker. He and his wife, who occupied the rear of the house with their two small girls, rented to sportsmen in the hunting season. Fanny struck a bargain: she would take the cottage for fifty dollars a month and pay extra for the two face-cords of wood stacked in the kitchen. The Bakers were pleased; Fanny dispatched a wire, and Louis, his mother, and Valentine followed on the riverboat that connected with the Hudson River Railroad, part of the Delaware and Hudson line. Like Fanny, they were spellbound by the russet mountains, the topography so like that of the Highlands.

Even here, Louis's fledgling fame outran them. Before leaving New York, Margaret Stevenson had attended a Presbyterian church, hearing a sermon employing Jekyll-and-Hyde imagery; in Plattsburg she went to church and the minister spoke of the perils of succumbing to evil so that "in the end Hyde would conquer Jekyll." Saranac, however, appeared untouched by literature, a haven. The village streets — some no more than dusty cow paths — were comfortably removed from Baker's where Fanny and Lloyd had already settled. When the buggy turned off the dirt road above the Saranac River and proceeded toward the solitary cottage on the knoll, the Stevensons glimpsed split-rail fences, tall pines, a verandah, and misty peaks. "The country is a kind of insane mixture of Scotland and a touch of Switzerland and a dash of America and a thought of the British Channel in the skies," Louis would write two months later to John Addington Symonds, whom he had met at Davos; but at that particular moment the landscape was pure Scotland, a grateful mixture of woodsmoke and rain and the figure of Fanny in petticoat and jacket cooking dinner.

Was Robert Louis Stevenson in fact tubercular?

The question may seem pointless, most definitely unanswera-

ble. The evidence indicates he was, and the Stevenson legend —
for every major writer accumulates a legend — concerns heroic
struggle against illness. The legend is not inaccurate; still the
evidence remains presumptive.

Tuberculosis did not claim Stevenson; he died seven years
later on Samoa after a stroke. Dr. Karl Ruedi, Louis's Davos physician, suspected an arrested case of consumption and so did Dr.
Trudeau when he presently examined the patient. Trudeau's diagnosis is impressive since his laboratory investigations were the
most advanced of his day, but there will always be a margin of
uncertainty. That Louis suffered a malady or combination of
maladies of the respiratory tract is evident; his case, however,
does not rule out the possibility of bronchiectasis, an acute and
chronic bronchial condition similar to and sometimes mistaken
for tuberculosis. The symptoms, including high intermittent fever, usually follow a bronchial infection or a complicating factor
such as mumps, measles, or the various childhood ailments, especially colds, to which Louis was subject. J. C. Furnas, who ex-
haustively investigated the subject in the definitive Stevenson biography, *Voyage to Windward* (1952), concluded that Stevenson
probably had TB:

> The histories of his mother and grandfather hint that he had
> inherited inadequate resistance to the bacillus. Then — for a well-
> founded guess — the combination of physical debility and shat-
> tering emotional problems that had heaped themselves on him
> since he had left Edinburgh [in 1880] finally opened the way for
> a major infection.

His heavy consumption of cigarettes probably contributed as
well. Both Louis and Fanny rolled their own. "Cigarettes without
intermission, except when coughing or kissing," he declared in
a lighthearted description of himself to J. M. Barrie. Mrs. Baker
considered Stevenson the most habituated chain smoker she had
ever met, careless with his ashes and scattering them during his
voluble moments, and she thought it a wonder he did not set his

mattress on fire. Several times, almost succeeding, he put gaping holes in the bedsheets. Indeed, nearly a century afterward, the gullies left by unheeded cigarettes smoldering on the mantel above the Baker fireplace still betoken the impulsive romantic, a votary of tobacco lost in his vision of the South Seas. Stevenson's smoking was even memorialized in bronze. During the brief stay in their New York hotel the young sculptor Augustus Saint-Gaudens had modeled a bronze medallion of Louis and depicted him characteristically writing in bed, red poncho wrapped around thin shoulders, a book open on his knees, in his hand a cigarette from which an elegy, "Youth now flees on feathered foot" — from the 1887 volume of poetry, *Underwoods* — ascends like smoke. St. Giles's Cathedral in Edinburgh received a larger (and lesser) version of the medallion, but, conscious perhaps of ecclesiastical rectitude, Saint-Gaudens changed the cigarette to a pen. As for the Baker mantelpiece, Louis's landlords exhibited commendable restraint since theirs was only the second open brick fireplace built in Saranac and they were proud of it.

Louis approached a Saranac winter in the ebullient spirit with which he launched every new project. On either end of the much-abused mantel he placed a red tobacco-box and, as center ornament, a whisky bottle. He had a history of beginning enterprises (and literary projects) with enormous zest. After his initial ardor melted inertia prevailed. This does not mean he failed to complete manuscripts; indeed his oeuvre, impressive for such a brief literary life, testifies otherwise; but his method of coping with writer's block, disillusionment, or waning enthusiasm was to avoid proceeding methodically toward the objective in the manner of an army marching in formation with fixed bayonets; rather, employing guerrilla tactics, he won through. Stevenson often switched from one manuscript to another in order to husband his energies. His journalism, on the other hand, was produced, despite a dread of deadlines, on strict schedule. The *Scribner's* articles he wrote in Saranac — "Pulvis et Umbra," "Beggars," "The Lantern Bearers," among others — are succinct and straightforward in comparison with his earlier impression-istic essay style. Having achieved the status of a writer whose opinions carried weight, he possibly felt less necessity to speak through a literary mask — Hazlitt, Browne, Lamb, or the es-teemed authors of his "sedulous ape" apprenticeship. The Sar-anac essays contained some of his most felicitous writing, and not all were as homiletic as "Pulvis et Umbra" or were motivated by "the ungenuine inspiration of an income at so much per es-say, and the honest desire of the incomer to give good measure for his money." The major project of Louis's Adirondack winter, however, would be a novel in which the narrative skill of the author was evidenced by characters who presented the story from their psychologically complex points of view. The shape of *The Master of Ballantrae* became clearer in Stevenson's mind that fall. Although he had been mulling over the work for six years, his novel of fraternal antagonisms refused to fall into place eas-ily. In fact, the Adirondack scenes, ultimately composed in Hon-olulu, would prove the story's weakest section. The trouble sprang from the impossibility of resolving the tensions of a sub-tle psychological study through the melodramatic conventions of the romantic novel (Stevenson was keenly aware of this and of the story's point-of-view inconsistencies), yet, notwithstanding the author's structural problems, the Adirondacks contributed to the book an indirect, almost imperceptible texture. The fam-ily in *The Master of Ballantrae* was not Stevenson's immediate his-toric family; into his design, all the same, he incorporated the father-and-son conflicts of his youth, the darkness of a Saranac winter, and the ferocity of internecine emotions that narrow the world's dimensions to the hatreds of brothers.

The October air was tonic; Louis compared the intense tints of the trees to the colors of the cutout sheets for the toy theater he had received for his sixth birthday, the miniature stage and contoured patterns sold as Skelt's Juvenile Dramas. Margaret Stevenson thought the air delicious, "with a sweetness that again and again reminds me of the Highlands." Driving their buckboard into the village, they explored the piney backroads that dipped and rose among the hills. On one of these rides they almost certainly passed the seven cottages of Dr. Trudeau's sanatorium, which stood on the sheltered side of Mt. Pisgah, less than half a mile away.

Trudeau in 1887 had spent five years raising funds and performing missionary tasks on behalf of his project, "the Adirondack cottage cure," as it was first called, his experiment based on the example of Brehmer and Dettweiler. Although TB was not at that time regarded as a transmissible disease, Trudeau conjectured that an abundance of fresh air and the mutual interests of a closed society of other consumptives provided the optimal conditions of treatment. The best interests of his patients would be served by voluntary segregation. He first examined a site in nearby Bloomingdale, but the land proved too expensive. Then Saranac's guides donated boulder-strewn "Preacher Smith's Pasture" on the site of the old fox-run, ten acres purchased at $25 an acre. They grumbled it was a pity to spoil a good fox-run to build a sanatorium; nevertheless, they sensed what the enterprise meant to the doctor. If he fancied the view, why not help him? Saranac Lake was feeling the rudiments of civic pride; Trudeau, the community's leading professional citizen, no less zealous a hunter than the guides themselves, deserved support.

With the encouragement of Anson Phelps Stokes, who shared the doctor's vision of an institution that would care for the tubercular poor, Trudeau began fund raising. In a pocket notebook he entered the names of donors. "Most people couldn't understand just what I wanted to do, because they always argued consumption couldn't be cured," he afterward recalled. "An aggregation of such individuals would be so depressing that no one would stay in such a place." People donated anyway. When he returned from a trip to New York, he totted up his list and realized he had raised three thousand dollars. What sort of staff was necessary? Whom should he consult? There were no precedents; Trudeau was on his own.

Daniel W. Riddle, one of the founding members, supervised the initial building arrangements, while M. J. Norton, who had a small farm in the vicinity, agreed to furnish a horse and cart, and to do odd jobs. By 1884 the foundations and frame of the first cottage sanatorium in the United States were in place — the "Little Red," a one-room structure built for $350 and donated by Mrs. William F. Jenks of Philadelphia. "Little Red," with its slanting roof and functional carpentry, seemed temporary, soon to disappear among the boulders. Fifty years afterward the single-gabled cottage, bright in the paint that had become its trademark, would assume symbolic status on the 1934 Christmas Seal, but in 1884 its plain boards looked bleak and provisional.

The cottage remained unfinished throughout the rest of the year. Late that fall, however, Dr. Alfred Loomis in New York recommended the first patients, Alice and Mary Hunt, sisters from a crowded tenement, who had a sponsor willing to pay their railroad fares. The sisters had to wait until the structure was completed in February 1885 — evidence of the improvisatory character of the sanatorium's pioneer days — but finished it was, finally. The single room measured 14 by 18 feet, and the porch was so cramped that only one patient could sit out at a time. The furnishings consisted of a wood stove, two cots, a washstand, two chairs, and a kerosene lamp. Dr. Trudeau had envisioned a building on a grander scale as his first-year goal, but accepted the outcome philosophically:

I can distinctly see the Adirondack Cottage Sanatorium [he declared in 1915], in all its incongruous details, in the midst of its beautiful natural environment of mountains and unbroken forest. The grounds were a rough hillside covered with scant grass, through which everywhere jutted boulders of varying sizes, a few rising four or five feet above the ground. Not a sidewalk, not a path anywhere! The buildings, a small rough-board and shingle barn, one unpainted wing of the main building without any porch, and one small unpainted cottage! The patients, two frail, ill-clad factory girls! The staff, a farmer, his wife and two daughters . . . Truly, I must have been an optimist by nature, and the joy of life and youth must have run in my veins then, for I was not in the least discouraged.

When the Stevensons first glimpsed Dr. Trudeau's village within a village, the sanatorium retained its makeshift origins. "Little Red" was occupied by a different pair of sisters, the Misses Pentland; walrus-mustachioed M. J. Norton still served as farmer-manager, while his wife and daughters took care of the cleaning. Everything exhibited an air of improvisation. The doctor belatedly realized the property lacked a water supply, but a donation of supplemental acreage supplied the sanatorium with a spring. The water had to be carried to the cottages; primitive toilet facilities were provided in the Administration Building, where patients went for their baths; the drainage was a perpetual cause of complaint. The entire medical staff consisted of Trudeau, who in summer hitched his buggy and drove fourteen miles to Saranac Lake and back to Paul Smith's daily. He had no infirmary, not a single nurse, and hired lumberjacks and guides to care for the bedridden. These formidable woodsmen confronting for the first time an acute episode of hemorrhaging would sometimes bolt from the room and no amount of cajolery would induce them to return. On the rare occasions when somebody died, Trudeau was obliged to take charge of the situation in person; the sanatorium staff was always thrown into a state of panic so contagious he feared they would all quit at once. The patients paid five dollars a week for room and board, and even at those rates found the food atrocious.

To the Stevensons, of course, the institution's struggle for existence was indiscernible. If Dr. Trudeau's cluster of cottages hardly looked as imposing as the chalets of Davos, the sanatorium echoed the high-minded rigor of the Swiss establishment, and in all likelihood Louis regarded the buildings with interest, as he regarded every brave beginning.

A celebrated photograph of the Stevensons in Saranac Lake shows them bundled to the ears and standing on their snow-spattered verandah. Margaret Stevenson in the era's obligatory widow's weeds, the dark dress and white muslin wimple that lend her an incongruous resemblance to Queen Victoria, is out of the picture. (Resilient observer of the family drama, she is not averse to an offstage role.) Lloyd, Fanny, and Louis wear bulky fur coats, but curiously the two maids on their right, Valentine and a local "help," face the camera wearing the black dresses and starched aprons of their indoor calling. Lloyd's toque is pulled down upon the milky blankness of his eyeglass lenses; he looks weighted like a wobbly inflatable beach toy that always resumes an upright position whenever it is pushed, and vulnerable, too, as only a twenty-year-old can be vulnerable, teetering between adolescence and manhood. Fanny bends forward to pat the large, part-Newfoundland black-and-white puppy that Louis gave her as a Saranac present, while Louis himself, casual and half-smiling, gazes quizzically at the camera. The speckled print doesn't show Louis's nicotine-stained fingers, Fanny's piercing gaze "like the sighting of a pistol," or Lloyd's destiny as a light novelist, pioneer automobile buff, and mainstay of the Lambs Club in New York. The spectator follows the frieze of faces until the most significant element of the photograph is reached, a thermometer hanging on the wall over Louis's left shoulder.

Baker's, "a hatbox on a hill" and "a house in the eye of many winds," had an elevated view of the swift currents of the Saranac River. The twin-chimneyed L-shaped cottage is smaller in ac-tuality than it seems in an 1890s mezzotint. Late-Victorian do-mestic architecture often took the form of a commodious resi-dence done in eclectic period styles, but Baker's was as summary as the speech of the Saranac guides. The half-dozen rooms ac-commodated the traffic of eleven persons — the Stevenson mén-age, the Bakers, their two small daughters and pet kittens, the servants, Valentine and an Irish-American maid supplied by the Fairchilds, plus a juvenile handyman who slept in the sloping woodshed at the rear of the house, which also incorporated an outhouse enclosure. One entered the Stevenson portion through the kitchen. Beyond lay the ample sitting room, with its open brick fireplace, then the bedrooms, and a nook that served Louis as a study. An abrupt staircase led to Lloyd's room and a slip room for Valentine. Sliding double doors separated the Ste-vensons from the Bakers and the arrangements preserved a nominal privacy.

In any event, much coming and going occurred. During the six and a half months of their occupancy the Stevensons were in constant flux, escaping at intervals to warmer, less isolated, places, such as Philadelphia or Boston. (At the latter, in March, Aunt Maggie met William James, who told her he was writing Louis a fan letter; alas, she did not at the time realize Professor James was related to the family's close and valued friend, Henry James.) First, Fanny was away to visit her still-energetic mother in Indiana, returning by way of Montreal, where she purchased a stock of "extraordinary garments" fashioned by Canadian In-dians — furs and fur caps, buffalo robes, rugs, coats, snowshoes, and fleece-lined Indian boots. She had heard about and taken to heart local stories of the brutal Saranac winter. Not all the stories were ominous. Margaret Stevenson "went one day to visit a lady who has been here for four years, and she says she de-lights in the winter, and is longing for the frost to set in; the air is delicious then, and you don't feel the cold nearly as much." Fanny, however, sided with the pessimists and proved foresighted.

"Zero is like summer heat to us now," Louis observed the fol-lowing March. Before the snow closed in, though, the ailing man of letters admired by Meredith and James was referring to himself as "a rank Saranacker and wild man of the woods." He reveled in the conceit of Baker's as a hunting lodge similar to the "Hunter's Home" built by Paul Smith on the north branch of the Saranac River in 1852. The accommodations were rustic enough to sustain that whimsy. When Margaret Stevenson proposed covering a damaged deal table in the living room, Louis responded with mock dismay. "What have hunters to do with tablecloths?" he cried. She also complained of the lack of footstools among the furnishings and the drafty floor bothered her, so they had a log sawed into sections to serve the purpose.

The cottage lacked coffee- or teapot (coffee and tea were locally brewed in saucepans) and finding an eggcup in the general store proved impossible. The widow Stevenson took pleasure in the peculiarities of the village, especially the old-fashioned shop signboards, like the shoemaker's long black wooden boot with his name across it in yellow, but Louis rapidly acquired a reputation as standoffish.

Considering the state of his health and his commitment to *Scribner's*, this is scarcely surprising. The outpouring of his work, however, was prodigal; Fanny remembered, besides the two novels and *Scribner's* articles, "the inditing of innumerable letters — one day twenty, another thirty-five, another thirty-two." Integral to Louis's process of writing was thrashing out the problems of the story or essay during an outdoor walk, and he hated meeting anyone then. Furthermore, in flight from his own celebrity, he dodged people who persisted in dropping in; Fanny had to put aside a visiting day once a week. Admirers like the young man who traveled fifty miles on snowshoes to meet the author were unaware of the social ground rules.

The inhabitants had a case, nevertheless: despite his American-born family, Stevenson was baffled in his efforts to come to grips with the American character. Emerson viewed the Adirondack woodsman as an instance of natural man uncorrupted by social institutions, but Stevenson, a product of the Edinburgh professional middle class, tended to look at Americans through socially conscious eyes. His sporadic attempts to draw credible American characters met with failure despite his fervent admiration of *Huckleberry Finn* and Mark Twain. The sensibility that captured the essentials of Scots, British, French, and colonial European behavior faltered when it came to Americans. Stevenson took an authentic interest in American manners and idiom, enjoyed the country, appreciated the people, but when he essayed an American portrait he fell back on stereotype and his dialogue turned hollow. "His opportunities had been too cramped," Furnas suggests. "Even the Americans he knew well consisted too much of Brahmins like the Fairchilds or expatriates like James and Sargent."

Although there is considerable truth in this, Stevenson had firsthand acquaintance with Americans as diverse as an old bear hunter who nursed him at an Angora goat ranch near Monterey in 1879, Mrs. Mary Carson, his San Francisco landlady, and the Reverend Dr. William A. Scott, the Presbyterian divine who married Fanny and Louis in San Francisco and then bestowed on the groom as wedding gift a ponderous theological tome, *Answer to Bishop Colenso,* written by himself. Stevenson on his earlier American visit had even begun a novelette, *Arizona Breckinridge, or A Vendetta in the West,* in which he might have been a precursor of Zane Grey. The hackneyed tone of his title indicates how self-consciously he approached American subject matter. Off-target as usual, he settled upon the Sicilian *vendetta* rather than the American terms, *run-in* or *shoot-out.*

Louis preserved his distance from the village in general. Since he did not fish or hunt and opposed blood sports on ethical grounds, he was a Saranac Lake anomaly. Still, he hit it off with the Bakers. There were late night tête-à-têtes with Andrew Baker, who sometimes fell asleep in his chair; but notwithstanding these sessions Louis maintained his lifelong custom of early rising. The servants lit the stoves around six-thirty. After breakfast Louis and Lloyd, who was typing *The Finsbury Tontine; or, The Game of Bluff,* a first draft of the black-comedy novel about a corpse in a barrel — destined to become *The Wrong Box* — settled into their writing routines.

> The sun (which has long been a stranger) shines in at my shoulder [Stevenson wrote Henry James]; from the next room the bell of Lloyd's typewriter makes an agreeable music as it patters off (at a rate which astonishes this experienced novelist) the early chapters of a humorous romance; from still further off — the walls of Baker's are neither ancient nor massive — rumours of Valentine about the kitchen stove come to my ears.

Fanny usually spent the mornings reading or writing or supervising the sealing of the front door and windows. She resumed work on a play, *The Hanging Judge,* an abandoned project of Louis and W. E. Henley in Bournemouth, and with her husband's assistance completed it, though the play was never produced. Margaret Stevenson kept to her room and went to extremes not to interrupt the authors in midsentence. "I get out by the window; I wish you could see the performance, for as the aperture is only the size of four small panes of glass, and the frame is held up by a stick, you may fancy it requires careful engineering to get through it."

By twelve-thirty, work over, the family assembled for lunch, after which the buggy arrived, and two members went for a drive while Louis ventured forth on his solitary ramble. Upon his return he went to bed until six and then had dinner, which was followed by cards or general conversation. Around ten everyone retired. It was a regimen that suited Louis. In addition to his writing he often read aloud during the evenings. Lloyd recalled him declaiming in a melodious voice from *Othello, The Tempest, Julius Caesar,* and *Macbeth.*

> Once Stevenson laid down the copy of *Don Quixote* he was reading, and said, with a curious poignancy that still lingers in my ears: "That's what I am — just another Don Quixote." . . . In conversation I can recall his referring to it often — "that it was the saddest book he had ever read"; "that Don Quixote was the great-

est gentleman in fiction"; "that the Duke and Duchess were a pair of detestable cads to make sport of the old fellow and he their guest." Moreover, he had even stumbled through the original in his halting, laborious Spanish.

Louis also read Henry James's *Roderick Hudson,* which, he said, "took my breath away," and ought to be brought to the attention of George Meredith. The seventh book of the *Aeneid* and Robertson's *Sermons* proved challenging; George Bernard Shaw's novel about pugilism, *Cashel Byron's Profession,* sent by William Archer, delighted everyone. ("Tell Shaw to hurry up: I want another," Stevenson wrote Archer.) On the shelves of the Franklin County Library Louis rediscovered the novels of an old but by now slightly faded favorite, G. P. R. James; from the small desk under the eaves of his study, the *Scribner's* essays flew southward. The major Saranac enterprise, *Ballantrae* (pronounced, Stevenson carefully indicated, with a long *a,* as in "ale" — an admonition ignored by his new American public), awaited colder weather.

It was not delayed. October brought bitter winds and occasional snow, but the fundamental characteristic of the climate was its uncertainty. One morning would promise a false spring, the next day would dawn in howling arctic whiteouts. By mid-November the temperature sank to twenty-five below zero Fahrenheit. Water froze in the basins, ink froze in the well, the wood stoves throbbed the clock around. Louis woke dreaming that a rat was gnawing on his ears. Valentine drew forth her handkerchief rolled up in a ball beneath her pillow, and the handkerchief was solid as a stone. When she scrubbed the kitchen floor the hot water froze, and despite the glowing stove, the vitreous boards gleamed like a skating rink.

Out of doors, metal burned at a touch. Lloyd, wearing three pairs of gloves — kidskin, fur-lined, and leather — drove the buckboard, but felt the cold more than the others and escaped to asylum with the Fairchilds as soon as he could arrange a face-saving departure. Louis considered the temperature shifts harsh but healthful: "I walk on my verandy in the snaw, sir, looking down over one of those dabbled wintry landscapes that are (to be frank) so chilly to the human bosom . . . and the wind swoops at me around the corner, like a lion, and fluffs the snow in my face; and I could aspire to be elsewhere; but yet I do not catch cold, and yet, when I come in, I eat."

In January, Louis and his mother endured further tribulations, Fanny having fled to New York and Lloyd to Boston. The thermometer plunged to forty below, and while the stove was boiling throughout the night, Louis's buffalo coat congealed tight against the kitchen door. Valentine still tried to scrub the floor. The edge of her skirt brushed against the suds, immediately froze, and did not melt all day. Venison and bread formed a staple diet since groceries in general still came through distant Ausable. Thawing out the venison was difficult; even when the roast had been in the oven for an hour it reached the table frozen and crunching. There was always venison soup: Valentine stirred constantly, but never could seem to eliminate the ice floating in the pot.

> You should hear the cows butt against the walls in the early morning when they feed [Louis wrote the family's Bournemouth friend, Adelaide Boodle]; you should also see our back log when the thermometer goes (as it does go) away — away below zero, till it can be seen no more by the eye of man — not the thermometer, which is still perfectly visible, but the mercury, which curls up in the bulb like a hibernating bear; you should also see the lad who "does chores" for us, with his red stockings and his thirteen-year-old face, and his highly manly tramp into the room; and his two alternative answers to all questions about the weather: either "Cold," or with a really lyrical movement of the voice, *"Lovely —* raining!"

The extreme cold was preferable to fitful winter. Earlier, Louis had acquired a pair of skates and, in place of his daily walk, took to gliding over Moody Pond, not far from the rear of the cottage. An excellent skater, and in his buffalo-skin coat and hat a picturesque one, he swooped and circled beneath the squat triangle of Mount Baker, which rose from the shores of the pond. Soon he was joined on skates by the tireless S. S. McClure, also a native of Scotland, and more than ever determined to secure Stevenson's name for the pages of the *New York World*. *Scribner's* had beaten McClure, but he was a go-getter who would later serve as the model for the unconvincing character of Jim Pinkerton, the "advertising American" in *The Wrecker*. Perhaps Pinkerton didn't come off because McClure was too idiosyncratic; he and Louis became friends as well as professional associates, although the friendship caused an embarrassing contretemps with *Scribner's*.

Louis, to understate the case, did not have a head for business: "He was so sensitive to the opinions of others that an office-boy could influence him for the moment," McClure observed. "And yet, in the long run, he could not be influenced at all." While Fanny was visiting her Indiana relatives, McClure came to Saranac Lake with an offer to publish in syndicate form Stevenson's medieval romance, *The Black Arrow*. During their conversations Louis let slip the news that he was planning two other novels, one a sequel to *Kidnapped*. McClure pounced. How much would Louis want for serial rights? Eight hundred apiece, Louis said. McClure countered. Instead of eight hundred would you take eight thousand dollars? Louis blushed and stammered and then, completely forgetting his agreement with *Scribner's,* said yes. Hitherto his commercial transactions had been the province of Fanny or friends familiar with the literary marketplace, Charles Baxter, Sidney Colvin, and W. E. Henley. "I am offered 1600 Pounds ($8000) for the American serial rights on my next story!" Louis jubilantly informed Baker. "I'm awfu' grand noo, and long may it last!"

Forty-eight hours later, contrition reigned. He penned an apology to Charles Scribner:

Saranac Lake, November 20–21, 1887

My Dear Mr. Scribner, — Heaven help me, I am under a curse just now. I have played fast and loose with what I said to you; and that, I beg you to believe, in the purest innocence of mind. I told you that you should have power over all my work in this country; and about a fortnight ago, when M'Clure was here, I calmly signed a bargain for the serial publication of a story. You will scarce believe that I did this in mere oblivion; but I did; and all that I can say is that I will do so no more, and ask you to forgive me. Please write to me soon as to this.

Scribner was vexed and Louis begged editor E. L. Burlingame to intervene. Should Scribner mention the matter, "try to get him to see this neglect of mine for no worse than it is: unpardonable enough, because a breach of an agreement; but still pardonable because a piece of sheer carelessness and want of memory, done, God knows, without design and since most sincerely regretted. I have no memory."

Ultimately the oversight was redressed and Baxter assumed responsibility for Louis's contractual arrangements, serving in effect as his agent. McClure's skating trips continued, however, nor was he bereft of additional visionary sugarplums — the possibility of lectures (booked by the McClure lecture syndicate), travel articles (to be published in installments by the McClure syndicate), and whatever could be gleaned through travelogues using the recording phonograph (newly invented and supplied by McClure), which would document the voices of faraway lands where the author and his family might choose to visit.

Louis, however, didn't need a phonograph cylinder, for he was already listening to voices of his own contrivance. Contrary to his plea to Scribner, he had an excellent memory when the recollection mattered. The memories would come unbidden, but he had to be ready, like all authors, to heed them wherever he was, whatever he was doing.

The verandah of Baker's Cottage suggests the quarterdeck of a small yacht. The boards meet the foot with a positive creak and thrust as though careening against the wind, and the illusion is enhanced by the bubbling proximity of the Saranac River. On a night in late fall (Stevenson refers to "winter" but this seems unlikely since he had completed ninety-two pages of his first draft by Christmas Eve), Louis stepped out on his verandah after reading for the third or fourth time Captain Marryat's *The Phantom Ship.*

> ... the night was very dark; the air extraordinarily clear and cold, and sweet with the purity of forests. From a good way below, the river was to be heard contending with ice and boulders: a few lights appeared, scattered unevenly among the darkness, but so far away as not to lessen the sense of isolation. For the making of a story here were fine conditions. "Come," said I to my engine, "let us make a tale, a story of many years and countries, of the sea and the land, savagery and civilisation; a story that shall have the same large features and may be treated in the same summary elliptic method as the book you have just been reading and admiring.

Extraordinary things were happening within Louis at that moment. First, he addressed his imagination as an "engine." This in itself is not exceptional. Writers of fiction, particularly before 1914, often deploy industrial metaphors in their memoirs — seldom, though, do they have as their father an actual engineer. Next, the engine obliged: an arresting image flashed into Louis's consciousness, that "of a buried and resuscitated fakir," a case related to him by an uncle, Dr. John Balfour, who had served the East India Company as physician before returning to Edinburgh, where he devoted himself to battling outbreaks of cholera. Astonishingly, the Indian's image superimposed itself on the Adirondack darkness, and Louis began speculating how he might resolve these opposites, how the notion of the resuscitated fakir might fit the design of a tale of many lands.

> And while I was groping for the fable and the characters required, behold, I found them lying ready and nine years old in

my memory. Pease porridge hot, pease porridge cold, pease porridge in the pot nine years old. Was there ever a more complete justification of the rule of Horace? Here, thinking of quite other things, I had stumbled on the solution, or perhaps I should say (in stagewright phrase) the Curtain or final Tableau of a story conceived long before on the moors, between Pitlochry and Strathardle, conceived in the Highland rain, in the blend of the smell of heather and bog-plants, and with a mind full of the Athole correspondence and the memories of the Chevalier de Johnstone. So long ago, so far away it was, that I had first evoked the faces and the mutual tragic situation of the men of Durrisdeer.

The writer's imagination — not in the final analysis a mechanical engine but a vital power sustained by magical skill and endurance — was disinterred, and from a different perspective the origin of *The Master* also anticipates the multiple transformations of the village of Saranac Lake, a place where the dead will be restored to life.

Stevenson dedicated *Underwoods* to the doctors who treated him on two continents. The roll call of physicians, cited with cheerful aplomb and not without irony, exposes the conditions under which the poems were made. In general, Louis appreciated the medical profession and populated his fiction with sympathetic doctors, such as Dr. Livesey in *Treasure Island,* but of all the medical practitioners encountered "on cis-Elysian river-shores" during the author's short life, Dr. Trudeau proved the least congenial.

They maintained superficially cordial relations. After all, standing out in a hamlet settled by loggers and guides, they exemplified the community's aspirations. It does not seem likely that, as a recent biographer of Stevenson has indicated, Trudeau was unaware of his patient's literary eminence. Louis, on his part, had come to Saranac Lake to take advantage of proximity to a doctor-researcher gaining a national reputation because of his work on tuberculosis. Nevertheless, they were temperamental foils: Trudeau, cautious, utilitarian, and proper; Stevenson, emotional, visionary, and though outwardly genteel, still somewhat bohemian — the scientist and the artist, textbook representatives of alien modes of experience. Of course, no personality fits a mold so easily; everything was more complex, less clear-cut, than a contrast of opposites like Jekyll and Hyde, though to reduce it to essentials, their differences may have been inflamed that winter by a plain case of cabin fever.

Stevenson and Trudeau seem to have gotten on each other's nerves. The doctor was irritated by Louis's chain-smoking and prescribed moderation. Had the writer not been a private patient a more healthful regimen might have been devised. Louis's fatalism also proved annoying. Ill health was, in his opinion, like original sin: nothing could be done about it. An indication of the coolness of the relationship lies in the Trudeau *Autobiography*. Out of three hundred twenty-two pages, six are devoted to Stevenson, with considerable padding, and this at a time when Dr. Trudeau's name was twined with Stevenson's in the popular imagination:

> It is hardly to be wondered at that we did not agree on many topics, for our interests and our points of view on many subjects were utterly at variance. My life interests were bound up in the study of facts, and in the laboratory I bowed daily to the majesty of fact, wherever it might lead. Mr. Stevenson's view was to ignore or avoid as much as possible unpleasant facts, and live in a beautiful, strenuous and ideal world of fancy.

The friction shows. Stevenson and Trudeau met infrequently because Louis had no illness while he was in Saranac; but when they did, the conversation, which had started off enchantingly, often ended close to acrimony. They quibbled about trumpery issues before the open fireplace while the snow fell outside and the rest of the family were away. One of their arguments, reconstructed by Trudeau, concerned the relative merits of the American and British baggage systems. According to Trudeau, Louis, puffing agitated clouds of cigarette smoke and striding back and forth, proclaimed the superiority of the British individual porter over the American brass-check system: "That is just you Americans all over! Checks! Checks! Checks! You eat on the check system. You hang your hat on the check system. Why an American can't speak of dying without saying that he 'hands in his checks.'"

Other encounters were less disputatious. Notwithstanding their schedules, Stevenson and Trudeau were in social demand. At Mrs. George Cooper's dinner party for General George Armstrong Custer's widow, Elizabeth, both men were present along with upper-crust Saranac Lake. Elizabeth Custer twitted Louis by asking him "why he never put a real woman into his stories." With "twinkling gravity" Louis promised her one in his next book. (She turned out to be Alison Durie in *The Master,* a stick figure who should have made Mrs. Custer sorry she asked, though it marked the beginning of Stevenson's progress toward creating a wholly dimensional female character like the elder Kirstie of *Weir of Hermiston.*) Afterward Louis confided in Trudeau about the difficulty of inventing a woman under the prevailing conditions of Victorian male propriety: "When I have tried, I find she talks like a grenadier."

On another occasion Louis visited the doctor in his laboratory. As Trudeau explained the research that would affect the future course of international tuberculosis treatment, Louis bolted out the door and onto a porch. Trudeau followed. "You don't look well," he said. "How do you feel?" To which Louis reportedly answered: "Your light may be very bright to you, Trudeau, but to me it smells of oil like the devil."

This bellicose comment stressed the gulf between Trudeau and his patient and provoked rumors that Stevenson had witnessed frightful laboratory experiments in vivisection. The Dr. Frankenstein myth dies hard, and years later Trudeau, having heard an embroidered account of the incident, felt obliged to issue a retraction:

> Stevenson saw no mutilated animals in my laboratory. The only things he saw were the diseased organs in bottles and cultures of the germs which had produced the disease. These were the things which turned him sick. I remember he went out just after I made this remark:
>
> "This little scum on the tube is consumption, and the cause of more human suffering than anything else in this world. We can produce tuberculosis in the guinea-pig with it, and if we could learn to cure tuberculosis in the guinea-pig this great burden of human suffering might be lifted from the world."
>
> Stevenson, however, saw only the diseased lungs and the disgusting scum growing on the broth, and it was these things that turned his stomach, and not any suffering animals which he saw.

Which was the dreamer? Trudeau, carried away by clinical passion and oblivious to the responses of his audience, or Stevenson, revolted by diseased organs? All the doctor and his visitor perceived was their differences. Yet, as G. K. Chesterton realized in his commentary on *Jekyll and Hyde*, "The real stab of the story is not in the discovery that the one man is two men; but in the discovery that the two men are one man . . . The point of the story is not that a man *can* cut himself off from his conscience, but that he cannot." Without Jekyll, Hyde could not exist; without Hyde it is impossible to hypothesize Jekyll. Trudeau and Stevenson suffered from the same affliction, found refuge in Saranac, demonstrated a similar intrepid will, but were unable to see that as scientist and poet they complemented each other.

McClure's effervescent proposals for a cruise that he would finance finally bore results:

> On Monday, if she is well enough, Fanny leaves for California [Louis wrote at the end of March]; it is rather an anxiety to let

her go alone; but the doctor simply forbids it in my case, and she is better anywhere than here — a bleak, blackguard, beggarly climate, of which I can say no good except that it suits me and some others of the same or similar persuasions whom (by all rights) it ought to kill.

The Saranac pattern, Fanny serving as scout, was repeated; this time she would charter the schooner-yacht *Casco* in San Francisco harbor, opening the Pacific chapter of the author's life. Meanwhile a falling-out between Louis and his friend and ally W. E. Henley marred Stevenson's waning days in the Adirondacks. The break, one of the century's most obstreperous and melancholy literary quarrels, left no reputation untarnished.

In brief, a letter from Henley arrived in Saranac; he had read *Scribner's* for March 1888, which contained Louis's essay "Beggars" and Fanny's third published short story, "The Nixie," and detected in the latter a plot devised by Louis's cousin Katharine de Mattos. Henley had tried to place the original manuscript without success, then Katharine had given Fanny permission to take over the story. To be more precise, Fanny had asked if she could try out her version of the plot, and Katharine had said Yes when she meant No. Supplying such flourishes as a heroine who is a water sprite, Fanny produced a tale that probably would have been rejected too but that displayed the inestimable editorial advantage of her surname. "It's Katharine's, surely it's Katharine's?" Henley asked, as though astonished by his discovery. ". . . I think it has lost as much (at least) as it has gained; and why there wasn't a double signature is what I've not been able to understand." PRIVATE AND CONFIDENTIAL preceded the letter, and the pages closed: "Burn this letter."

Stevenson interpreted Henley's comment, rightly so, as malicious attribution of plagiarism. Their friendship was already severely strained that winter; Henley's younger brother, Teddy, a scenery-chewing actor, was touring America in the leading role of *Deacon Brodie,* the melodrama Stevenson and W. E. Henley had collaborated upon in 1878. The fulminating Teddy had become involved in a barroom brawl in Philadelphia and was living lavishly wherever he went, but this did not indispose him to ask Fanny for a loan when she visited New York. Stevenson's usual forbearance boiled over: "The drunken whoreson bugger and bully living himself in the best hotels, and smashing inoffensive strangers in the bar!" Louis raged in a letter to his friend Charles Baxter. "The violence of this letter comes from my helplessness: all I try to do for W.E. (in the best way) by writing these plays is burked by this inopportune lad. Can nothing be done? In the meantime I add another £20 to W.E.'s credit."

Henley, who resented Louis's charity, grudged his success, and patronized Fanny, waited thirteen years to procure revenge. When Graham Balfour's official *Life of Robert Louis Stevenson* in two volumes appeared in London in October 1901, the editor of *Pall Mall* magazine commissioned Henley's review. Titled "The Two Stevensons," the review was notable for its unbridled and gratuitous savagery. Henley wrote,

> To me there were two Stevensons: the Stevenson who went to America in 1887; and the Stevenson who never came back. . . . At bottom Stevenson was an excellent fellow. But he was . . . incessantly and passionately interested in Stevenson. He could not be in the same room with a mirror but he must invite its confidence every time he passed it. [The Stevenson of legend, Henley went on] this faultless, or very nearly faultless, monster . . . this Seraph in Chocolate, this barley-sugar effigy of a real man . . . is not my old, riotous, intrepid, scornful Stevenson at all.

Readers wondered why a supposed friend would go to such lengths to disparage a long-dead comrade. Fanny surmised Henley must have been drunk when he wrote the review; Henry James supposed the diatribe was "rather a striking and lurid — and so far interesting case — of long discomfortable jealousy and ranklement turned at last to posthumous (as it were!) malignity." Irving S. Saposnik speaks for many modern scholars, however, by maintaining that Henley, for all his spite, did Stevenson's reputation a service: "Despite his characteristic petulance, he at least partially restores Stevenson's identity" — an image varnished in 1901 almost beyond recognition.

Charles Baxter, in any case, sent an emollient response to Louis in Saranac. Baxter attributed Henley's aspersions to disappointment over the theatrical flops he had written with Louis, and pointed out that "the presence of pecuniary help" might heighten the "bitter contrast between success and failure." Louis and Henley, Baxter suggested, should cease corresponding for six months and allow their passions to cool.

Brooding about the quarrel and Fanny's whereabouts, Louis played his penny whistle and stared out the window at the melting snow.

> It is odd that now, the beginning of April, we feel the cold much more than we did in midwinter [his mother noted]. We have had many showers of snow, interspersed with thaws, and there is a generally dirty look everywhere; last night it froze again, the thermometer was down to six degrees above zero, and today it has never been higher than twenty degrees; and that is really too much of a good thing on the seventh of April.

Louis agreed. On Friday the thirteenth, ignoring superstition, he decided at nine-thirty in the morning he could no longer stand quarantine and by twelve-thirty the family had finished packing. The weather again was "simply detestable, rain and sun by turns," but had Saranac proved such a poor bargain? Healthier than he had been in years, Louis had even gained weight, thanks to the kumiss recommended by Trudeau. The winter was an ordeal, but once again disclosed that creativity and physical equipoise are more intimately related than creativity and illness.

Arguably, the Saranac months had been the most productive

of Stevenson's life. He was not completely estranged from a literary existence, as he would be in Samoa; and the cares of his family, such as Fanny's later breakdown, hadn't begun to fray his spirit. "We have much reason to be grateful for what Saranac has done for him — it certainly is a wonderful place," Margaret Stevenson said in valediction. They had arrived by buggy but left on the afternoon train.

"The Country of the Free in Thought"
1914

A NAMELESS YOUNG MAN is traveling over the trunk line from Hamburg to Davos-Platz. His stay in Davos will be brief, three weeks, no more. The countryside flashes past the windows of his compartment: the plateau of southern Germany, the marshes near Lake Constance. Reaching Swiss territory, he not only changes trains but merges into the reader of Thomas Mann's novel *The Magic Mountain:* "You mount a narrow-gauge train; and as the small but very powerful engine gets under way, there begins the thrilling part of the journey, a steep and steady climb seems never to come to an end." The climb seems never to come to an end because Hans Castorp — his name appears in the fourth paragraph, bearing the overtones of its possible Latin source, *castus* or innocent — anticipates the imperishable spell that mysteriously envelops his objective, the International Sanatorium Berghof. The month is July, the year 1907, seven years before the outbreak of the First World War (we must concentrate upon the symbolism of the number seven), and he intends to visit his soldier-cousin, Joachim, a sanatorium patient. As the panting engine ascends, Hans is "carried upward into regions where he had never before drawn breath." Indistinguishable from the preliminary stages of a pilgrimage or initiation, his education has begun. Behind him stretches what Mann with a touch of disparagement calls the Flatland, the sphere where time — and order, reason, quotidian moral dogma — prevail. Ahead, set apart from orthodox society, lies the ambivalent Magic Mountain, the sphere of darkness, sin, and death, its name implying the site where Tannhäuser fell under the amorous spell of Venus. There in microcosm a decaying Europe congregates.

Only by comprehending the meaning of death does Hans achieve the fullness of life. Only by entering the dance of opposing forces does he experience their authentic multiple relationships. Lacking durable values, European civilization appears used up; on the other hand, its depletion portends renewal. Through a persistent dialectic Mann generates a cohesive design. His antagonisms express the interplay of the spiritual (art, illness, love, death) and the material (nature, health, materialism, logic). If Flatlanders try to make the most of time, the consumptive patients at the Magic Mountain squander it; the temporal sphere is invaded by the timeless; Hans, the callow young Hamburg engineer, evolves into an unsuspected artist; Joachim, the military cousin who embodies Prussian esteem for duty and authority, ignores doctor's orders and returns to the Flatland where he perishes. (Ultimately, Hans fulfills Joachim's ambition to be a combat soldier, and whistling Schubert amid the futile assaults of trench warfare, an inferno generated by Flatland mentality, he flounders across Joachim's putative field of glory.) Hofrat Behrens, medical head of the sanatorium, decrees that disease has exclusive corporeal origins; on the other hand, his assistant, Dr. Krokowski, proclaims, "Symptoms of disease are nothing but disguised manifestations of the power of love; and all disease is only love transformed."

The oppositions multiply: bourgeois Europe and colonial Asia, chaos and form, corruption and renewal. Hans Castorp, embodiment of Germany, "the country between," stabilizes the relationships of patients from the East and the West; others on the Magic Mountain also alter its equations, notably a voluble Italian named Settembrini, whose clothes are as slapdash and frayed as his humanistic idealism, and his alter ego Naphta, a baleful authoritarian who represents the absolutist neo-Fascist attitudes of a conservative-radical. They contend for Hans Castorp's soul even though he gives his heart to a slovenly siren, Clavdia Chauchat. As her Gallic last name indicates, she's a "hot cat" and is associated with feline imagery just as Hans is a sort of blundering puppy. Another and even more magisterial figure completes a trinity of the liberal and the reactionary and the apolitical — Mynheer Peeperkorn, a wealthy Dutch imperialist-planter who, though ill, inarticulate, and impotent, embodies the principles of the *élan vital*.

Hans Castorp is entering into the domain of night in order to fathom shadowless day. His sojourn on the Magic Mountain, the three weeks expanding into seven years, will duplicate the spirit-journeys of the shamans of primitive peoples. The mythological significance of his quest unfolds as he proceeds toward self-iden-tification. A delusively rational order requires healers brave enough to confront demonic powers. The energies of illness cre-ate a world as dreamlike yet durable as the energies of health.

In spite of the obvious fact that Davos and Saranac contain intricacies outside the scheme of Mann's novel, the initiatory rites of patients entering the Adirondack Cottage Sanatorium were no less rigorous. As befits a culture that has outgrown the mechanisms of magic, however, these rites were claimed to be in every respect scientific. Unfortunately, science was not enough: tuberculosis, like civilization and its discontents, still withstood investigation. Koch had discovered the cause, not the cure: treat-ment required devout faith in the mystique of bed rest, diet, and the nourishing air. Between the Stevensons' departure and America's entry into the First World War, countless afflicted pil-grims streamed into Saranac Lake and repeated, if not in precise detail, the bold substance of Hans Castorp's ceremonial passage into the dominions of death. Most would never return.

For Edward Livingston Trudeau, too, the early 1890s were years of tragedy. His sixteen-year-old daughter, Chatte — Charlotte, attending a girls' boarding school in New York City — had never disclosed signs of illness, but in January 1888 she wrote home that she was unwell and during the Easter vacation, when she stepped off the train, Trudeau immediately perceived the symptoms of tuberculosis. Toward Charlotte he managed to mask his feelings, then told his wife at once. She clung to hope; Trudeau knew better. "I felt from the first this was the same type of disease my brother had; the type that progresses rapidly and against which treatment is of no avail." The diagnosis proved all too accurate: Charlotte, after enduring alternations of confidence and despair, died in March 1893.

Trudeau immersed himself in laboratory research. Having learned of Koch's discovery of the tubercle bacillus, the American doctor had performed his celebrated 1885 rabbit experiment at Paul Smith's — out of three lots of rabbits, one inoculated with pure TB cultures and permitted to run free, another inoculated but confined in boxes and cellars, and a third not inoculated and at liberty, the first and third lots survived. This supported the fresh-air theory, yet was by no means conclusive. To effect a cure Trudeau realized he must train himself in bacteriology (thanks to Koch, he realized what bacteriology was, but had never heard the name before), notwithstanding his isolation from the centers of medicine.

At his old New York medical college he was taught how to stain and recognize the bacillus under the microscope, and in Saranac Lake he established a rudimentary laboratory. Never mind that he knew nothing about a laboratory's requirements:

> If I could learn to grow the tubercle bacillus outside of the body and produce tuberculosis at will with it in guinea-pigs, the next step would be to find something that would kill the germ in the living animal. If an inoculated guinea-pig could be cured, then in

all probability this great burden of sickness could be lifted from the human race.

Dr. Trudeau's clinical zeal was decidedly different from the philosophical approaches of Mann's fictional physicians debating the relations of soul and body.

The tiny laboratory Trudeau devised in his office at the corner of Church and Main streets contained a minimum of equipment — microscope, stains, slides, a dry and a steam sterilizer, glassware, a diminutive homemade thermostat heated by a kerosene lamp. The thermostat stood on a bracket-shelf beside a sink that the doctor had to fill from a bucket, since Saranac still lacked running water. High temperatures were necessary for growing bacteria, but on extremely cold nights the fire in the wood stove went out, the room became frigid, and the thermostat temperatures dropped with it. Trudeau then improvised an apparatus of four wooden boxes, one inside the other, packed with wool and sawdust, and grew adept at opening or shutting the box doors in order to regulate the thermostat. Using this primitive contrivance, he succeeded in growing the germ in pure cultures.

His papers on tuberculosis were beginning to appear with frequency in medical journals, yet he had no one with whom he could discuss his research. Handyman John Quinlan saw to the chores around the lab, the care and feeding of rabbits and guinea pigs, but during the winter nights Trudeau, focusing the barrel of his microscope while the thermostat fluttered and the stove logs crackled into ash, felt as isolated as Stillman struck in the wilderness by the vertigo of infinity. Physicians usually rejected Koch's theories outright or considered them of paltry diagnostic significance, and even allies like Trudeau's friend Alfred Loomis, who had first sent him to the Adirondacks, continued to spurn the germ theory. One morning, however, the doorbell rang and Trudeau greeted a gaunt young visitor, Dr. Edward R. Baldwin from New Haven. Baldwin said he had contracted tuberculosis. What makes you think so? Trudeau asked, and Baldwin replied that his microscope confirmed it. Trudeau was stunned by this affirmation of Koch's postulates. The older physician arranged to have his colleague admitted to the sanatorium at once.

Baldwin, despite Trudeau's blessing, waited six weeks for admission. The pace of institutionalization was accelerating; although the death rate in the United States had dipped to 200 per 100,000, tuberculosis remained a plague unchecked. A sanatorium could not guarantee miracles, but at least it provided an alternative to despair, and desperate patients were struggling for a place on the waiting list. Dr. Trudeau's Adirondack Cottage experiment, founded on Emersonian optimism, did not resemble the Davos of *The Magic Mountain,* where the profit motive flickers in the background and the board of directors returns dividends on death; all the same, the institution like any other was subject to the law of supply and demand. Between 1889 and 1894, nine new cottages were built as well as a partially enclosed open-air pavilion equipped with billiard tables, an infirmary for serious cases, and a large house attesting to the dignity of the resident physician who ruled this medical fiefdom. Constructed with the amplitude of 1890s domestic architecture, the cottages sported turrets, gambrels, and ubiquitous porches. Inside each building ten rooms opened onto a sitting room with a fireplace; every room had a transom but no carpets or hangings. The décor was austere yet not unattractive.

As a believer in early diagnosis and treatment, Trudeau did not wish the sanatorium to become a hospice. Accordingly, he refused to accept terminal or hopeless patients, a policy that attracted criticism from bitter rejected applicants and from physicians who accused Trudeau of trying to make a name for himself by treating only selected cases. In rebuttal he declared,

> The tuberculin test, the X-ray and the autopsy table all confirm the well-observed facts which prove that after forty years of age

most human beings have at some time in their lives had a little
tuberculosis and recovered from it without ever having been
aware of its presence. After the disease has gone beyond a certain
stage, or is of an acute type, sanatorium or any other known treatment may prolong life, but it rarely brings about a permanent or
even a satisfactory arrest.

Experience had taught Dr. Trudeau to respect his limitations.

His policy of triage, however, had the effect of intensifying
hierarchy, of distinguishing degrees of illness and degrees of
cure. Trudeau himself suffered from "the onus of these thank-
less and unpaid examinations," which as a sensitive and compassionate man he abhorred. If his approach to TB was inflexible,
he was a combatant in a war of annihilation.

Such a military outlook was too Spartan for most people,
whose reflexive response to an appalling reality was to put it out
of sight, and for them the Trudeau Sanatorium assumed the
attributes of an elite school. The enrollment was limited to one
hundred twenty, the applicants unlimited. "The Trudeau Sanatorium is to be considered fundamentally an educational institution," states "an illustrated souvenir pamphlet" issued in the
twenties, "and like all public institutions for education, the receipts from students — who are after all patients receiving an
education — are insufficient for its maintenance." A school was
a more comforting metaphor than a battlefield; how could Trudeau, for example, cope with the epidemic among the Plains
Indians? Tuberculosis was extremely rare among the Sioux until
nearly three thousand were moved into prisoner-of-war camps
during the 1880s. By 1913, the incidence of the disease among
the tribes had risen to almost ten times higher than the worst of
the nineteenth-century epidemics of Europe. The first graduating class (it was so designated) from the Adirondack Cottage
Sanatorium included a Sioux Indian named Herbert Zit Kola
Zee.

The community and the sanatorium enjoyed a reciprocal

growth. Descendants of Pliny Miller, builder of the Saranac River dam and owner of the village's original three hundred acres in 1821, were still prominent citizens in 1892 when Saranac Lake became the first incorporated village of the Adirondacks, with Dr. Trudeau as its president. A bank, organized by three tubercular financiers, was soon to materialize. (Alfred L. Donaldson, one of the triumvirate, would establish himself as the region's pioneer and preeminent historian.) No longer did the barber on crutches noted by letter-writing Margaret Stevenson make his tonsorial rounds. The Ausable Forks veterinarian, founder of Bull's drugstore, from which telephone service originated, sold his interest in the phone exchange to a consortium. Saranac Lake's assessed valuation soared in a decade from $136,000 to more than a million. The success of Dr. Trudeau in demonstrating that Adirondack air could relieve pulmonary disease prompted the New York state legislature in 1900 to appropriate funds for a tent sanatorium at Ray Brook, halfway between Saranac Lake and Lake Placid — the first institution of its kind. Out of Ray Brook's tent city and plank walkways mushroomed a complex of bland brick buildings that expressed the spreading bureaucracy of TB care. (Ray Brook became the site of the 1980 Olympic Village and then a state prison.)

A great-great-grandson of Pliny Miller rode a float in Saranac Lake's first Winter Carnival in 1898. The parade alternated storybook themes with celebrations of the village's hunting and fishing past. Seaver Rice, Miller's five-year-old descendant, was Little Boy Blue on a float entered by his father's cure house business.

During the first year of the new century Stephen Crane died of tuberculosis in Germany; American authors less celebrated — indeed, unknown — came to Saranac Lake. "Minor" writers they remain, minor even to the specialists who read and analyze them — it is absurd to pretend otherwise; nevertheless, listening attentively we might hear them speak past their grief and pain, from the depths of the human psyche, where those faithful to art have named their own freedom.

Thomas Bailey Aldrich in 1900 cut a considerably larger figure than he does now, a revered man of letters to whose career clung the aura of the midcentury, when Emerson, Longfellow, and Holmes wrote the country's literature; Adelaide Crapsey was a Vassar undergraduate with intimations of a poetic vocation, though she would never see her poems in print save in school magazines, newspapers, and yearbooks. Her impact on her own generation, however, proved greater than Aldrich's on his: Edmund Wilson, Carl Sandburg, and, above all, Yvor Winters praised her unique voice. Curiously, she has had no comparable contemporary acknowledgment. In an era marked by critical rediscoveries of talented women, she remains as she was in life, fugitive, original, and obscure.

Aldrich and his wife, Lilian, arrived in Saranac Lake in the autumn of 1901 to rally around their thirty-three-year-old son, Charles, one of their twin sons, who had been married on the previous Christmas Day. The parents spent the next summer on the Devon coast and, on returning, received word that Charles, suffering a severe and unexpected hemorrhage of the lungs, had been rushed to the Adirondacks.

At sixty-five, Aldrich was savoring an expansive and leisurely retirement of travel and writing. He had long since made his mark. The nine years of his editorship at the *Atlantic Monthly*, where he succeeded William Dean Howells in 1881, had brought forth such contributors as Thomas Hardy and the Connecticut poet Edward Rowland Sill in addition to the fixed stars of the New England pantheon. His own fame rested largely on a single book, *The Story of a Bad Boy*, though he was also renowned at the time for *Marjorie Daw*, a charming sentimental romance. *The Story of a Bad Boy*, his most spontaneous fiction, reanimated his childhood in the seaport town of Portsmouth, New Hampshire, becoming the harbinger of a flock of similar tales, notably *Tom Sawyer, Huckleberry Finn,* and *A Boy's Town,* by his friends Clemens and Howells. In *The Story of a Bad Boy,* readers found relief from the surfeit of the postwar era by returning to a pastoral, manifestly more innocent, America. Aldrich too seemed an emissary from that nostalgic time. With his waxed blond mustache, his ruddy countenance, and elastic step, the little man's aplomb conveyed dapper resilience. He had never shared the anxious introspection of the New England Calvinist tradition. The light French novels he relished and the bric-a-brac celebrated by his verses were decidedly un-Bostonian. His formative experiences had not only taken place in Portsmouth, but offstage at his family home in New Orleans; furthermore, Aldrich was a product of New York's casual literary life, having served his editorial apprenticeship with N. P. Willis on the *Home Journal* and covered the Civil War as a New York–based correspondent. Only when he married in 1865 did he settle in Boston, where he liked to quip that he was not the genuine article, he was Boston-plated. His predecessor Howells, more conscious of the shifting center of the nation's literary gravity, steered an opposite course, from Boston to New York.

Under pressure to maintain the lofty intellectual standards of the *Atlantic,* Aldrich was temperamentally not inclined to grapple with the urgent social, political, and economic issues of the day. Instead, he emphasized his undoubted strength, fastidious literary taste. His were the gifts of the miniaturist, the polished light verse poet; he was clever rather than profound, craftsmanlike rather than inspired, urbane rather than innovative. Fortunately, he knew it and exhibited in prose the poise of a tightrope walker who stumbles on the high wire only for the sake of showmanship, every step executed with breathtaking technical finesse. He was a consummate professional, never less than accomplished; yet when the occasion demanded, as in his elegies for the New England authors who were the last leaves on the tree, year after year spinning away, he demonstrated how eloquently he could sound universal emotions. He claimed that he would "rather be censured in pure English than praised in bad," which was probably a wire-walker's feint, but his writing still retains its limber appeal. "The neat-handed Aldrich, who was very seldom commonplace, always knew when to stop, an unusual virtue," states Van Wyck Brooks. "He was more consciously an artist than Holmes or Lowell, though he lacked their moral force and their wealth of perception, and he soon outgrew his early faults of style." The *Atlantic Monthly* during his editorship ceased to voice bold opinions about national affairs and became a magazine that defined literary standards for an elite readership.

The poetry of Thomas Bailey Aldrich belonged to his youth. After the success of *The Story of a Bad Boy*, in 1870 — also the year in which his twins were born — he devoted himself to prose. Was there a connection between the twins and his fictive Portsmouth boyhood? Intrigued by the concept of an eidolon or shadow self, Aldrich was to remark in a letter from Saranac Lake to Howells: "I've a theory that every author while living has a projection of himself, a sort of eidolon, that goes about in near and distant places and makes friends and enemies for him out of folk who never know him in the flesh. When the author dies this phantom fades away, not caring to continue business at the old stand." The reference was to Mark Twain, whose public-relations image was then busily girdling the globe; but it does not require a great leap to imagine Charles, a projection of his father's recollected self, as a literal eidolon. The apprehensive parents rented a house and Aldrich plunged into writing projects, concealing his foreboding behind an epistolary façade of jokiness.

> We are very pleasantly settled and like the quiet life here. We are on the edge of the village with the mountains for our immediate neighbors. Our house, a new and spacious villa which we were lucky to get, stands on a plateau overlooking the Saranac River. Two or three hundred yards away at our feet is the cottage in

which Stevenson spent the winter of '87. He didn't like Saranac
Lake, and I fancy was not very popular. It is a beautiful spot,
nevertheless. The sunsets and the sunrises compensate for the
solitude, which moreover has a charm of its own.

Of all places in the world this is the place in which to read.
We've taken an overgrown cottage on the outskirts of the town,
which at night looks like a cluster of stars dropped into the hollow. The young Aldriches have a cottage near by, and there are
two or three other houses visible — when it doesn't snow. It snows
nearly all the time in a sort of unconscious way. I never saw such
contradicting, irresponsible weather. It isn't cold here, for human
beings, when it is 20 degrees below zero. Everything else is of
course frozen stiff. The solitude is something you can cut with a
knife. Icicles are our popular household pets. I am cultivating one
that is already four feet long — I am training it outside, you understand, on a north gable. I feel that all this is giving you a false
idea of our surroundings, which are as beautiful as a dream.
Every window frames a picture of bewildering and capricious
loveliness. If our dear boy only continues to gather strength we
shall have a happy winter in this little pocket-Switzerland. He is
very thin and white and feeble. At times I have to turn my eyes
away, but my heart keeps looking at him.

The contradictory tensions of Aldrich's feelings intensify his
despair. Saranac Lake, a pocket-Switzerland, also belongs in a
dream, possibly a nightmare; first the solitude has an individual
charm, then it becomes oppressive; the view from every window
is lovely, a loveliness qualified by bewilderment and caprice.
When the letters to Howells succumb to gloom, as they do during the emotional nadir of the holidays, Aldrich falls back on
mournful badinage:

Why did Hutton go to Jerusalem for "Literary Landmarks" when
he might have found plenty of them in the Adirondacks? Among
those who have left footprints on the sands of time of this neighborhood are Stillman, Emerson, and Stevenson . . .

Dec. 24–25. For the past few years I have had a suspicion that
there is something not at all merry in Merry Christmas — that

sinister flavor which one detects in one's birthdays after one has had fifty or sixty of them . . . This morning our boy was able to come downstairs and watch the revealing of a pathetic little Christmas tree in his front parlor. When he was brought up here on the 1st of October he was not expected to live through the journey. And now we have seen him sitting in his armchair and smiling upon the children as the gifts were plucked for them from the magical branches.

Throughout the winter Aldrich distracted himself inventing plots for stories he would never write. "Our boy" fluctuated between illusory health and ebbing strength, and as the days stretched onward and Aldrich "sometimes mistook Thursday for the previous Monday," he took up his pen once more. Stevenson in Saranac Lake had recovered the health necessary to continue writing; Aldrich wrote out of professional habit and the need to escape into a more comprehensible universe. Eventually, he and Lilian built a house, which he named The Porcupine, "because it had so many good points and was occupied by a quill-driver." To Howells he declared,

> *You* would get a book out of these surroundings. The village of Saranac is unique and the natives are — uniquer! Their lives are very simple and accumulative. The rent for two years' occupancy of a cottage pays for building it. No style at all. The Saranacers like the folk described by David Harum, don't dress for dinner, they dress for breakfast. A thrifty people, with very large ideas of the lavishness becoming in foreigners — i.e. persons from New York and Boston and other partly civilized centres. There is much wealth and little show among this part of the population, which consists of invalids and their families, and an occasional misguided guest. When all is said there is a charm in the place. There's something in the air to heal the heart of sorrow.

On the sixth of March 1904, Charles succumbed to tuberculosis and the vitality of his father died with him. Thomas Bailey Aldrich had always associated Charles with that shadow self preserved in memory, a perpetual boy. Three years remained before Aldrich's own death at the age of seventy. Among his last Saranac tasks, the four-act play *Judith of Bethulia* was culled from the Biblical Apocrypha as a vehicle for the illustrious actress Nance O'Neil, then celebrated for her Lady Macbeth. Gaudy with the trappings of the spectacle stage, the drama opened in New York that fall. The critics were unenthusiastic but O'Neil kept it in her repertory, and a young member of her troupe, D. W. Griffith, selected the piece for his transition, in 1913, from one-reel to four-reel film direction. Aldrich had adapted the story of Judith, depicted as a courtesan who saves her city from besieging hordes by seducing the Assyrian leader Holofernes and decapitating him, but the adaptation had given the tale a neat twist. The new Judith was a refined widow, an adornment of the genteel tradition, authentically in love with Holofernes. Griffith, fascinated by the underlying theme of the nature of sexual respectability, created a film about which present-day critical opinion is divided, though critical opinion is all but unanimous concerning the high quality of the performances, in particular Lillian Gish's portrayal of a mother's desperate attempts to find food for her child as the siege of Bethulia wears on.

Had not her publisher's wife received a spectral nudge, Adelaide Crapsey's poems might well have slipped into oblivion. Claude Fayette Bragdon, the publisher, who was also an architect and later a prominent stage designer, lived in 1915 across from Mount Hope Cemetery in Rochester, New York, where in a family plot Adelaide's ashes were buried. A man of broad and varied cultural accomplishments, Bragdon gave Rochester — though upstate unconventionality yielded fewer rosebuds and thorns than the thickets of Greenwich Village — a dash of bohemianism. Manas Press, his own imprint, issued books and broadsides on theosophical topics; and he evidenced an eager interest in the occult and the Orient that he retained throughout his life, publishing his final book, *Yoga for You*, in 1943 at the age of seventy-seven. His second wife, Eugenie, to whom he ascribes paranormal psychic powers in his autobiography, *More Lives Than One*, was the vehicle through whom Adelaide allegedly spoke. "One morning in the summer of 1915 I was awakened by my wife Eugenie, who asked me if I knew anyone by the name of Adelaide." Since Bragdon and Adelaide had indeed been friends with common literary sympathies, he put forward her name and that of her mother, also Adelaide. "Take me to see Mrs. Crapsey," commanded Eugenie; "I was awakened by the sound of her name, repeated over and over: Adelaide! Adelaide!" According to Bragdon, he and Eugenie proceeded to the Crapsey home, where they discovered the Reverend Algernon Crapsey and his wife pondering their daughter's poems in a manuscript assembled with the editorial advice of her friends and colleagues, Mary Delia Lewis of the Smith College English department, and Esther Lowenthal, an economist and later dean of the college.

Bragdon contradicts this colorful version elsewhere, stating only that the Crapseys had approached him with the poems, which had been rejected by several firms, and asked for advice. In any event he agreed to publish them, and during the editorial process, whenever a question arose concerning the text, he communicated with his author's spirit via Eugenie's automatic writing. The result surpassed everyone's expectations and on the eve of publication Adelaide expressed her satisfaction:

"It is well, I am pleased, accept my gratitude. You have done me a great service; I thank you from the country of the free in thought; so good bye, Adelaide Crapsey."

She had reason, even as a shade, for gratitude. Bragdon, a devoted editor, preserved the poet's original punctuation, consulting her Smith College associates and recognizing the value of possibly her finest poem, the anguished free-verse *cri de coeur* that stands apart from anything else she wrote, "To the Dead in the Grave-Yard Under My Window." The slender volume, *Verse*, had decorative lozenge-patterned end papers and a binding in Adelaide's favorite gray on which had been stamped in gold a mystic device not unlike an Egyptian ankh. *Verse* almost at once found adherents among the coming generation of poets. Less than two years after her death Adelaide was legendary, a cult figure. The Alfred A. Knopf edition, in 1922, altered her punctuation to fit orthodoxy and added seven poems. There were two reprintings and further enlarged editions in 1934 and 1938.

Susan Sutton Smith, the foremost Adelaide Crapsey scholar, whose *Complete Poems and Collected Letters* (State University of New York Press, 1977) constitutes the definitive edition, deplores, and rightly so, "the fondness some admirers have for examining the poems as 'human documents,' which substitutes inaccurate and sentimental thoughts about her life for any consideration of her work." Critics of the Manas Press edition of *Verse* seldom overlooked the tragic circumstances of Crapsey's poignant final *annus mirabilis* that links her with Keats as a youthful genius doomed by tuberculosis. The commentary on the poetry generally misunderstood it, following the lead of popular anthologist Louis Untermeyer (he seemed to think her invention, the cinquain, was based on Japanese syllabic verse), who for fifty years published warmhearted but misguided biographical and critical information about Adelaide Crapsey. And yet the work and the life often coincide too, and the single year she spent writing in Saranac Lake secured her place in American letters. *Verse* was patently intended as a personal testament.

> *Wouldst thou find my ashes? Look*
> *In the pages of my book;*
> *And as these thy hand doth turn,*
> *Know here is my funeral urn.*

If the quatrain shows that she never entirely escaped the floridities of turn-of-the-century poesy, it also raises a lapidary inscription under which the poet is interred. A bibliophile, she would have delighted in Claude Bragdon's edition just as she would have been skeptical about his psychic messages. Her regard for her publisher did not include endorsement of his mystical views. Agnostic and rational Adelaide simply wasn't the sort of woman who would accede to an afterlife as a burbling spirit; her courage, intellectual brilliance, and refusal to capitulate to self-pity distinguish an exceptionally attractive personality. Furthermore, she had a jubilant, often self-deprecatory, sense of humor. A Bragdon pamphlet on the fourth dimension, sent her in Saranac by way of consolation, was retitled in a letter to Esther Lowenthal as "another Man the Cube." Adelaide speculated it would soon have a sequel, "*A Primer of Higher Space* 'hot from the press.'"

The major themes of Adelaide's thirty-five years of life were her poetry and metrical studies, her inspiriting friendships with other women, especially Lowenthal and Jean Webster, and her closeness to her gentle, gifted, and exasperating father, Algernon, who was placed on trial for heresy by an ecclesiastical court of the Episcopal Diocese of Western New York in 1906. A heresy trial in the early twentieth century sounds like a throwback to the seventeenth, and indeed, as the Reverend Dr. Crapsey's entry in the *Dictionary of American Biography* has it, on the Christmas Eve before his death in 1927 he might have heard "the same teaching in regard to the Second Person of the Trinity broadcast over the radio, quite without criticism, by one of the leading Episcopal clergymen of New York City," but his was a celebrated trial of the period and widely publicized. The twenty-seven-year-old Adelaide returned home from Europe in order to attend.

Dr. Algernon Crapsey impressed parishioners by his sincerity and benevolence. A small, slight man, five feet six inches tall and weighing no more than 120 pounds, he brought to his pulpit a rhetoric all the more commanding because of his soft-spoken demeanor. The social prestige of the nineteenth-century American clergyman was in his case augmented by a lively social conscience. Ordained a priest in 1872, he was so successful on the staff of Trinity Parish in New York that a special position was created for him, but he wanted a parish of his own, and in 1879 — the year after Adelaide, his third child and second daughter, was born in Brooklyn Heights — he assumed the rectorship of St. Andrew's, in Rochester, an ailing and sparsely attended church. Through an energetic social program, the Reverend Dr. Crapsey transformed St. Andrew's into a potent communal force. The principal products of late-nineteenth-century Rochester were men's clothing and women's shoes, industries that employed unskilled immigrant labor and paid penurious wages, and Dr. Crapsey felt a crucial obligation to kindle a religious flame among disenfranchised working men and women. The antimaterialistic spirit of the gospel blazed in him after his first European trip, to which he was treated by his parishioners in the summer of 1889, a tour in which he noted the majesty of the cathedral towns of England against the squalid slums of the industrial counties.

Alas, the Reverend Dr. Crapsey, subject to a generalizing idealism, that occupational hazard of clergymen, perceived the problems of the world more easily than the problems of a family of eleven children. It was not that he was a tyrannical or willfully negligent parent, only that his authority in the family emerged through a haze of philanthropic ambiguity. The mother, Adelaide, occupied the same exalted plane. Unquestionably the children had difficulty coping with conflicting signals of affection and neglect. A family photograph depicts nine of them arranged by height on a diagonal (Adelaide third from the top), which is undoubtedly merely a photographer's stunt but which shows them in varying degrees of astonishment at having been caught in a symmetrical moment. Families of that size, while conforming to a Victorian ideal, are simply not tidy, and finding out who you are in them is hardly a matter of height. Adelaide Crapsey spent her adult life either as a student or a teacher at schools serving as surrogate families. In Rochester, too, she was surrounded by books, for in addition to his unorthodox opinions in rejecting the Virgin Birth, Dr. Crapsey produced a steady flow of pamphlets and volumes of his own (he was even a Lloyd C. Douglas–like novelist). The cloistered bookishness of her environment, Edward Butscher believes, both nurtured and inhibited Adelaide's talent. On one hand she had continuous access to an abundance of English and American literature and criticism, but the school environment

> also encouraged a somewhat reclusive concept of aesthetic commitment, as an historical rather than an experiential function, and quite effectively cut Crapsey off from extended contact with the greater number of her fellow Americans in their various degrees of social and vocational interaction, and from most men — all the schools she taught at were exclusively for women.

Was she so different in this respect, however, from any other conventional female academic of the period? Within her family she found in her older sister Emily the first of the confidantes and allies who would prove so important to her intellectual and social development. Opportunities to teach men were virtually nonexistent. Instead of constricting her gifts, women's colleges provided, in addition to jobs, stability and the sense of self that ultimately allowed Adelaide to confront and achieve transcendence over a fatal illness. She welcomed sibling support: the dinner table over which Dr. Crapsey presided was also a forum for current events, Scriptural interpretation, and commentary about art and literature, but Adelaide and her father held center stage. In his autobiography, *The Last of the Heretics,* she is the only one of his children he mentions by name. Significantly, however, when she began to write poetry she showed it to neither parent but to her maternal grandmother. Poetry was too important to trust to a blurring forbearance. Significantly, too, it was the daughter rather than the mother whom Dr. Crapsey took to the anachronistic ecclesiastical trial in Batavia, New York, and who accompanied him when he was a delegate to the 1907 Hague Peace Conference, which they combined that summer with a walking tour of Wales.

Adelaide's future depended on eluding the smothering influence of her formidable father. Of course it was impossible not to admire his ardent attempts to align Christian dogma with modern life. Like a new Agassiz, he preached the science of religion and the religion of science. "In successive stages of my career," he said, "I have been influenced by the master minds of Newman, Darwin, and Karl Marx." Dr. Crapsey did not shrink from applying to Rochester his sense of their generalizations. A vacant-lot gardening project, started as a relief measure for out-of-work families during a period of industrial layoffs, was maintained for several years. When Emily and Adelaide were sent in 1893 to Kemper Hall, an Episcopal boarding school in Kenosha, Wisconsin, they volunteered for the staff of the newspaper-magazine, the *Kemper Hall Kodak;* and among sixteen-year-old Adelaide's contributions was an article upholding Charlotte M. Yonge, the English novelist who defended the reforms of Anglicanism promulgated by Cardinal Newman and others in the Oxford Movement.

Also from Kemper she wrote: "What do you think I have done, Mamma? It will please you and Papa, I guess. I have stopped curling my hair and wear it parted in the middle just as straight as yours. Marjorie says I look exactly like you." There is a strong familial resemblance. Identifying with and later substituting for her mother, Adelaide tried to adopt the tone of a child seeking to please both her parents, but the qualifying comment indicates how unsure of herself she felt. The family's photo discloses that *all* the children parted their straight hair in the middle — an absurd point, except that in Adelaide's case she treated this as a sign of her singularity. She was her father's favorite. A number of photographs catch a gaze alert with pent-up intellectual energies missing from the dreamy and unfocused emotions in her mother's face. Perched on a U-shaped thronelike chair and wearing a formal gown décolleté enough to accentuate her torso and pale shoulders, the diminutive Adelaide stares away from the camera. In her deep-set eyes and full lips, expansive brow, and determined chin are mingled the claims and contradictions of sensuality, stoicism, delicacy, and a lurking innocence.

Part of the appeal of her image derives from her typicality as an emblematic young woman of her day, a coltish but cultivated undergraduate destined to discard her inevitable hair ribbon and enter the codified world of a female college faculty where prosody takes precedence over poetry; but she also conveys a concentrated detachment, the essence of something held back, to surface in those same poems in which she is unlike anyone else at all.

The reality of the struggle of Adelaide to be herself would appear in its most painful form during the final months of her life. While she was in a private nursing home at Saranac Lake in January 1914, her parents, without her knowledge, resigned her cherished teaching position at Smith. So outraged was Adelaide, and so crushed, that in April, upon learning what had happened, she permitted herself to express feelings ordinarily suppressed:

> When it comes to saying what I think of the whole thing I'm simply bereft of words. It seems to me utterly unbelievably [unbelievable] that such a decision should have been made without consulting me — and that it should have been "kept from" me for two whole months. Now I've not only got to face what I dreaded beyond anything else — another year without work — but instead of making the decision for myself like a reasonable human being (and I knew perfectly well that such a decision loomed pretty threatenin[g]ly before me) I've just been arbitrarily sand-bagged with it. That is the worst thing that could have happened — has happened in the worst possibly [possible] way — and I feel utterly disheartened and discouraged.

A letter from M. L. Burton, the president of Smith, had arrived in Rochester, inquiring about the effect of Adelaide's illness on her plans for the next year, but instead of forwarding the letter, the parents had consulted with her doctors and then had written Burton. Thus they removed Adelaide's principal motivation for staying alive in her struggle against tuberculosis, and to make matters worse, seemed blissfully unaware of their blunder:

> Father, as far as I can make out, forgot all about the transaction and Mother put the letters away (forgetting about them too probably!) — and by no breath or sign of any description was it intimated to me that anything had been done.

Adelaide's misspellings convey her emotional agitation and the shock of betrayal. The realism behind the decision may have been fair to Smith; nonetheless, it left her dazed, vulnerable, and panicked by the proximity of death.

> Father turned up on Saturday and I've explained to him with some lucidity (though truly Esther, I wasnt horrid about it) how it all seems to me. I think I converted him to my view of the matter — But of what use is that now.

Back at Kemper, however, the Crapsey sisters had only wished to excel, and excel they did. Adelaide had followed Emily as editor of the *Kodak*, played basketball (despite her height), finished four years of Latin in two, won the school's French prize, and also followed Emily as class valedictorian. In Emily's senior year, their father delivered the commencement address.

In 1897 Adelaide entered Vassar, where she duplicated her Kemper Hall academic and extracurricular distinctions, was named class poet for her last three years, won election to Phi Beta Kappa, and graduated with honors. The motivation to excel suggests another poet at a women's college fifty years later; but Sylvia Plath at Smith resented the absence of her dead father, whereas Adelaide still hoped to impress a father who condemned England's Transvaal policies.

Impress him or not, she incorporated many of his views in herself. Adelaide's typewritten thesis, "The Social Democratic Party of America," seems even today a remarkably mature sociopolitical analysis, despite a tendency to partisan argument. Still, she is also shrewdly impersonal: "In many causes of the Socialist Party the principles of socialism are thoroughly grasped and an application to American conditions is intellectually made, but in many others there is nothing but a glib use of catchwords, a meaningless array of statistics and an hysterical denunciation of everything in existence." The prevailing decorum of Vassar is indicated by the fact that she and her roommate, Jean Webster, the sole undergraduate supporters of Eugene V. Debs, were considered the campus radicals. Jean was as original in her own right as Adelaide; together, they gave their class a special cachet.

Alice Jane Chandler Webster, a grandniece of Mark Twain from Fredonia, New York, wanted to be a popular writer. She fulfilled that aim virtually out of college in a series of novels based on a breezy and ingenious college heroine named Patty. *Daddy-Long-Legs,* Jean Webster's 1914 Broadway hit, and its sequel, *Dear Enemy,* have few admirers today when Jean's brand of sentiment seems forever trapped in its saccharine period, but *Daddy-Long-Legs,* starring Ruth Chatterton, enjoyed one of the year's longest Broadway runs. Translated into several languages, the play was adapted for the screen, where it proved exceptionally durable. Mary Pickford played in it in 1918, Janet Gaynor and Warner Baxter in 1931; as *Curly Top,* in 1935, it became a vehicle for Shirley Temple and John Boles; and with revisions that left only vestiges of the plot structure, it was turned into a 1955 song-and-dance film for Leslie Caron and Fred Astaire.

Daddy-Long-Legs is the story of a rich playboy who sponsors the education of an orphanage drudge, and once she blossoms into a comely young woman he is smitten. The Cinderella motif is unmistakable; around the sentimentality of the piece, however, the orphans ("the small, blue-ginghamed lonely ones of earth"), and the thinly disguised Oedipal undercurrents, flickers a genuine humanitarian impulse. Visits to orphanages and to soup kitchens — Jean was a stringer for a Poughkeepsie newspaper — undoubtedly strengthened her sympathies for the underdog, and it appears likely that Adelaide would have joined her. The somberness of these visits was unrepresentative of the high spirits palpable in their surviving correspondence. They were simply Best Friends and would always remain so, and when Jean wrote Adelaide's valedictory in the March 1915 *Vassar Miscellany* it was her bubbling sense of humor that came back to her roommate.

Jean's trajectory between 1901 and 1915 constituted a steadily rising curve; Adelaide's arc was wavering and hesitant. *When Patty Went to College,* published serially in 1903, attracted attention; Jean declared that her sparkling heroine was based on Adelaide. Novels poured from Jean's prolific pen, including more Patty adventures, *The Wheat Princess* (1905), *Jerry Junior* (1907), and *Much Ado About Peter* (1909); she spent long periods in Italy and purchased an old house on West Tenth Street. There is no evidence that Adelaide resented those tokens of success; on the contrary, she relished Jean's good fortune as vicarious relief from the disturbances within the Crapsey family. Emily at twenty-four died suddenly of appendicitis, while an elder brother, Philip, died in 1907 of malaria contracted during the Spanish-American War. The heresy trial of the Reverend Dr. Crapsey resulted in his formal deposition from the ministry for preaching his secular views about the Virgin Birth, and the family survived on the bounty of an admirer, William Rossiter Stewart, a Rochester philanthropist, who built them a new house. Adelaide returned to Kemper Hall, where she taught for two years, and during this period began to think of herself as a scholar rather than a poet. Inspired by the inexhaustible metrical resourcefulness of Milton, she decided to make her lifework the application of phonetics to English metrical problems.

A Study in English Metrics, published in 1918, became her passionate fixation. It was intended as a major intellectual statement, a highly technical treatise in which scientific methodology was applied to English poetry just as the same methodology was applied by her father to religious doctrine. The work is crammed with charts and percentages and scrupulous syllable computation, but, as Butscher remarks, "It is saddening to admit that so much of the laborious syllable counting could be done in a fraction of the time and effort today by computer." Like Trudeau in medicine, she worked within the limitations of the technology of her day; and if the results seem monotonous and barren to us, her concepts promised to yield an art of infinite possibility. On the positive side, the study refuted the popular notion that English prosody evolved from a lower state to a higher, according to the principles of the idea of progress; and Adelaide was able to demonstrate why Gilbert Murray was wrong in holding Swinburne more "classical" than Milton. Were there ancillary creative benefits? The study of metrics may have convinced her that stress rather than feet can determine a line. The monotonous tiers of unrevealing statistical evidence, though, present an image of Adelaide walling herself away in this abstruse and barren study as a medieval nun might retreat into the shadows of the cloister. From 1902 to the middle of 1913 she worked ceaselessly on the project, counting, counting. Her decision to construct a scholarly magnum opus undoubtedly was influenced by the narrow range of roles open to the women of her day, but it had the effect of sequestering her from her poetic contemporaries as effectively as Emily Dickinson had been sequestered in Amherst; and until Adelaide's year in Saranac, it made her regard the making of her own poetry as incidental.

The sole affectation that might mark her as a poet was a propensity for dressing in gray — gray dresses, gray capes, gray shoes. First remarked when she was teaching at Smith, this may have begun years before. Gray became her; the color of twilight and of self-denial, her habit symbolized the rigorous duty to which she felt consecrated. Then again, on a much simpler bias, gray demonstrated undoubted style. Adelaide had male friendships, after all, and though she seems to have spent her adulthood in relative emotional isolation, evidence of sexual passion exists in her poetry. "Birth Moment," the early poem that ends on a vocative injunction to Aphrodite, celebrates desire.

(Ah, keenest personal moment
When mouth unkissed turns eager-slow and tremulous
Towards lover's mouth . . .)

The apprentice-work poem has a striking physicality. "I offer myself to you as cool water in a cup of crystal," begins another youthful rhapsody, but Adelaide's actual love affairs, if any, are a matter of conjecture.

Separate European periods, 1904–5 and 1909–11, bracketed by periods of teaching at Kemper Hall and Miss Lowe's Preparatory School, in Stamford, Connecticut, added substantially to her poetic development. Extreme poverty characterized her European travels, days spent in libraries and probably in bed, for at Kemper she began to disclose symptoms of protracted fatigue. In view of her shyness, her absorption in her metrical analysis, and the state of her health, it is hardly surprising that in London she did not meet Ezra Pound, T. E. Hulme, Hilda Doolittle, or other English members of the group with whom she was later associated under Pound's label "Imagism," yet she reached many of their conclusions independently. Poetry required hard-edged images as corrective to the lush diction of the Georgians. Poetry must say as much as the short lyrics of Walter Savage Landor and Emily Dickinson, strong influences on Adelaide together with the language of the Bible on which she had been reared.

Astonishingly, she antedated Pound in exposing Western verse forms to Oriental influences. Like Pound, Adelaide did not speak Japanese or Chinese — about 1904 she had read translations from the Chinese in Rome — and her principal contact with haiku and tanka techniques derived from French translation, notably Michel Revon's *Anthologie de la Littérature Japonaise*, published in Paris in 1910. Another source was Yone Noguchi's collection of originals and translations, *From the Japanese Sea*, published in London in 1903 and New York in 1910. (Pound did not begin to study the manuscripts of the Orientalist Ernest Fenollosa until 1913.) Revon, containing explanations of the layers of meaning implicit for the Japanese reader, is by far the superior work, free of the lacquered mannerisms that mar Noguchi's selections.

The influence of Japanese literature upon the English form she came to devise, the cinquain, remains problematic. As the word *cinquain* suggests, it has five lines and so does the classical waka, which during the Meiji era came to be called the tanka, but there the technical resemblance ceases. The tanka is a syllabic, rhymed form, having thirty-one syllables; the cinquain, developed by Adelaide in 1911, is built on stresses, one for the first line, two for the second, three for the third, four for the fourth, and then, like a plucked string fading into silence, one for the fifth. Although Adelaide copied eleven tanka and eight haiku into her notebooks, Sister M. Edwardine O'Connor, a pioneering textual critic of the cinquain, rejects any Japanese influence: "This verse form grew out of a deliberate effort on her part to find the shortest form of English verse." The result made "the most condensed metrical form in English that would hold together as a complete unit." Later discovery of the direct links between Adelaide Crapsey and Japanese literature — while examining her manuscripts, Hideo Kanawami recognized passages of Basho as translated by Revon — would seem to invalidate this. Perhaps both inferences are correct: in creating an English form meant to have a tensile clarity and a mood of evanescence, Adelaide discovered her temperamental affinity to Japanese poetry. A more basic question is *why* she fashioned such a taut exacting pattern, a form that proceeds with the meticulous ceremony of the Japanese tea ritual or Anglican worship. The self-control brought to her study of prosody is evident, the same self-control demonstrated during the outwardly passive terminal months at the nursing home; but there is also a natural disposition toward classical reticence. The grays of her imagination blend unobtrusively into a landscape of wintry tones; moreover her technique demonstrates the view, presented in a letter to Jean Webster, that people have a right to unexplained motives.

The invention of the cinquain coincided with a worsening of Adelaide's condition at Smith College, where, after two years in Europe, she had become an instructor in poetics. Her progress toward academic recognition, the syllable-and-accent counting, continued in a cramped and virtually airless English seminar room. Tired by mechanical, repetitive labor, she sought relief in writing poems. As a flowering plant about to die sometimes begins to bloom, her creative powers seemed more assertive as her health declined. Still she did not consider herself a poet, although she had created a vehicle related to her interest in prosody. She did not have a voice of her own, a voice identical with its subject. How aware was she of death? The college doctor prescribed fresh air; Adelaide spent too much time indoors. A daily walk and plenty of fresh air ought to take care of her fatigue, he said. It was so obvious, he did not bother to conduct a physical examination.

In the summer of 1913, while a house guest of Jean Webster in Tyringham, Massachusetts, Adelaide collapsed.

"On the 8th of July as I got out of my bath I leaned over quickly felt a remarkable pain and after a second found it more discrete [discreet] to drop full length on the bathroom floor than to stand up. After a while I got up grabbed a nightdress — and retired again to the floor."

The defense mechanism of humor was her last resort: "It was awfully funny," she informed Esther Lowenthal, but the joke failed to deflect her pain or the anxiety of her friends. To Glenn Ford McKinney, Jean wrote of finding a private hospital for Adelaide in Pittsfield, a hospital to which she went only under duress. Until that point she had managed to conceal the truth, even from herself, and in Pittsfield also there were doctors who, after examining her lungs, held contradictory opinions. Toward the end of the summer, however, the medical evidence became impossible to misinterpret.

"I got back to Tyr. yesterday to find the most distressing news about Adelaide —" Jean wrote Glenn.

> She has been examined by two throat & lung specialists and they both say that she has tuberculosis in rather an aggravated form. She has had it for 3 or 4 years in a lurking hard to diagnose way, but it has suddenly burst out into a well developed unmistakable case. She must give up Smith and go to Saranak immediately for two years at least.
>
> There is a very good Sanitarium about a mile & a half out of the village where it isn't so depressing nor abnormally expensive. I am hoping to be able to get her in there but there's a big waiting list & it requires some pull. I have written to everyone I know of who has any interest with the head doctors. I may have to take her up to Saranak myself & make sure that she is comfortably installed with all the queer things she needs for a winter in the open. Her family are not awfully efficient about putting things like that through and of course they are most dreadfully upset. She was their last hope. All the rest of them more or less have had accidents or illnesses or operations & they are nervously worn-out with 12 years of that strain. Nine children are too many in a nervous family! There is always something awful just going to happen.

Was Jean meeting Adelaide's expenses? The bare cupboard of a defrocked clergyman dependent on a patron's generosity seems an unlikely place to furnish the costs of a protracted illness. Adelaide's salary at Smith was inadequate to cover her care in those days before health insurance; so it is not unreasonable to assume that Jean, whose popular successes augmented her family money, aided her friend. In any event, by early September Adelaide was installed in a Saranac cure cottage at 39 Clinton Avenue rather than in the sanatorium proper. The latter's waiting list may have prompted this decision. The cottage faced Pine Ridge Cemetery, thick with the shadows of tall pines falling across the well-kept grass.

The grim sight of the cemetery would confront Adelaide daily that winter while she lay motionless in sub-zero temperatures on the porch. "I'm down flat — don't get up at all — do nothing — one letter a day + that frowned on . . . I'll write as soon as I can — got a temperature yesterday settling Eng A marks + such — so I'm lying low today —

"Really everything is being done — It's just a matter of keeping still + waiting . . ."

Her physician was Dr. Edward R. Baldwin, the same Dr. Baldwin from New Haven who had knocked on Trudeau's door. At the sanatorium he had recovered sufficiently to resume a practice and make himself invaluable in the older doctor's lab research. Adelaide immediately established a rapport; she responded to his youth and obvious compassion, and so impressed him that he left a memoir of her Saranac ordeal. As she wrote to Esther Lowenthal, the Smith economist:

> Dr. Baldwin is very nice indeed, very quiet — and very cautious. It's a great relief to me to find that he is as careful about his greys as I am. Grey overcoat, grey other things, grey tie and a scarf pin of some cloudy grey crystal — All of this I am sure will be a great help. (These frivolous comments for your ear alone) — I seem to be going on very well — whether it's fundamental or not I'll tell you when I know. I'm still on this silly "absolute quiet" regime — I'll be glad when I can at least brush my hair and take my own bath.

Throughout that cruel year of fluctuating hopes, a year in which she would discover her identity as a poet, her letters — with the exception of the incident of the loss of her job at Smith — never register bitterness. To her friends she is unfailingly cheerful; she insists on keeping up with the New York and London *Times*, her customary fare; the *Atlantic;* the *Nation; Poetry;*

the latest in belles-lettres and novels. At the same time she is never far from the pages of a lifelong devotional text, the pages of what she called her Simon-pure King James Bible. Dr. Baldwin thought of her as invalidish, so sensitive she was "unsuited for association with the other patients," so he was unprepared for the explosion of fury when he informed her that she must abandon her prosodic inquiry.

Here was a woman, after all, whose reflective yet detached attitude toward language made every overtone matter, like the gray wash and curve of brushwork in a Zen drawing; and, in fact, she punctuated poetry with an ellipsis of only two dots.

> *Just now,*
> *Out of the strange*
> *Still dusk . . as strange, as still . .*
> *A white moth flew. Why am I grown*
> *So cold?*

Here was a woman who, despite a lifetime of restraint, suddenly burst into a vehement spun-out line more reminiscent of Whitman than of waka, whose monologue carried the cadences of Browning, and who spoke for herself rather than for a fictive character. The very title, often rendered as "Trudeau's Garden" because of a subsequent penciled addition, proclaims her subjectivity: "To the Dead in the Grave-Yard Under My Window: — Written in a Moment of Exasperation."

> *How can you lie so still? All day I watch*
> *And never a blade of all the green sod moves*
> *To show where restlessly you toss and turn,*
> *And fling a desperate arm or draw up knees*
> *Stiffened and aching from their long disuse;*
> *I watch all night and not one ghost comes forth*
> *To take its freedom of the midnight hour.*
> *Oh, have you no rebellion in your bones?*
> *The very worms must scorn you where you lie,*
> *A pallid mouldering acquiescent folk,*

Meek habitants of unresented graves.
Why are you there in your straight row on row
Where I must ever see you from my bed
That in your mere dumb presence iterate
The text so weary in my ears: "Lie still
And rest; be patient and lie still and rest."
I'll not be patient! I will not lie still!
There is a brown road runs between the pines,
And further on the purple woodlands lie,
And still beyond blue mountains lift and loom;
And I would walk the road and I would be
Deep in the wooded shade and I would reach
The windy mountain tops that touch the clouds.
My eyes may follow but my feet are held.
Recumbent as you others must I too
Submit? Be mimic of your movelessness
With pillow and counterpane for stone and sod?
And if the many sayings of the wise
Teach of submission I will not submit
But with a spirit all unreconciled
Flash an unquenched defiance to the stars.
Better it is to walk, to run, to dance,
Better it is to laugh and leap and sing,
To know the open skies of dawn and night,
To move untrammel'd down the flaming noon,
And I will clamour it through weary days
Keeping the edge of deprivation sharp,
Nor with the pliant speaking on my lips
Of resignation, sister to defeat.
I'll not be patient. I will not lie still.

And in ironic quietude who is
The despot of our days and lord of dust
Needs but, scarce heeding, wait to drop
Grim casual comment on rebellion's end:
"Yes, yes . . . Wilful and petulant but now
As dead and quiet as the others are."

And this each body and ghost of you hath heard
That in your graves do therefore lie so still.

There is a magnificence in it. Yes, it may be too long, too theatrical, too showy; the language may veer from the casual interior monologue to the archaic inversion and near-cliché, but no
matter. The poem, acquiring headlong eloquence, addresses a
spiritual crisis as unequivocal as T. S. Eliot's dark night of the
soul in "The Dry Salvages." The defenses Adelaide found so
protective were in ruins, her notion of herself demolished.
Nevertheless, she remained her father's daughter, a heretic in a
secular world of sickness, surrounded by doctors rather than
priests.

Saranac made her a writer. Unlike Stevenson or Aldrich, she
had no literary reputation to bother about, but all at once she
confronted a searing subject, her imminent death, and developed a new flexibility of manner. Parallels to the art of Emily
Dickinson grow marked, not only in Adelaide's isolation and the
extreme compression of her lines, but in her off-slant vision, an
originality influenced by her mounting distrust of gaudy diction.
"Lines Addressed to My Left Lung Inconveniently Enamoured
of Plant-Life" manifests mordant humor, and if the poem's in-
clusion in a letter accounts for its black mirth, Adelaide had no
hope at that point of seeing any of her lines in print. By the
fourth of February her increasing debility prompted Dr. Baldwin to try collapse therapy, the artificial pneumothorax treatment developed in the late nineteenth century by the eminent
physician Carlo Forlanini. She submitted to the grueling surgical
procedures with her customary gallantry:

Everyone was very gay — my "pnemo thorax party" it got called
— and chatted most sociably — the patient occassionally [sic] laps-
ing into silence (after her usual fashion) — I report one nice retort — It was getting to be pretty clear that the 3d try was not
going to be successful — and I heard Dr. Price say gaily — "Well,

you know, with one man we tried 57 times" and placidly Dr. Baldwin's voice remarking — "Oh, Price is thinking of pickles" (I couldn't see them you know first because my back was turned to them and my arm up (to draw the ribs apart) and second because I always screw my eyes tight shut when any one does anything to me.)

The following week Esther Lowenthal visited Saranac Lake, perused the manuscript poems, and fetched them to the typist who had served in a similar capacity for the metrical study. And Jean Webster, in the role of informal literary agent, took time away from the hectic progress of her first Broadway production to interest editors in Adelaide's work. Her interminable hours on the cottage porch (*"I'll not be patient. I will not lie still"*) were for Jean, now engaged to Glenn Ford McKinney, incandescent and brief. Nevertheless she journeyed to see Adelaide periodically. There were good days and bad days, and on one of the good days Jean brought Adelaide a special delivery letter of acceptance from the *Century Magazine*. The weather that spring was chill and rainy, however, and she fought a gathering depression. She was resolved to get well, but chafed at her setbacks, her perplexing fevers. Could she begin teaching again? Had Esther heard about Wheaton College? Might another sanatorium produce better results?

"I have just written to Dr. J. Alexander Miller to see if he won't be able to suggest a place where he could take charge of the case," Jean wrote Glenn. "He has a wide variety of noncharity patients and he must know some nice places for them to live . . ." The reports from Europe at the outbreak of the First World War augmented Adelaide's foreboding. In late August she departed Saranac on a train ride in sweltering heat to Rochester. The days remaining until her death on October 8 were marked by swift decline. Her first biographer, evoking Adelaide's poem "Incantation," gives an account of the poet's final night that suggests the potency of her legend — and the depths of the romantic mist still veiling the pathology of tuberculosis.

The nurse came downstairs, looking rather frightened, her arms filled with flowers. "I don't know what to do with these. Miss Crapsey told me to take them all away." She was moved to a porch over the garden. There she spent her last night. She remembered Italy and a little Italian moon-charm about which she had written a poem years ago. ("You must say it nine times, curtseying, and then wish.") She looked up at the moon and tried the charm. "*O mia Luna! Porta mi fortuna!*"

Jean Webster's version differs. Having left the tumult of her hit show to be at Adelaide's bedside, she wrote on stationery from the Hotel Seneca:

> Dear Glenn,
>   Adelaide is terribly weak. I doubt if she can live through the night — and the most horrible thing is that I don't want her to. She hasn't slept for four nights. She isn't able to lie down, but sits huddled in the nurse's arms gasping for breath.

Nearly a year later, September 7, 1915, Jean and Glenn were married. Their only child, a daughter, was born the following June 10, and because of complications attending the birth, Jean died twenty-four hours later. Adelaide's letters to Jean were subsequently cleaned out of Mrs. McKinney's New York apartment.

When Adelaide died her mother remained unaware of her daughter's talents as a poet, but Dr. Crapsey with unconscious irony commented, "For fifteen years she had been a sick woman doing the work of two well women." Only that May, Adelaide, writing Esther Lowenthal from Saranac, had asked if she would mind doing an errand and buying some clothes for her not in the customary grays but "pretty powdery flowery designs . . . I've had so many just plain colours," she said. "I look less ill in pink."

CHAPTER SIX

"The Hour of Counterfeit Bliss"
1915–1926

IN ALFRED MURGER'S *Scènes de la Vie de Bohème*, the source of Puccini's opera, the heroine Mimi is told she might die with the falling leaves. "Why should the falling leaves worry us?" she replies. "Let us spend our days among pine trees where leaves are always green."

With every passing year Edward Livingston Trudeau seemed readier to heed those words. He was haunted by his inability to eradicate tuberculosis, but hunting and fishing still yielded satisfaction, the trees and ponds a mystical source of strength. More and more he resembled his father, that dedicated and obsessive sportsman who preferred the campfires of Osage Indians to the burdens of city life. Trudeau was gradually relinquishing active medical practice: Edward Baldwin assumed the responsibilities of the laboratory while Lawrason Brown took charge of the sanatorium. A dedicated palace guard — doctors Trembley, Price, Blanchet, Mayer, and Kinghorn, in addition to Baldwin and Brown — exhibited, like their leader, firsthand experience of the disease. Tuberculars who had salvaged their lives and careers, they authenticated the miracles of a cold climate and resin-laden air. By now Dr. Trudeau was a monument, a mythical founding father. Anecdotes clustered around him, the time, for instance, he informed a patient, "The worse you are, the less the bill." When the examination was over, the patient wanted to know, "How am I?" "I owe you ten dollars," the doctor said quietly.

To be sure, he still radiated his fabled optimism. Age brought out a latent streak of vanity, as it sometimes does in men who suspect themselves superannuated and are anxious to demonstrate otherwise. Perhaps it was as simple as having an auditor; Trudeau retained the eloquence of his convictions, but time was claiming the friends of earlier days in Saranac Lake. Holding court at teas, salons, and dinners, he basked in the praise of hero-worshiping dowagers before pretending the ladies bored him with their prattle. Nothing gave him keener pleasure on such occasions than recounting the exploits of his eldest son, Ned — Edward Livingston Trudeau Jr. The terminal months of Chatte had been brightened by Ned's undergraduate triumphs at Yale. (Once he came into a baseball game as relief pitcher, Princeton leading, 7–1, and Yale won the game, 8–7.) President of his class at his father's Columbia College of Physicians and Surgeons, Ned was a doctor of unusual promise who, upon completing his training, had married an artistically talented Chicagoan before joining a flourishing New York practice. "I rejoiced I had not let him assume a more obscure career with his father in the remote Adirondack village, with its ever-present burden of chronic illness," Trudeau recorded, not without a touch of paternal self-congratulation; but, while convalescing from pneumonia, Ned died suddenly at the age of thirty-two.

Of the Trudeaus' children only one would survive to become a physician. Ned's death sapped his father's resilience, and tuberculosis, so long quiescent, flared anew. Lung collapse therapy provided fleeting relief; the doctor's migraine headaches refused to subside, however, and his health was obviously declining. Bedridden with increasing frequency, he developed a contemplative fatalism on the subject of death, which he called "the grip of the tiger."

"When you've been in the game as long as I have, you'll come to regard sickness as part of the day's business and something to be expected," he told a visitor. Nevertheless, despite a certain prosaic inevitability, death for Trudeau assumed tantalizing moral dimensions.

> This business of life and death puzzles me [he went on]. Why should there be such a thing as suffering in the world? I don't understand the scheme. It all reminds me of this suffragette "Cat and Mouse" bill in England. They put a militant in jail and then when she is likely to die of starvation they let her out. Getting back her strength, she goes back to a cell and nearly starves to death again. And again they let her out, and — so the grim comedy goes on!
> It's just the same in this world of sickness. Death's the cat; life's the mouse. Death comes along and paws you about till life's at its last ebb. Then Death, like the cat, goes into a corner and waits until the victim recovers enough strength to suffer some more, when the cat comes pawing again.

His favorite guide, Fitz Greene Hallock, cut paths, removing brush and logs, so that Trudeau could hunt. Presently the doctor became unable to walk and Hallock designed a portable chair that guides lugged through the woods with Trudeau swaying between the poles. The sedan-chair effect was regal — and it was enhanced by the duplicate chair Hallock built for Charlotte Trudeau — moreover, it was representative, for in Saranac Lake the Trudeaus reigned over the medical hierarchy and were revered as though they comprised an actual dynastic succession.

During the autumn of 1913, two years before the doctor's death from the complications of tuberculosis, Hallock took Trudeau on a hunt over the old trails. Other guides bore a sofa that they placed near a juncture of logging roads, and Trudeau, rifle across his knees, sat on the sofa, waiting. The earth was moist from ground fog and rank with the odors of lichens and fallen leaves. Light trickled from the pale sky, but the emaciated doctor betrayed no impatience, though he was obviously expectant as he had been expectant forty years earlier, spreadeagled across the balsam boughs of the guide boat outside Paul Smith's. Appolos was gone; he had died the year before and was buried beneath a massive granite marker near the crosses of Trudeau's children in the pine-sheltered cemetery of St. John's in the Wilderness. The shrieking of birds vanished amid the evergreens, chipmunks dodged the sofa's legs, but before all shapes dissolved, there was a distant crackling of branches and a ten-point buck stepped from the brush onto the road. Trudeau raised his rifle, sighted along the barrel. The crash of his shot ruptured the darkening air.

American folk heroes and heroines of the past could be measured by the yardstick of work, but the folk heroes of the future, prototypes of leisure like the baseball player or the gangster, diverted the increasing spare time of industrialized society. The work ethic no longer commanded automatic respect. Dr. Trudeau's America was slipping away — an era of materialism, greed, and conspicuous consumption, yet also a time of reactions against those values, the late nineteenth century retaining odd, elegiac traces of the pieties of earlier generations. Saranac's shift from work to play accompanied two historical circumstances: the proximity of the Canadian border, which made the village a haven for bootleggers once Prohibition arrived, and the abrupt upturn in tuberculosis cases accompanying the First World War.

Mortality rates from tuberculosis increased markedly in every combatant country by 1915 and did not slacken until the Armistice. This statistical profile followed the curve of past experience: TB was as integral to warfare as patriotism. Hardship, unfavorable living conditions, and stress caused the death rate in England and Wales to soar from 125 per 100,000 population in 1914 to nearly 250 in 1918, and the same rate of increase occurred in Prussia. The war created an entirely new class of patients; and symbolic of the twentieth-century folk hero as disabled veteran was a ballplayer of genius, right-handed pitcher

Christy Mathewson, who arrived in Saranac Lake in 1920 after contracting tuberculosis as a result of his service as assistant gas officer of the Rainbow Division in France.

The Mathewson house on Park Avenue — it is still called the Mathewson house today, almost sixty years after his death — is a substantial gray-shingled building on a large balsam-shrouded corner lot. Elite residences line Park Avenue, ending at the field-stone gates of the Trudeau Institute (Saranac makes a distinction between "upper" Park and the presumably less elegant lower portion), but amid the Tudor estates built for doctors and the assertive mansions erected by millionaires with tubercular rela-tives, the Mathewson house, like the man himself, is unostenta-tious. Here Matty spent his final years, dying at forty-five after the first game of the 1925 World Series between Washington and Pittsburgh. The following day at Forbes Field the players wore mourning bands and W. O. McGeehan of the *New York Herald Tribune* voiced a widespread sentiment in calling Matty "the best loved of all baseball players and the most popular of all Ameri-can athletes of all time."

Accounts differ about the mishap — either it took place in a gas chamber stateside or during training at Choignes in France — that caused Mathewson's early death. Branch Rickey, who served with Matty in the newly organized Chemical Warfare Ser-vice, insisted no accident occurred overseas. Together they com-pleted an identical course at Choignes, and after the final field exercise, Matty, then thirty-eight years old, won an impromptu broad-jumping contest against all comers. Rickey's testimony is interesting, for when he and Matty were gas officers in France, Wesley Branch Rickey himself was a decade away from Saranac. Although his playing talents were lackluster — a catcher for the New York Americans, he once surrendered thirteen bases in a single game, still a major-league record — he would nonetheless leave his mark on the sport as coach, manager, general manager, father of the farm-team system, and the owner who, with Jackie Robinson, broke baseball's color bar in effect since Cap Anson threw a tantrum in 1887 over the proposed signing of a black player named George Stovey. At law school in Ohio State University in the fall of 1908, Rickey had strained his health through all-night study and extracurricular work. The doctors diagnosed tuberculosis and that winter he went to Saranac Lake, where his condition improved enough to permit enrollment at the University of Michigan law school in 1909.

Whether or not Rickey was right about Mathewson's accident, exposure to gas in the Army of Occupation — he had volunteered on August 28, at the close of the 1918 season — weakened his resistance. "He had to train the boys in the use of gas masks and in the tricky ways of the deadly gases," one contemporary said. "It was the sort of job no life insurance company would recommend. It left Christy Mathewson's strong lungs impaired." A newspaper report of his funeral was not off the mark: "Capt. Christy Mathewson was buried yesterday, a victim of the World War."

Matty officially neither smoked nor drank, and if he indulged himself with a drink or cigarette on occasion, he favored abstinence. He was handsome and blond — not craggy baseball-player handsome, but as handsome as a square-jawed Arrow Collar Man or the romantic lead of a Broadway musical. Six feet one and a half inches, 195 pounds, with regular features and an open, candid expression, he unquestionably possessed physical magnetism. More than that, his triumphs were based on a blend of prowess and gallantry: he was arguably the greatest control pitcher in the game's history, and beyond argument a gentleman who made baseball couth. Indeed, Matty represented a throwback to the homespun virtues of Dr. Trudeau; the twenties antihero was about to come into style, the Chicago Black Sox were harbingers of postwar disillusionment, but Matty was chivalry wearing an unpadded leather glove, a Galahad among Neanderthals. The teams he played for were populated by tobacco-chomping bozos so superstitious they'd spit in their hats at the sight of a cross-eyed man. They had names like "Tacks" and

"Bugs" and, in the case of the intrepid deaf-mute New York Giants pitcher, Luther Hayden Taylor, "Dummy." Outfielder "Turkey Mike" Donlin, the batting star of the Giants, missed the greater part of the 1902 season because he was serving a prison sentence for drunken assault. In this company Matty seemed as august as a vestryman. He would not play on Sundays. While he had no personal objection to playing Sunday baseball, he realized that would distress his sabbatarian mother, so he never did. (Branch Rickey, who actually made a similar promise to his mother, never personally participated in or attended a Sunday game, but became the inventor of the Sunday double-header, prompting John Lardner to dub him "a man opposed to Sunday baseball except when the gate receipts exceeded $5000.")

Foremost among Matty's skills, however, was his problem-solving ability. His mind worked like a slide rule, calculating fast and slow, hit and field, pause and feint. Baseball is not a game of inches, Rube Bressler told Lawrence S. Ritter in the classic oral history *The Glory of Their Times,* it's a game of *hundredths* of inches. Furthermore, baseball is a game of deceit. Extreme precision — measurement, analysis, method — disclosing the patterns of the game as consistent and sensible, contrasts with elements of guile showing that nothing is exactly what it seems. Matty's study of the logic of games became as indispensable to him as his fast ball; he had a temperament that responded to the challenge of abstract puzzles.

Sportswriters always mentioned his college background (Bucknell ex-'02) as though it was unique, but that was part of his role as the player chosen to lend decorum to the raffish national game. He was not a singular product of higher education: during Matty's active career (1900–16) there was no scarcity of college men in baseball. Indeed his battery mate, Chief Meyers, had matriculated at Dartmouth. Among Matty's colleagues were Harry Hooper, with a St. Mary's degree in civil engineering; Eddie Plank, who pitched against Mathewson at Gettysburg College; and Eddie Collins, former quarterback of the Columbia football team. Branch Rickey collected two undergraduate degrees from Allegheny while playing in the American League, and Miller Huggins, a protégé of future President William Howard Taft, received his law degree before entering baseball. College, however, doesn't certify a passion for recognizing thematic patterns in games, and in identifying and remembering such patterns Matty was unsurpassed. Checker champion of a half-dozen states, he often played and won simultaneous matches. He was a potential grandmaster at chess, a middling golfer, better than average around a billiard table, and deadly in whist, poker, and bridge. For years, he met his road expenses by playing poker but preferred to spend his evenings in chess clubs challenging top-ranked competitors. Like the virtuosi of the clubs, he played tournaments blindfolded. While his teammates caroused, he was often contesting a score of opponents in stark subbasement rooms. He applied the same mental habits to other pursuits. Curiosity about poetry caused him to ask sportswriter Langdon Smith, who had written "Evolution, or The Tadpole and the Fish," how to do it. "I know there's a trick in this verse writing," he said to Smith, "and I want you to give me the key — the mathematics of it. I can see the lines run in regular combinations of syllables." Smith supplied an instant course in verse forms and gave Matty a book on the subject. Although he subsequently wrote poems and became an avid reader of them, Matty's verse did not meet his own standards and he suppressed it. Fiction, on the other hand, never attracted him; he distrusted what he regarded as make-believe and read until he felt he had a tangible grasp of a specific subject. (The essays of Charles Lamb, his favorite author, provided the exception to this puritanical rule.)

Science, typically, rather than chance brought him into baseball. Matty's account of his start reveals his lifelong problem-solving aptitude and his methodical engineering approach. Someone else might have thrown a stone casually; Matty saw it as a challenge of aerodynamics:

When I was a boy about eight or nine years old I lived in Factoryville, Pennsylvania, a little country town. I had a cousin older than myself who was always studying the theory of throwing. I used to throw flat stones with him and he would show me (what I suppose almost every boy knows) that if a flat stone is started with the flat surface parallel to the ground it will always turn over before it lands. That is, after it loses its speed, and the air cushion fails to support it, the stone will turn over and drop down. The harder it is thrown the longer the air sustains it and the farther it will carry before it drops. If the stone started with the flat surface at an acute angle to the earth, instead of parallel to it, a stone, instead of dropping, would curve horizontally. I began to make all sorts of experiments with stones.

I got to be a great stone thrower, and this practice increased my throwing power and taught me something about curves. When I was nine years old I could throw a stone farther than any of the boys who were my chums.

From this I became interested in baseball games, and before long I was allowed to stand behind the catcher when the Factoryville team was playing and "shag" foul balls or carry the bats or the water.

They called him "Husk" in Factoryville because he was strapping, yet he was not a product of the soil; his mother had inherited a modest fortune and his father was a gentleman farmer. A younger brother succeeded in breaking into the majors, too, worked eleven innings, never won a game, but attained dubious immortality through one of the trick questions of early baseball statistics: "What pair of pitching brothers have the highest total of major league victories?" To refute anyone who mentioned the legitimate fraternal feats of the Coveleski brothers, Harry and Stanley, winners of 297 games, the answer was Christopher (373) and Henry Mathewson (0). Since 1974, Jim and Gaylord Perry have replaced them.

The afternoon Matty made his home-town pitching debut (the regular pitcher was suddenly indisposed) he was only fourteen, employing a fast ball, a change of pace, and two types of curves against men twice his age. His prep school, Keystone Academy, did not object if he pitched for a dollar a game against semi-pro teams from the coaltowns of northeast Pennsylvania, and by the fall of 1897, when he reached Bucknell, he was a baseball veteran. Not only did he star on the pitcher's mound, but in basketball and football, where he became an All-American fullback; he took an active part in two literary societies and the glee club and was elected class president. Doubtless he would have completed this illustrious campus career, but he had fallen in love with Jane Stoughton, a coed from Lewisburg, Pennsylvania, whom he later married, and professional baseball seemed the best chance of accumulating a nest egg. In 1899 he signed his first professional contract, for $80 a month, with the Taunton club of the New England League.

Competing against professionals, he failed to meet their standards. His glory days seemed over; he did not dazzle the league; in fact he seemed inept. Matty's principal problem as a pitcher always had been his motion. There was a slight jerk to his delivery that he could never entirely eliminate and that he admitted was hard on his arm. Nor had he perfected the control that later became his hallmark. In the New England League, more often than not, he was plagued by wildness.

A Taunton teammate, however, showed him the secret of a reverse curve or "fadeaway," a pitch now called a screwball; Matty's fadeaway broke outward from left-handed hitters, and he used his new acquisition with devastating effect. His 1900 season began at Norfolk, Virginia; by July he had won twenty of twenty-two starts. The New York Giants and Philadelphia Phillies courted him. The Giants, a bumbling club headed for a last-place National League finish, looked appalling on paper, but Matty, perusing the rosters of both teams, reasoned he'd have a better chance in the pitching rotation.

He was nineteen and his new teammates, unimpressed by his minor-league record, studied his work and dismissed it. When he had been with the club a few days, a sportswriter asked who he was, and the manager of the Giants, George Davis, replied, "Some kid who's supposed to be a pitcher. I don't think much of his motion, though. It's too hard on his arm, and if he shows anything, his arm won't stand the big league racket long. He's awkward." That season Mathewson appeared in only six games, lost his three starts, and walked twenty men in thirty-four innings. The Giants returned him to Norfolk, where he was drafted for $100 by Cincinnati, then hawked back to the Giants for Amos Rusie, a once-formidable, over-the-hill, sore-armed pitcher.

Matty's time had come, however. The fadeaway was increasingly manageable, while the obstinate arm jerk allowed him to place sharp, deceptive breaks on the ball. The Giants finished seventh in 1901, but Matty won twenty games, including a no-hitter against St. Louis. Suddenly he was a superman, the "Big Six" of legend, a sobriquet that derived from his physique rather than his field number. There were twelve other twenty-game seasons to come in sixteen years, and four with more than thirty wins. In 1903 he and "Iron Man" Joe McGinnity, who three times won both ends of a double-header and set a National League record of thirty-one wins, lifted the Giants from last place to second. In 1905 Matty gave an epic World Series performance, which still inspires awe — three shutouts against the Philadelphia A's in less than a week, fourteen hits scattered across twenty-seven innings, eighteen strikeouts, and one walk. Unquestionably his greatest season was 1908, when he pitched an astounding fifty-six games, winning thirty-seven, losing eleven, posting twelve shutouts, and fanning two hundred fifty-nine batters.

"They could sit in a rocking-chair and catch him," Chief Meyers, Matty's customary catcher, remarked about his control. The Chief, a devoted admirer, could never understand why Matty disdained to threaten batters with an inside fast ball; neither could another close friend noted for his combativeness, John

("Muggsy") McGraw, manager of the Giants throughout most of Matty's pitching career.

"All those guys are up there crowding the plate because they know you won't bean them. Why don't you cut one loose for the old bean once in a while — dust them off?" Meyers pleaded. "They'd back up then and wouldn't stand up with so much confidence. Just watch them stick their foot in the water bucket when Rube Marquard is working."

Matty shrugged and refused to throw at hitters, even when his baseball luck turned sour. Two of the most famous lapses in the game's annals — Fred Merkle's dash for the dugout when he should have touched second base, an oversight that cost the 1908 Giants a pennant; and center fielder Fred Snodgrass's muff of a lazy fly ball in the tenth inning of the 1912 World Series — turned victory into defeat despite Matty's flawless pitching performance, and in both instances his comments were magnanimous, totally free of rancor. Self-pity was not his style.

Diagnosed as tubercular at the age of forty, he reacted as though TB was another blindfold adversary. At Saranac Lake his wife recorded his response to feverish, painful nights:

"Never mind that, Jane. That's all over and we can't do anything about it. Let's forget it and start over."

Chess and checker problems preoccupied him in bed. He improved sufficiently to become ambulatory, and he and Jane strolled along the village roads in search of his favorite wild flower, the blue gentian. Then, in an uncanny paralleling of Dr. Trudeau's final years, the woods became Matty's sanctuary: he took up quail shooting.

> He was not permitted to do much walking [Jane remembered], but he devised a way to enjoy quail shooting without the usual physical exertion required. We would drive along the mountain roads in an automobile. We watched the sides of the road closely. If signs of a covey of quail or grouse were observed, the car would be stopped and Christy, with his shotgun, would step on the

ground on the side of the car away from the quail. Then he would slowly walk toward the birds until the covey flushed. He never shot one except upon the wing. By this method, which I am told was rather ingenious, he often secured the bag limit.

Toward the end of 1922, John McGraw, manager of the New York Giants, George M. Cohan, composer and showman, the Giants' attorney, Judge Emil E. Fuchs, and Harry M. Stevens, who with his brothers ran a noted baseball commissary, were dining together at the Lambs' Club in New York. Opposite them sat George Washington Grant, owner of the Boston Braves.

McGraw said, "There's George Washington Grant. His club's for sale for a half-million."

Cohan said that he hadn't heard the Braves were on the market.

"Yes, the Braves can be bought," McGraw told him. "Now there's a club you should own, George. You've always wanted a team. Here's your chance."

Cohan shook his head. "No, I guess not: I'm just a trouper, after all. I haven't time for a baseball club. I'll stick to something I know."

McGraw turned to Fuchs and asked, "Judge, why don't you buy it? You know the game and have the interest."

Fuchs didn't hesitate. "Sure I'll buy it," he said. "But on one condition."

"Which is?" McGraw said.

"Christy Mathewson will help me run it."

Perhaps the most insidious characteristic of TB lies in its fitful capacity to mimic good health; when patients feel better they suppose they have been cured. McGraw arranged a meeting between Fuchs and Mathewson, and Matty was euphoric over returning to baseball. Hadn't he seen his first big-league game in Boston? He recalled that in 1899, on his way to join the Taunton club, he had paid seventy-five cents to watch Kid Nichols of the Beaneaters pitch against Cleveland's Cy Young at the Beaneaters' Walpole Street grounds. Fuchs brought up the question of Matty's health and was informed it was amazingly improved.

Fuchs gave Grant $50,000 for a thirty-day option and on February 11, 1923, announced that the three new owners of the Boston Braves were himself, Mathewson, and James MacDonough, a New York banker. Matty had been elected president while Fuchs, owner of most of the stock, was vice president. Meanwhile, Matty sought an opinion about the state of his health from Dr. Baldwin and received a dismaying response.

"You'll last about two years if you go back to baseball."

Nevertheless, Matty went back, and served the two years as the Braves' figurehead president. Judge Fuchs ran the club, gaining a reputation as a Good Time Emil who grabbed checks and wined and dined the press at costly dinners in the Copley-Plaza Hotel. "Is it any wonder," declared sportswriter Harold Kaese, "that the Braves' binge of 1923–35 left Boston fans with the worst hangover they had ever known? For picking up checks, the Judge was in a class by himself."

Understandably, Matty might have yearned for the golden age of McGraw's Giants. The Braves in his charge were an eccentric, free-wheeling lot, and that fall they picked up Charles ("Casey") Stengel, a thirty-four-year-old outfielder and later the team's manager. Informed that he had been traded, Stengel, who a few weeks earlier had hit two home runs off Yankee pitchers in the World Series, is reputed to have said, "The paths of glory lead only to the Braves." There was acrid truth in this adage (it would apply to Babe Ruth, ending his major league career), for Matty became as disliked among the Braves as he had been admired among the Giants. The club's resentment stemmed from his accountancy of the players' meal tabs. The players were limited to four dollars a day, which at the time was sufficient to feed even the most dedicated trencherman. Four dollars wasn't enough, the team contended, and following the judge's liberal example, began signing checks for all comers. Matty carefully went over the tabs himself. The precision that guaranteed him baseball immortality struck his players as the cheese-paring of a sleeve-gart-ered auditor. It may have been merely the difference between the diamond and the front office, yet Matty's Boston period proved anticlimactic. The man who had struck out two hundred fifty-nine batters in a season was reduced to haggling with pee-vish overfed athletes.

Matty's gas-chamber accident also cut short a potential post-baseball business career. Whatever his talents were as an admin-istrator, he displayed a sophisticated flair for marketing. Precur-sor of athletes who peddle lotions, salves, and apparel on television commercials, he lent his name to a variety of products, and even appeared with Chief Meyers and actress May Tulley in an off-season vaudeville sketch titled "Curves."

The author of the sketch was sportswriter Bozeman Bulger, one of Matty's ghostwriters (the most assiduous was John N. Wheeler, author of *Pitching in a Pinch*). Bulger, who, in those easygoing journalistic years, saw no conflict of interest, now and then joined his reportorial subject for commercial side ventures. Once, through the newsman, Matty heard about a safety-razor endorsement, and responded with a directness that expressed his incorruptible pragmatism.

The razor's manufacturer had promised to pay Bulger $100 and Matty $200.

> I approached Matty on the proposition [Bulger recorded]. He was interested immediately, being at all times a good businessman.
>
> "We certainly can't afford to let that money get away from us," he remarked. "But, say, is it really a good razor?"
>
> "I use one myself," I told him. "Anyway, what difference does it make? The other players make money boosting products."
>
> "Yes, that's true, but, you know, the reason they are willing to pay me $200 to recommend that razor is because when they put the ad in the paper people will take my word for it. Isn't that right?"
>
> He was assured that such was the general idea.

"Wait a minute — you say you use that razor? Let me have it. We've got to get this money, but I want to be sure."

Without the least hurry he walked to the bathroom, lathered his face and then proceeded carefully to shave himself with the razor in question.

"Seems to work all right," he decided.

He then walked over and signed the testimonial which had been previously prepared by the company. We collected the money that afternoon.

At Matty's funeral Mrs. Mathewson requested his James A. Matthews American Legion post not to participate in the service. She feared that involving the Legionnaires, consumptives to a man, would risk lives unnecessarily. Many ballplayers attended, however, and there were tributes from Larry Doyle and "Home Run" Baker, who sent a massive bank of blue gentians.

"Laughing Larry" Doyle, the Giants' brilliant second baseman, had almost assured Matty of victory in the perfectly pitched decisive game of the 1912 World Series. His first time at bat Doyle smashed a certain home run pulled down by Harry Hooper, tumbling over the center-field barrier. Doyle's World Series feats conveyed the gusto of his once-celebrated exclamation: "It's great to be young and a Giant." By 1942 he had contracted tuberculosis himself. He would return to Saranac Lake, enjoy a friendship with author Walker Percy, and twelve years later move into a room in the village, the last patient discharged from Trudeau.

THE KISS IS NO LONGER A SURE PRELUDE TO MARRIAGE, mused the *Adirondack Daily Enterprise* in 1923. The *Enterprise*, with its syndicated features, sports section, and stock market coverage, resembled a big-city newspaper just as the sleek high-rise 100-room Hotel Saranac, designed in 1925 by William Scopes, resembled a big-city hotel. The foyer of the Hotel Saranac contained small, exclusive shops; one flight up, the palmy Florentine lobby overlooked Main Street, and a cabaret band played "Yes Sir,

That's My Baby" and other "song hits that meet with instant approval." Scopes, a designer of handsome cottages at the sanatorium, had been a patient who, while taking the cure, completed a correspondence course in architecture.

The village streets were paved and lit by electricity; taxi stands conducted a brisk side trade in bootleg liquor; and the Fox Pontiac and the Colonial theaters booked vaudeville acts as well as motion pictures reviewed by the ubiquitous "Fan," in the *Enterprise,* and by anonymous staffers of the competing *Saranac Lake News.* The movies often included local landmarks. Directors of early adventure films found Saranac an ideal location for stories with arctic backgrounds like *The Call of the Wild,* or for cliffhangers like *The Perils of Pauline* (also filmed in Fort Lee, New Jersey) featuring Pearl White. A studio complex sprang up on Edgewood Road. When a Klondike was required, the cameras went to Lower Saranac Lake or Franklin Falls before producers began to realize it was cheaper to build a studio Klondike than to wait on the vagaries of weather and light. (Oddly enough, tuberculosis helped establish the movie industry in Southern California. In 1907, Francis Boggs, having read a Chamber of Commerce claim that Los Angeles enjoyed 350 sunny days a year, led a barnstorming group of players from Chicago's Selig Company across the country. En route they filmed single-reel dramas. One of the actors left the troupe when it reached Los Angeles and was replaced by Hobart Bosworth, a stage director who had been a Broadway actor until the onset of TB affected his voice. Boggs assured him his delivery was satisfactory for pictures, so Bosworth assumed the lead in *The Power of the Sultan,* believed to be the first dramatic film made entirely in California. During the open-air filming Bosworth regained his strength, but to his dismay Colonel Selig wrote, recalling the company to Chicago. "I couldn't go to Chicago," Bosworth protested. "I'd be dead in a year." Boggs suggested Bosworth write Colonel Selig and extol California as the best place to make movies. The letter must have been persuasive because the colonel immediately entrained for Los Angeles and soon built a small studio there.)

For all its facets of urban culture, Saranac Lake at the start of the twenties still had only seven hundred fifty-three private residences. Boom times lay ahead. The decade's hectic changes had three sources: the health industry, outdoor recreation, and booze.

Double-headed trains chuffed into the depot as the hopeful and the decrepit converged on the renamed Trudeau Sanatorium. Assuming they failed to qualify or refused to accept the rigorous regulations — husband and wife were separated if both suffered from the disease, and the sanatorium, still practicing the policies of triage, demanded a chance of recovery — they were dispersed to cure cottages throughout the village. The dead left Saranac by night when the depot platform was stacked with pine boxes. It was a mundane occurrence, only a shade less bizarre than the situation described in Mann's *Magic Mountain* where the deceased made their last journey lowered on sledges to the Flatland, but it was no less melancholy. Conversations in Saranac paused as the New York Central pulled out of the depot and gathered speed between miles of silent trees, its whistle keening through the dark.

The wilds of the region were an incalculable asset. However, unlike the village of Lake Placid, nine miles away, Saranac adopted a laissez-faire attitude toward nature. Lake Placid pursued an aggressive policy of recreational development; Saranac, giving priority to the business of tuberculosis, evolved into a single-industry community. Lush resorts and imposing estates dotted the shores of Placid's Mirror Lake; Saranac, with its continuous demand for sanatorium space, left nature more or less alone. The village was, first and foremost, a spa, a sanctuary for the sick. Consequently, tourists avoided Saranac under its various rubrics, City of Hope, City of the Second Chance, as though the place was bewitched; at the same time, ironically, the latter-day Adirondack Murrays, the owners of rustic lodges, the hunters and fishers and vacationers who built humbler camps around the region, could count on returning year after year to find the landscape unaltered.

President Calvin Coolidge gazed over that consoling landscape from his summer White House at Paul Smith's in 1926 (ever the joker, Paul had christened the resort's main thoroughfare Easy Street) and predicted that Prohibition would remain a permanent feature of American life. The law could not be modified; strict enforcement of the Volstead Act was necessary. Coolidge's words were welcome. Sixty miles from the Canadian border, Saranac profited from a bootlegging traffic that flourished as it did across northern New York. The market appeared limitless — tubercular veterans who had acquired two-fisted drinking habits overseas, moneyed patients, the owners, staff, and guests of the Great Lodges sprinkled throughout the region. The proportion of illicit enterprises to the seven hundred fifty-three houses of the village is impressive. *In the Shadow of the White Plague*, a memoir by Elizabeth Mooney, whose mother was a patient at the Santanoni Apartment House for Health Seekers, estimates that Saranac Lake had a dozen speakeasies and seven stills; drugstores sold alcohol in nursing bottles, and a dry-cleaner tucked pints into the pockets of garments returned to the customer. The serpentine "Rum Trail" (Route 9) ran from Champlain near the border to Glens Falls, Saratoga, and Albany. Avoiding roadblocks at Poke-O'-Moonshine, rumrunners dodged through the mountains and reached Saranac on the dirt roads of Franklin and Clinton counties. They used a convoy system, sending a pilot car ahead of the shipment. The scout car carried no contraband, and if the driver was detained that too warned the caravan.

"For the most part northern New York was spared the gang warfare that scarred the metropolitan areas during the Twenties and early Thirties," observes Allan S. Everest in *Rum Across the Border*. Tire-squealing chases without headlights, however,

Above: W. J. Stillman's painting *The Philosophers' Camp,*
in which Emerson, Agassiz,
Lowell, and other New
England intellectuals enjoy
the wilderness. This was the
group that "discovered" the
Saranac region in 1859.

Left: Jeffries Wyman in
Cambridge, taken by
Oliver Wendell Holmes
on August 11, 1865.

Before and after going into the Adirondacks. From *Harper's New Monthly Magazine*, August, 1870.

A magazine spoof aimed at "Adirondack" Murray's famous book. Murray's claims for the beneficial climate of Saranac brought it widespread attention as a health spa in the late 1860s.

The Reverend William Henry Harrison "Adirondack" Murray, pastor of the Park Street Congregational Church in Boston.

Dr. Edward Livingston Trudeau, who
came to the Adirondacks to die and,
instead, lived to battle TB for some
forty years.

Robert Louis Stevenson *(far right)* and his family at Saranac Lake during
the hard winter of 1887−88.

The poet Adelaide Crapsey a few days before her
death from tuberculosis in 1914.

Christy Mathewson with his son, about 1920.
Mathewson, a New York Giants pitcher for
seventeen seasons and a member of baseball's Hall
of Fame, died at Saranac in 1925.

Norman Bethune was one of Saranac's most
colorful patients. A Canadian doctor, Bethune
was a romantic idealist who was badly wounded
in the First World War on the Western Front,
was a volunteer with the loyalists in Spain,
and died while serving with Mao Tse-tung's
army in the caves of Yenan.

A Chinese lithograph of Bethune's fateful midnight encounter with Mao.

Right: Sara and Gerald Murphy at Camp Adeline in the summer of 1936. A painter of promise, Gerald along with Sara had a talent for friendship, and in *Tender Is the Night* F. Scott Fitzgerald used them, in part, as his models.

Below: A Man Ray family portrait of Baoth, Sara, Patrick, and Honoria Murphy during the mid-twenties.

Above: Albert Einstein with physicist Leo Szilard at Saranac Lake, 1945.

Left: Béla Bartók, the eminent Hungarian composer, at Saranac in 1945.

Lawrence "Laughing Larry" Doyle, New York Giants second baseman
from 1907 to 1917, the last patient at Saranac after the conquest of
tuberculosis, leaving Trudeau Sanatorium in 1954

proved as dangerous as gun battles with troopers and rival gangs. Bootleggers familiar with every detour and short cut, natives who knew how to squeeze the last ounce of horsepower from a heavily laden Auburn 120 or souped-up Hudson, matched wits with the seventy-eight-man Troop B of the New York State Police led by swashbuckling Captain C. J. Broadfield astride his mount, Border King. To call Border King a mere horse understates the case; he was a steed in every sense of the word, but no match for the internal combustion engine. The hapless Border Patrol, wearing colorful Mountie uniforms that might have been issued to the chorus line of *Rose Marie,* galloped after suspicious-looking hearses and roadsters and tried in vain to cover the territory; in 1923 there were only sixteen officers strung along the northern border, and Troop B didn't receive its first car, a Model T, until 1925. The officers patrolled in pairs and on horseback, and many remained on horseback until Repeal in 1933. Roadblocks, inadequate as these were, provided a token countermeasure.

Saranac Lake officials maintained that plowing snow-clogged roads to hardpan was good for rumrunners, bad for horses. Leave the roads untouched, the budget-conscious village fathers argued, and give mounted patrolmen a passable chance. The proposal was defeated. The caravans of cars and trucks that rumbled north and south gurgled with an assortment of alcoholic beverages, but usually carried beer. A trade in hard liquor sprang up at the start of Prohibition; by 1923, however, a notorious "Rum Row" flotilla of offshore craft was supplying New York and the East Coast with whiskey at Montreal prices. Northern New York bootleggers specialized in beer and ale, although during the winter months they carried liquor, less likely to freeze. Molson's or Carling's Ale could be sold at an enormous profit; moreover, the traffic went two ways. From the north sluiced a torrent of illegal alcohol, while from New York City in return flowed stolen goods, especially silks, on which Canada placed a 42 percent duty, and industrial alcohol recooked in the

United States and sold to Canadian distilleries. Prohibition stimulated the Canadian economy, financed highways, schools, and federal programs; but Prohibition also sabotaged Canadian goods and bequeathed to Canada and the United States an underworld in which one glimpsed skewed reflections of the behavior and language of legitimate society. Even as Saranac's high school students vied for five-dollar essay prizes awarded by the Women's Christian Temperance Union, the *Enterprise* reported on a local repair-shop owner who used double-speak to conceal his activities. "Send me down five inner tubes and six boxes of patches," he would instruct his Montreal dealer by telephone. On a tip, police tapped the line and discovered that "inner tubes" were whiskey and "patches" Canadian ale.

John Thomas Nolan, or Noland, alias "Legs" Diamond — thief, bootlegger, narcotics peddler, extortionist, bank robber, highjacker, murderer, hoodlum, and scoundrel — visited Saranac regularly, though not on business. Gangs from Buffalo and Rochester conducted haphazard clashes over the territory; Jack's gangland principality lay southward, in Greene County, where the drowsy streets of Tannersville provided a façade for his racketeering operation. The Catskills gave him a hideout from the New York mobsters he had repeatedly double-crossed. Jack's object in visiting Saranac was his brother Eddie, curing on Shepherd Avenue and later at Lynch's Cottage on upper Riverside Drive. Eddie was dying from what he called "the con" and Jack felt close to him, possibly closer than to anyone else. Against the law and rival mobsters they presented a united front. They had run away from Philadelphia together after their mother's death when Jack was twelve, and outside their ties of family and mutual criminality had another bond — they were tubercular, the price of a racketeering apprenticeship on the squalid streets of New York's Lower East Side.

In Jack's case, the disease was dormant. Permitted a few more years, however — he was thirty-five when he was shot to death in an Albany rooming house early in the morning of December 18, 1931 — he might have discovered that TB was as inflexible as the killers presumably hired by his rival, Dutch Schultz. Anyway, Jack never expected to die in bed. There were too many people calling for his blood. The dawn he died a gangster's death he was trying to make a comeback, peddling dollar gin in Watervliet, gradually easing back into the big time. Alice was living with him and Eddie's widow and her boy. A real family. If the D.A. let them alone everything would fall together again. Why didn't Tom Dewey lay off? What would it take to fix Dewey? What was his price?

Jack understood the stirrings of ambition. From obscure origins as a petty crook, he had reached a perverse pinnacle of success as a well-publicized mobster. He was manicured and spiffy, his shoes gleamed and his ties matched, but his wardrobe did not disguise his gauntness, and when he was arrested and the flash bulbs went off, newspaper photographs revealed him in a high-crowned fedora and unbuttoned dark overcoat, crumpled like a puppet between burly marshals. There were no stains on the fedora and, of course, no blood on the overcoat, and it was difficult to believe this forlorn man, for all his snarl and swagger, was linked to no fewer than twenty-five murders.

More than most hooligans he possessed a dark glamour. Literary critics have speculated that he was one of the sources for the character of Jay Gatsby in F. Scott Fitzgerald's novel *The Great Gatsby*. A Byronic veneer, the reckless stoicism of the lone wolf, may have been responsible, but for whatever reason Jack exerted a spell. His wife, Alice, and his showgirl mistress, Kiki Roberts, tolerated his repeated infidelities and homicidal wrath. To a degree, the three tolerated each other. Alice's resentment, however, found expression in the chair she wired in their house at Acra in the Catskills. Visitors who sat down received a mild shock. When Jack initially sat in it and she turned on the current, he leaped up and swore. Alice told him he'd better get used to the hot seat "because you may have to sit in one yourself sometime." Jack was amused, and the living room electric chair became a feature *chez Diamond*. The sadomasochistic spirit of gallows humor presided there.

His myth was so imperious that more than a half-century later Charlie Green, a Saranac grocer, could recall Legs's visits to his Main Street store. Charlie's store still has a sawdust tang in the air and apron-clad clerks who use long poles with levered clamps to hook the boxes on the top shelf. Generations of tigercats have drowsed in the window, and the day that Legs became a customer an Ur-tigercat lay curled in a patch of sun. Charlie in his tenth decade remembered Legs clearly. He and Kiki strolled into the grocery and Legs recited the order in a low, well-modulated voice. The gangster could have been mistaken for a customer's man; he wore a navy blue suit and matching bow tie, and his manner was diffident. On the other hand, comely redheaded Kiki — born Marion Strasmick in Boston — created a stir. Most women would choose a fancier occasion than a trip to a grocery for an ermine coat, and Kiki seemed somewhat overdressed. Across the street, Saranac Lake's police chief, James Couglin, perambulated back and forth with a cordon of officers, watching Legs and Kiki select breakfast cereal.

Even Jack may have come to believe in Legs. The myth began with the nickname itself: No one seems entirely sure of its origins. Jay Robert Nash (*Bloodletters and Badmen*) states that Jack acquired it on the first rung of the criminal ladder. As a sixteen-year-old sneak thief and member of a gang called the Hudson Dusters, he specialized in "wagon bouncing" — that is, he would pilfer packages from the rear of parked delivery trucks and outrun pursuing policemen. The *New York Times* attributed his name to his fondness for fox-trotting, since he had once been a gigolo and semiprofessional dancer. William Kennedy, whose novel *Legs* tells the truth of art, shows Jack in one of the book's scenes at a table in the Rain-Bo Room. He is poring over a *New York Daily News* interview by John O'Donnell:

O'Donnell explained that Eddie Diamond was once called Eddie Leggie ("Leggie," a criminal nickname out of the nineteenth-century slums) and that somehow it got put on Jack. Cop told a newsman about it. Newsman got it wrong. Caption in the paper referred to Jack as Legs. And there was magic forever after.

Jack's charisma had ethnic and sexual overtones; in the public mind he became a personification of the Irish-American gangster and, thanks to the compromises of his complaisant wife and chorine mistress, a vagabond lover with the instinctual reflexes of a lawless satyr. In the sociology text *Careers in Crime,* James A. Inciardi notes that in the eight-page pornographic comic books distributed during the 1930s and 1940s Jesse James along with Al Capone and John Dillinger are depicted as sexual supermen. Undoubtedly this was Jack's subconscious public image, too, though in reality he displayed the impotent disabilities of the psychopathic personality. The outstanding characteristic of the psychopath is a dreary predictability: racketeers always repeat the same clichés, and the historical Jack was never as engaging as his fictional shadow. Between 1914 and 1916 he was arrested and released fifteen times on various charges, ranging from assault to murder. Sentenced to five years in Fort Leavenworth in 1919 for army desertion and for stealing in the service, he served a year and received a federal parole. Among gangsters he was known as a killer who shot from ambush. His reputation for covert duplicity underwent revision, however, during the bravura Hotsy Totsy Club shoot-out in July 1929 when, shortly before dawn, two-score witnesses saw Jack and a hit man named Charles Entratta, alias Charlie Green (no relation to the Saranac Lake grocer), outdraw and cut down two minor hoods in the second-floor Broadway speakeasy. Entratta was Jack's protégé, just as he himself had been the protégé of Jewish gangsters like Arnold Rothstein ("Mr. Big"), the gambling czar reputed to have fixed the 1919 World Series, and Jacob ("Little Augie") Orgen, who controlled the garment industry through goon squads and intimidation. Orgen and Rothstein were slain while Jack was serving as their bodyguard, and on both occasions he was substituting for the ailing Eddie Diamond.

Little Augie and Jack on a mild October night in 1927 had just left the former's Delancey Street headquarters. Jack was explaining the arrangements he was making for Eddie to enter a Colorado sanatorium. Eddie was in jail awhile, but it was the next best thing to a hospital. He'd get plenty of rest. Jail was good for Eddie's lungs. As they turned into Norfolk Street, a cab careened past and stopped, and Little Augie, responding with the reflexes of a New Yorker incredulous at finding a cab on the Lower East Side, started toward it. The door opened and a machinegunner in the rear pumped a staccato burst. Orgen, riddled, fell dead on the pavement. Wounded in the arm and leg, Jack stumbled into a doorway and escaped. A year later, he was attached to the retinue of Rothstein, who backed the Diamonds in their bootlegging wars opposing Dutch Schultz, but internecine strife pitted the brothers against fractious elements within the gang. Eddie went to Denver in late October for the cure, and Jack went with him. On November 4, Rothstein was mortally wounded in Room 349 of the Park Central Hotel and died two days later, refusing to name his assassin. The day after Rothstein was wounded, Eddie was trapped in a Denver cabaret (he was not overly scrupulous about breathing fresh air) owned by Jack. Five thugs shot repeatedly, yet Eddie survived, and within the year the five gunmen, rubbed out one by one, met grisly and sudden deaths.

The struggle between Legs and the Dutchman blazed back and forth while each sought to control the lucrative upstate bootlegging routes. Twice more Jack was targeted. He and Kiki, pajama-clad, were dining in her eighth-floor Hotel Monticello suite when three killers, ignoring Kiki, burst through the door and wounded him five times. Miraculously, he lived. Then, during the spring of 1931, emerging from the Aratoga Inn, a Catskills roadhouse, he was struck by four slugs from a sawed-off shotgun: again he recovered. Headline writers dubbed him the Clay Pigeon. The legend of Legs celebrated his incredible luck.

Eddie's condition had deteriorated meanwhile, and he was transferred to Saranac Lake. During his final months he could not meet the standards of Trudeau, but in Lynch's Cottage he observed a similar regimen. Jack's visits prudently took place at night; the episode in Charlie Green's grocery store was the sole instance of a daytime appearance. Taking precautions of his own, Eddie brought to Saranac a bodyguard who was required to cure with his employer. They lay on the porch shivering beneath their blankets, they ate the same nourishing meals, they charted their temperatures, and the bodyguard kept his pistol tucked out of sight, as though each patient was a duplicate of the other, the sick and the healthy man.

"The consumptive is rather more prone to sexual excitement than the average normal individual," wrote John Bessner Huber in *Tuberculosis*, published in 1902, and enumerated the contributory factors: many hours in enforced idleness, nervous tension, the erethism of high temperatures, an occasional superabundant sense of well-being, the philosophy of *carpe diem,* and the erotic consequences of warm baths. Huber neglected to cite the caressable proximity of the opposite sex. Languid hours spent together (Dr. Hugh "Keep Them in Bed for a Year" Kinghorn placed absolute confidence in rest) doubtless accounted for Saranac's unusually high ratio of marriages and divorces.

There was a village term for it — "cousining." Your "cousin" might be your nurse, and a number of marriages between nurses and patients occurred in addition to predictable patient romances. Adirondack folklore maintained you left your spouse in Utica. The cousin, in fact, was a marital substitute. Allen Seager (1906–1968) records that when he was at Trudeau Sanatorium in the late twenties he knew half a dozen patients who had been divorced by their husbands or wives as soon as TB was diagnosed.

Seager himself was scarcely more than twenty-one, a Phi Beta Kappa graduate and Rhodes scholar from the University of Michigan, though he always claimed he had received his Rhodes because he was the only man who turned up for the examination in a stiff collar. Near the end of his second winter at Oxford University's Oriel College he found he couldn't get warm in front of a roaring fire, so he consulted a doctor and received a diagnosis of TB. "It all seemed hilarious," he recalled; the ambulance in which he departed Oxford courteously stopped at pubs en route to Southampton while a friend scrambled out and fetched sustaining pints of mild and bitter. Back in Ann Arbor, Seager submitted to a further checkup: he had cavitation, two holes in his left lung, and infiltration, a spot the size of a half dollar on his right lung. Treatment for an artificial pneumothorax commenced, and soon he was informed about a vacancy at Trudeau.

In later life Seager became an English professor on the faculty of the University of Michigan and wrote a collection of short stories, *The Old Man of the Mountain,* and several skillfully composed novels, *Equinox, Amos Berry, The Inheritance,* and *The Death of Anger,* which deserve reappraisal. His comic yet wistful depiction of Saranac Lake, possibly the most beguiling of all the sanatorium's portraits, belongs to a 1964 memoir, *A Frieze of Girls.* (The title derives from a remark at lunch: Seager's companion asked, "If you think of your life at twenty, what comes back first?" The writer answered, "It was a kind of a frieze of girls and long aimless car rides at night.")

The sanatorium routines reminded Seager of rejoining a fraternity. He was assigned to a cottage with space for a dozen men, and each patient had a dressing room and screened porch. Seager's porchmate was a hyperactive Swiss whose profession was making dentures:

> He had so many wool blankets on his bed that he used a bookmark pinched from the library to tell where to insert himself.

About eight o'clock at night he would start to prepare for bed. He would pull on the pants to a sweatsuit over a pair of flannel pajamas, tie the ankles, crumple the New York *Times* and *Herald Tribune* and stuff them down the legs until he looked like a tackling dummy; then he would tie the waist and stuff the top, put on a knitted cap, two pairs of wool socks, a pair of gauntlets, and he would jump into bed and rustle. This was enough to deter if not prevent sleep entirely. It got very cold there and these precautions, wool or electric, were necessary. It was often forty below at night and for two weeks it didn't get above twelve below at noon. Usually you slept on your back with two pillows crisscrossed over your face, the Adirondack Pack. You pulled the blankets up to the base of the nose, leaving only it exposed and greasing it beforehand so it wouldn't stick to the pillow.

The open air, ample meals, and rest had a happy outcome. Seager was able to resume his scholarship a year after leaving Oxford. Meantime he spent New Year's at Saranac, storing up memories of a celebration feverishly magnified to orgiastic proportions by invalids who had little to dwell upon except their waning mortality. Preparations started in October. Cousins flirted outrageously and arranged their holiday trysts. Labyrinthine negotiations with bootleggers commenced. In spite of mufflers, galoshes, and fur hats and coats, the patients shuffling toward the village speakeasies cast wraithlike shadows on the snow. The party itself, following such extensive overtures, might well prove anticlimactic, the spiked punch, the tissue hats, the tinsel horns, the nattering of a wind-up Victrola, the slack grin of an untuned piano. Consumptive flappers and sheiks tottered between the cottages. The merriment, of course, was confined to the "up" cottages, where patients were ambulatory though accustomed to head counts each morning. The reticences of a winter night yielded to the crunch of unbuckled overshoes, to laughter and persiflage about the next party down the line. If the gaiety was synthetic, it was also swift, vanishing beneath the snow-laden firs and abundant stars.

Josephine Herbst, the writer whose woebegone marriage took place in the twenties, called her honeymoon "The Hour of Counterfeit Bliss," and counterfeit bliss permeated the entire decade. The patients at Trudeau might simulate a hedonism that had in it more pathos than pleasure; so did society. The plight of doomed Jazz Age revelers astray was not unique to Saranac. And yet the contiguity of death heightened professions of love. Infidelity was impractical: there were no Don Juans in TB wards, only Tristans and Isoldes. The passion of cousins may have been monogamous for the most part; even so, their embraces inspired incendiary musings like those of Hans Castorp when he first glimpses Clavdia, the moody heroine of *The Magic Mountain,* dressed for carnival:

> Ball gowns he had seen, stately and ceremonial, cut in conformity with a fashion that exposed far more of the person than this one did without achieving a jot of its sensational effect . . . He was reminded of a theory he had once held about those arms, on making their acquaintance for the first time, veiled in diaphanous gauze: that it was the gauze itself, the "illusion" as he called it, which had lent them their indescribable, unreasonable seductiveness.

For Hans, "the utter, unaccentuated blinding nudity of those arms" is intensified by Clavdia's illness, and he is intoxicated by "these splendid members of an infected organism."

Who would dare predict that out of the decadent hankerings and emotional nuances of this febrile environment would one day emerge a proletarian hero revered by the Chinese as a secular saint?

CHAPTER SEVEN

Bethune

1927

HIS MARRIAGE WRECKED, his career stalled, his health blighted, Norman Bethune weighed the feasibility of suicide. The modest accomplishments of a straitened medical career fell short of his expectations of fame, success, and fortune. In a better-run universe he would have achieved eminence — he was confident he would — but brooding upon the upshot of his hopes, he realized he would know only humiliation, dismal tubercular decline, the death of a maimed animal. Of his despair he made no secret; fantasies of violence consumed him: he spoke of taking morphine, wading into a pond, and sinking beneath the water — a painless death.

Frances's letter, which had arrived in Saranac Lake that morning, changed his mind. To punish his wife by killing himself no longer sufficed; his morbidity exploded into rage. Since their separation Frances had been seeing a wealthy businessman, who — her letter revealed — maltreated her. Intent on murder, Bethune signed out of Trudeau, traveled to Pittsburgh, registered in a hotel under an assumed name, and bought a pistol though he felt too weak to pull the trigger. Under his alias he phoned Frances's friend and conducted a cordial conversation. Come on

over for a drink, Bethune said. Afterward he would notify the
police and surrender.

Something about Henry Norman Bethune, a thirty-six-year-old
Canadian surgeon, mesmerized people. His charisma was difficult to define: vigilant blue-green eyes and a self-confident bearing might account for it, or his custom-made Bond Street suits;
aside from his long, powerful hands, however, he seemed ordinary enough, a man of average height and build with a neatly
trimmed military mustache and thinning hair. Nevertheless, the
force of his personality was incontestable. Upon entering a room
he attracted attention as a popular actor commands a stage. Indeed there was a histrionic strain in his nature; the extravagant
gesture delighted him, his sense of performance. Most of all he
relished situations in which he became a romantic rebel flouting
authority, and he provoked those dramas gleefully.

Trudeau Sanatorium had never admitted a patient like him:
He chain-smoked cigarettes in defiance of cottage rules, winked
at bed rest, adopted the role of clownish rogue male. The day
he arrived, December 16, 1926, he unpacked a silver tea service
and candles, and every afternoon as fever began to smolder
throughout the cottages, Bethune served high tea. The nurses
were amused and faintly dismayed. Was he really a doctor? He
talked medicine with the doctors and they respected him, still
there was a hint of disapproval: Bethune didn't seem intellectually sound. Of course, one could tolerate a certain amount of
posturing from a chap in his condition, but he tended to make
a fool of himself. His behavior after his first month at Trudeau,
where he was automatically consigned to bed rest in Ludington
Infirmary, was appalling. Told he could get up, he jumped out
of bed, propped an opera hat over his brow and, still in pajamas,
strutted with a walking stick through the corridors like a song-
and-dance man. Vaudeville monkeyshines! Trudeau, faithful to
the decorum of its founder, jutted like an island of Victorian

respectability from a sea of bootleg liquor. Bethune's antics were gratuitous.

His frivolity masked despondency; it also diverted attention from a seriousness inspired by an unlikely source, the aesthetic theories of Walter Pater. "To burn always with a hard, gemlike flame, to maintain this ecstasy, is success in life." Pater's adjuration, the source of Bethune's philosophy, provided an immediate ideal; yet his ancestors upheld strong views of a decidedly similar bent. They too were unorthodox men and women, pugnacious visionaries who scarcely acknowledged the meaning of compromise. Once these true believers settled upon an absolute they stubbornly defended it against all odds. The earliest Bethunes, minor nobles from Normandy, went to Scotland during the eleventh century, and some gained ecclesiastical preferment, notably David Cardinal Beaton and James Beaton, Archbishop of Glasgow and Primate of Scotland. In the sixteenth century the Scottish Bethunes were joined by nonconformist relatives, French Huguenots. Bethunes became clergymen, entrepreneurial merchants, and Hereditary Physicians to the Lords of the Isle of Skye. Settling in Montreal, the Reverend John, Norman's great-great-grandfather, built Canada's first Presbyterian church. His competitive businessman son Angus achieved a partnership in the North West Company and, as Chief Factor, a voice in the councils of the Hudson's Bay Company when the two companies merged. Angus's brother John, an Anglican priest, was principal of McGill University; Angus's son Norman, an eminent Toronto surgeon, had been educated by his uncle, but clashed with the Anglican Establishment. Cofounder and dean of the Trinity Medical School, he was ordered in 1856 to bar non-Anglican students and resigned rather than obey; the faculty followed suit and the school closed. For the next fifteen years he rambled across Europe, a surgeon without portfolio aboard a North Atlantic steamer, an observer of the Franco-Austrian War, a doctor again in Edinburgh. Presently the school re-opened — without religious restrictions — and he resumed his faculty post and the practice of medicine in Canada.

His grandson-namesake, Norman Bethune, combined a medical vocation with his father's traits. The Reverend Malcolm Nicholson Bethune displayed the family's restive character. An obstreperous young man, he hoped to follow the example of Angus and become a tycoon, and upon graduation from Upper Canada College, traveled extensively in search of opportunity. Hawaii looked promising, Malcolm toyed with the notion of investment in an orange grove, and then in Honolulu at the age of twenty-three he met and fell in love with Elizabeth Ann Goodwin, a devout English evangelist and missionary. Dreams of founding a citrus empire faded; he realized how crass he must seem to a young woman of spiritual refinement, and he renounced materialism. From Toronto, Malcolm bombarded Elizabeth Ann with epistolary sentiment. She followed him to Canada, they married, and he entered Knox College in Toronto to study theology.

Malcolm Bethune's maverick ministry was marked by family tensions between duty, the individual conscience, and authority. He minced no sermons about rich men entering the kingdom of heaven or camels passing through the eye of a needle. Prosperous congregations did not savor his stern piety so he moved from charge to charge across the Ontario hinterland, spending brief tenures in small towns like Blind River and Aylmer. The first of his many flocks was in the lumber settlement of Gravenhurst near the Muskoka Lakes, one hundred miles north of Toronto. There he and Elizabeth settled in the Presbyterian manse, a modest two-story frame house beside a dirt road, and in this house (destined to become an international shrine) their first son, Henry Norman Bethune, was born on March 3, 1890.

Growing up among the wooded ponds of rural Ontario, Norman learned to swim, fish, and skate. He had an older sister and younger brother, each separated by two-year intervals. Despite the family's shabby-genteel domesticity — the Reverend Malcolm's ministerial pittance was supplemented by inheritance — Norman's insurgent spirit emerged almost as soon as he could speak. At the age of six he disappeared in Toronto, his frantic parents notified the police, and hours elapsed before he returned, having walked across and explored the city. A few years later, skating on a frozen river, he saved a boy who fell through the ice. That summer Norman himself narrowly escaped drowning in Honey Harbor of Georgian Bay, attempting to swim across the bay as his father had done the day before. Norman's juvenile heroics — efforts to defy, emulate, or surpass Malcolm — held a confrontational air, and emotional stress marked his paternal relations. The mother won her child's respect, but father and son frequently quarreled. Once Malcolm pushed Norman's face into the ground and made him eat dirt as a lesson in humility. Quickly repenting, Malcolm broke down in tears. A less brutal episode occurred with the boy's ceremonious announcement that he was no longer to be called Henry — Malcolm's name of choice — but Norman, the grandfather with whom he identified and whose surgeon's brass plate he hung on his bedroom door. Malcolm, the capricious father who vacillated between corporal punishment and tears, was regarded with scorn; but Norman's chagrin must have been profuse when at Georgian Bay he was hauled dripping and gasping aboard Malcolm Bethune's boat. His father arrived just in time; the following year the boy swam the harbor.

Bright, undisciplined, and volatile, he earned his tuition for the University of Toronto working first as a lumberjack, followed by a variety of jobs, including that of stoker on a Great Lakes steamer. During the winter and spring of 1909 he presided over the roughneck students of a one-room schoolhouse in a hamlet called Edgerly. Because he was not disinclined to spare the strap, his pupils brought in a tough older man who picked a fight on their behalf. Bethune, however, had learned how to box in the rough-and-tumble of the logging camp, and scored mul-

tiple knockdowns before his opponent fled. That ended Edgerly's discipline problems.

Two subsequent mediocre Toronto years at University College
implied a need for a change, and Norman enrolled in a novel
educational experiment, Frontier College, founded by the Reverend Alfred Fitzpatrick. The program, intended primarily for
immigrant manpower in the bush camps, mines, and construction projects of the far north, offered a simple education stress-
ing English. Canadian university students received free accommodations; by day Bethune worked as a lumber camp axeman
and by night as the proprietor of the camp's reading room. From
the fall of 1911 through the next spring he taught English to
Finns and Slavs, then drifted west for a stint as a reporter on the
Winnipeg Tribune and subsequently returned with fresh incentive
to Toronto and his medical studies.

This time he sailed through the courses. A year away from his
M.D., he enlisted at the outbreak of war and was assigned to a
field ambulance unit that arrived in France early in 1915. There
his military escapades acquired an apocryphal aura. Was he the
first Canadian to reach wartime Paris? Did he smash the unit's
motor ambulance? No evidence verifies either rumored episode.
Bethune, a stretcher-bearer, accompanied a mobile field laboratory to the trenches, and on April 29, 1915, at the Second Battle of Ypres, a burst of shrapnel ripped his left leg below the
knee. The leg did not require amputation, although he limped
noticeably during ensuing years. A period of convalescence in
England preceded his return to Canada, where he was invalided
out of the Royal Canadian Army Medical Corps in November
1915.

The demand for front-line doctors remained urgent, and with
other former medical students, Norman was asked to resume his
studies. Thirteen months after his army discharge he received
his Bachelor of Medicine degree, graduating in a crash-course
class that included Frederick Banting, a codiscoverer of insulin.
Roderick Stewart, Bethune's leading biographer, later inter-

viewed a Toronto classmate who recalled: "We used to think he had quite strong socialist ideas and no doubt many of them were well-founded. He was always very interested in the needs of the common man."

At the beginning of 1917 Bethune saw his first patients, but that spring on a Toronto street he was accosted by a girl who inquired why he wasn't overseas with the troops. Before he could reply, she had pinned the coward's white feather on his lapel. The incident impelled him to volunteer for the British navy, which, despite his wounds, accepted him. He spent the remainder of the war as a lieutenant-surgeon aboard H.M.S. *Pegasus,* one of Britain's original aircraft carriers.

Upon his second demobilization he launched his medical career in earnest, taking an internship at London's Hospital for Sick Children on Great Ormond Street. Bethune planned to specialize in pediatrics, but his training — interrupted by a Canadian visit and a nine-month tour of duty in the nascent Canadian air force, where he performed research on blackouts among pilots — inclined him to take up the scalpel. He completed a second internship in the West London Hospital where he was Resident Medical Officer, studied surgery intensively at the Royal Infirmary, Edinburgh, and took the fellowship examinations. In February 1922 he climaxed a steady progress through the medical hierarchy by election to the Royal College of Surgeons.

His professional ascent, as thorough an indoctrination as any contemporary surgeon could boast, had come about through the assistance of a benefactor, the wife of a wealthy English industrialist. A doctor herself, she ran a private East End clinic where Bethune was on the staff. (Throughout his life women responded to his expansive charm and teasing gallantries, and one woman described him later as the most aggressively male creature she had ever known.) Other interns were forced to scrimp; Bethune maintained a flat in Mayfair. He burned with a hard gemlike flame, cultivating sensations, entertaining writers, artists, and doctors in nightly sessions of drink and debate. The role of disillusioned idler symbolized the postwar years of Michael Arlen's *The Green Hat* and Noel Coward's comedies, and the aspiring surgical Fellow devoted himself to pleasure as well as the healing arts. "I soon found to my great amusement, that many people with a lot of money knew nothing about art," he said. "I put my critical faculties to work."

Thanks to his patron, he visited the Continent, where he haunted warehouses, auctions, and marketplaces, and collected objets d'art, selling the pieces at a considerable profit to London buyers. He found he had a talent of his own for painting and sculpture, but did not pursue it; charm and taste meant more. Spending freely, he coped with a blizzard of invitations — a gregarious, highly eligible bachelor, much in demand at parties. The rattle of the cocktail shaker and the sob of the saxophone were the leitmotifs of his internship. His fellow doctors gossiped. They said he was the heir of a wealthy Canadian rancher. He did not deny this, for if he was not an heir at least he acted like one — and then he encountered the woman who, through their two successive and vexed marriages, perennial quarreling, and the prospect of a third marriage occupied the hurricane-eye of his affections for the remainder of his life.

The style of Frances Campbell Penney's features, long-lashed dark eyes, slender bones, and tall neck festooned by pearls, was as exquisite as a likeness upon an ivory locket out of a previous century. Bethune, arrested by her voice, said of her musical Edinburgh accent, "It was love at first *sound*." The couple met in London during the fall of 1920. Once again a Bethune saga of courtship repeated past patterns: Malcolm Bethune, an enterprising colonial, had met Elizabeth Ann in Honolulu and changed his life. Elizabeth Ann symbolized a spiritual ideal for him, and Frances at twenty-two, with a comparable unworldliness and retiring disposition, exerted on Norman the same ethereal attraction. Fluent in French, she also revealed discerning

musical predilections. London in the 1920s, though, was separated by a vast gulf of sensibility from the Honolulu of the 1880s.
Malcolm was not inconvenienced by another woman in his life,
and instead of pursuing his business career, he conformed to
Elizabeth's gospel. Norman, on the other hand, had no intention
of submitting to anyone. The attraction of opposites exerted its
hackneyed claims. She responded to his masculinity, notwithstanding her sexual shyness and the inhibitions of a conventional lady reared in polite Edwardian society; he responded to
her sensitivity and breeding notwithstanding his impetuous bohemianism. His flamboyance and her passivity, his confidence
and her trepidation, his egoism and her conditioned inferiority
augured a difficult union; opposites attract only to the degree
that one or the other is not averse to compromise. Norman and
Frances had one conspicuous trait in common: they were fiscally
improvident. Her mother is reported to have exclaimed, "Oh,
my heart sank when I met him. I knew he was the kind of man
that would attract Frances."

The courtship lasted three years. It was a vertiginous affair,
Dr. Bethune chronically insolvent and supported by his fine-art
forays and the industrialist's wife; Frances's conservative upper-
crust Edinburgh family (her father was an Accountant of the
Court of Scotland) apprehensive about their only daughter's
brash suitor; the frictions of disparate personalities sparking fu-
rious disputes. The on-again, off-again affair sputtered while
Bethune passed his rigorous surgical examinations. There were
noisy rifts and penitent reconciliations. At the climax of one
squabble Bethune waded through a lashing gale into the English
Channel and nearly drowned; he afterward confessed that he
had always cherished an impulse to swim in stormy Channel
waters — a pseudoromantic comment, yet his behavior
seemed increasingly irrational and self-absorbed. Early in 1923,
Frances received an inheritance of some ten thousand pounds
from an uncle, and that August she and Norman were married

in a London Registry Office. Upon completion of the ceremony he turned to her and said, "Now I can make your life a misery, but I'll never bore you — it's a promise."

He kept his word. Hurrying to catch their honeymoon train to Dover, Norman refused to wait for the proper development of the wedding photograph, and Frances received "a sheet of blackness." The best man, seeing them off, sought to bolster their spirits by saying, "He really is fond of you, Frances," before the train pulled away for what were to be six extravagant months in Europe. Although Norman still exhibited a fondness for fustian romantic attitudes and proclaimed when looking at Giotto's *Life of St. Francis* that he should have entered a monastery, the newlyweds, conforming to the spirit of the age, manifested the antic mood swings of a Scott and Zelda Fitzgerald.

In the Channel Islands, their first destination, they went for a walk and came to a deep gully. Frances paused, they could easily detour around it, but Norman announced, "I would rather see you dead than funk that," and she jumped across. She felt coerced. The encouragements of their best man took on a mocking echo. Bethune's headstrong wooing had put him at risk, but his willingness to sacrifice her to an abstraction proved disheartening, and she recalled a legend from her finishing-school days about a knight who was asked by a lady to retrieve a rose she had tossed into a lion's den. The knight did so, then rode away alone.

That recollection was not an ideal note on which to start married life, so Frances concealed her foreboding. Heedless and debonair, the euphoric newlyweds romped across Europe. The ski slopes of Switzerland, the art galleries of Italy, the quayside cafés of Paris, flashed past like a travelogue; ten thousand pounds placed a festive Europe at their disposal; the horrors of the trenches belonged to a past buried as deep as the catacombs. Norman didn't neglect his medical studies; he observed master surgeons operating in the amphitheaters of Berlin and Vienna, but a gnawing and undefined discontent frayed his happiness.

Even surgical wizardry provided no bulwark against a growing nihilism. "I was like some butterfly batting its crazy wings against the light," he wrote to Frances when the party was long over, "blinded and stupid, going around in circles, with no purpose in life and no purpose in death." They ran out of funds in Vienna and he could hardly scrape enough together to send a telegram. Frances waited in their hotel room while he went to the telegraph office to collect money from the return wire. En route to the hotel with the money, he passed an art gallery that displayed a small statue he found captivating. Impulsively, he bought it. When Frances opened the door and saw him standing there abashed, holding the figurine and his change, she lost her temper. A row ensued, she threw the statue, Norman ducked, and the figurine broke. This seemed to revive Frances's customary composure and she asked Norman to bring some glue. Together they repaired the statue — Frances kept it throughout his lifetime — and that night they dressed and dined in an expensive restaurant.

The sexual malaise behind their escapades — the jump over the gully, the tense silences between bouts of hysterical quarreling — must remain, if conjectural, a strong possibility. Everything in Frances's background discouraged physical intimacy; furthermore, her submission to Norman was far from complete. Her behavior didn't take the form of outright revolt, yet she felt drained of identity. Unlike Zelda Fitzgerald, Frances was unable to compete directly with her husband, but only sought assurances that she was needed. Norman could not provide those assurances; the doctor committed to humanity was as yet too immature for one woman. His romanticism camouflaged self-love. The brilliance of his intellect was no compensation for the trials to which he subjected Frances — everything projected *his* opinions, *his* certitude of *his* distinguished future, *his* requirements in a wife. Frances might well consider herself *his* invention. Which, of course, she was — he perceived her as a mysterious romantic ideal duplicating his image of love.

Necessity at last prevailed and they reined in their expenditures. Norman decided to use the residue of Frances's money to establish a practice. But where? London, his initial suggestion, was vetoed. A tour of inspection through Ontario and Quebec eliminated those locales; Frances judged the provinces intolerably dreary. Detroit, however, struck Bethune as a proper place for an upcoming doctor. Far from the ossified British caste system that he had grown to detest, Detroit was close enough to Canada to seem relatively familiar, yet it was also throbbing with potential. Frances thought Detroit dirty and primitive; America, she declared, "was the only country in the world to have achieved decadence without civilization." A nostalgic glow bathed their memories of alpine idylls, but pragmatism carried the day. Norman Bethune hung out his shingle — his grandfather's plaque — at the corner of Cass and Seldon streets in the winter of 1924. Between them, he and Frances owned twenty-four dollars and a number of antiques picked up in European flea markets, including old pewter and a set of Louis Quatorze chairs.

Desperate to succeed, Bethune, a medical go-getter, within weeks established ties with Harper Hospital and the Detroit College of Medicine and Surgery. His credentials were impressive, and plainly he would accept any situation. The college had nothing open except a part-time instructorship teaching prescription writing in the Department of Pharmacology and Therapeutics. Bethune instantly accepted.

The new teacher was popular and devoted to his students. In polished, witty lectures he proposed, one student remembered, "the practice of medicine as a modern priestly craft." Despite that lofty doctrine, Bethune was no remote authority-figure and enjoyed conducting informal seminars over mugs of beer in a downtown speakeasy, where he uttered radical views that prompted conservative students to label him a communist. His left-wing principles, however, clashed with his careerism. On the one hand, his office-residence was in a squalid neighborhood, the red-light district of a factory town where Bethune dispensed his services virtually gratis to prostitutes and the poor; on the other, his fondness for the amenities of life, custom-made suits and shoes, haute cuisine, the cultivated environment of art, disposed him to mulct prosperous patients. His widening professional contacts brought in wealthy surgical cases, he purchased a new car, and soon he and Frances moved to a more fashionable address. Once again he began to collect paintings, though he maintained his consulting office on the wrong side of the tracks.

The improvement in his fortunes did not help his marriage; he reverted to the profligate style of their honeymoon. Living beyond their means, the Bethunes battled constantly over money. Norman's monomaniacal ambition frightened Frances; he was driving himself too hard, driving them both to exhaustion. In the fall of 1925, she left him. First she visited a school friend in Nova Scotia, then, without stopping in Detroit, proceeded to California for Christmas with her brother.

Bethune pleaded for her return. Frances responded to his entreaties and tried to make a fresh start, but their differences were not easily resolved. Once again they reached a point of total exhaustion. For Norman the exhaustion was physical as well as emotional; he blamed the domestic turmoil of the previous six months, his expanding workload. Fever, a racking cough, and fatigue suggested otherwise; his symptoms worsened; after a hemorrhage in the summer of 1926, a colleague examined him. The x-rays disclosed a large cavity in one lung and suspected areas in the other. "Pulmonary tuberculosis of moderate extent" was the verdict; try Saranac Lake for treatment.

Saranac had no available beds. That fall, mustering his strength for travel, he closed down his practice ("a gold mine if properly attended to, but thank god, I'm out of that shaft") and entered Calydor, the pioneer Canadian sanatorium, situated by an ironic twist of fate in Gravenhurst, his birthplace. He and Frances separated again, and he may have encouraged her to leave him — at thirty-six he was dying, but she had a life of her own and could return to her family in Edinburgh. The advice was in any event superfluous: she had decided on divorce long before. The abrupt halt of his budding career left the former surgeon dazed and resentful, but luckily, just before he learned of his tuberculosis, he had purchased an insurance policy that included a monthly disability allowance. His parents rode with him on the train from Toronto to northern Ontario, and when they got off they rode on a cinder street past the cluster of houses and the tiny church where Malcolm Bethune had so often denounced the laying up of worldly goods.

Treated by Dr. Charles D. Parfitt, a trailblazing TB researcher, Norman remained at Calydor until he received word in less than two months that a place had opened up for him in the Trudeau Sanatorium. Holly and tinsel wreathed the infirmary when he arrived that December, and he submitted quietly to his battery of tests. The tests yielded a favorable prognosis (he would otherwise not have been admitted), and he attracted another kind of intense scrutiny as the latest arrival within the gossipy orbit of Trudeau's diminutive world. During his weeks of confinement he wore a battered straw hat in bed (headgear was an important factor in creating the image of his eccentricity; other props included the top hat, a beret, and an ebony cigarette holder), and even the head nurse, thinking to humor him, served his "Canadian cup of tea daily."

In the middle of January he was transferred to the Lea, a patient cottage shared by five men. Three, including Bethune, were medical doctors, and a fourth (the artful foreshadowing of Time), a young Chinese named Nan Li. One of the oldest cottages in the sanatorium, the Lea Memorial Cottage (1887) was set back on the slope behind Dr. Trudeau's first cottage, Little Red, and provided close quarters. In the austerely furnished yellow-pine rooms stood each occupant's canvas cot. The doctor-patients rapidly came to know each other's idiosyncrasies all too well, but they made the best of the situation, and Bethune struck up a close and enduring friendship with an American Southerner, Dr. John Barnwell. Through whiteouts, icy dawns, and week after week of glacial temperatures, they resorted to subterfuges for the relief of tedium. A network of sympathetic Trudeau employees brought them forbidden delicacies, and from a "secret pantry" the quintet produced the ingredients of gourmet dishes the administration would forbid. The Lea's patients listened for hours to a "legal" phonograph. They threw parties. Other cottages were invited, and blithe nurses who could be trusted. Since there were nightly nurse patrols — patients received three ambulatory passes a month, which permitted them to leave the grounds — due caution was observed. To insure the success of one elaborate affair, the entire nursing staff was invited. Under Bethune's supervision the patients gathered spruce boughs and decorated the cottage. He had promised a surprise and no one was disappointed — at the proper moment he unveiled a cache of French wines that he had purchased in Montreal and smuggled across the border. Bethune and Barnwell also perpetrated a boarding-school ruse: they stuffed a ski-jacket dummy and propped it in the bed near the cottage window while they slipped past the patrols and the bronze frown of sculptor Gutzon Borglum's recumbent statue of Dr. Trudeau outside the gates, and headed for the village speakeasies.

Card games — especially their favorite, Russian bank — took place in the narrow bathroom under a dressing gown that Bethune tacked over the window. Often the five men sat up all night discussing tuberculosis, art, medicine, and politics. What did staying up matter? The next day they could always rest. The fraternity atmosphere that struck Allen Seager so forcibly was pervasive; but these were mature captives, and with burlesque "scientific detachment" they kept a chart of the dates they expected to die. The dates were transferred to the mural titled "The T.B.'s Progress, A Drama," with which Bethune ultimately papered the walls of the Lea. In the last panel, dominated by the Angel of Death, he included a churchyard with diagonal rows of stones bearing the terminal dates. For himself he selected 1932.

When the fatidic date actually arrived, two of the five cottagers were dead.

Winter burrowed deeper. While their tremors of breath dissolved in the claustrophobic chill of the cottage porch, Bethune lay with his blankets tucked against his chin and tried to thwart boredom. Inactivity sparked an explosion of fresh sensations and ideas. He thought of a Trudeau University. The physical plant was already in place, affiliation with other New York State campuses and McGill could supply a faculty augmented by patient-professionals. The idea derived from his own experience. The Trudeau administration, considering his qualifications, had asked him to conduct an evening series on anatomy at the sanatorium's D. Ogden Mills Training School for Nurses. The lectures were well received. Granted, they were abruptly canceled when reproduction was announced as Dr. Bethune's next topic, but the contretemps evidenced an insular prudery no intelligent person could take seriously. The university idea was another matter; it transcended personalities and would work. With mounting excitement he imagined the spacious Mills School, which had been donated by Mrs. Whitelaw Reid, adorning Trudeau University's campus . . .

His vision of the school proved so compelling that Bethune never assembled brick-and-mortar statistics. Nevertheless, he persuaded staff members to attend a formal demonstration in which he remolded the institution in his own image and refashioned, like his missionary parents, an imperfect society. The administrators considered his plan harebrained. (A decade afterward, however, they incorporated a Study Craft Guild as a direct result of it.) Exercise was prohibited, they pointed out; how did the doctor expect student-patients to cross the campus between classes? On the spot Bethune improvised a solution — escalators and moving sidewalks — fiscally impossible but otherwise logical.

The rejection of his university idea brought about a militant response. Ignoring official reaction, he hired an orchestra for a dance to which he invited his critics and the leading citizens of Saranac Lake. At the dance he staged a florid presentation to the sanatorium's medical director — a traveling bag.

Irony seldom wins friends, and Saranac Lake doubtless felt relieved when Bethune returned to Detroit in the spring of 1927 and resumed lecturing at the College of Medicine and Surgery. Frances still sought a divorce, Norman still wanted her back — no idealistic abnegation, no return to Edinburgh, no divorce — but she had become involved with another man. This emotional disaster was compounded by a physical relapse; his TB more acute than ever, Bethune realized his departure from Saranac had been premature. Early that summer he sold his practice in anticipation of heavy expenses and reentered the Lea. Gone was his cocky self-reliance; never had he faced such despondency. Now he was merely a man without hope who had received a letter, gone to Pittsburgh, and purchased a gun.

The phone rang and Bethune answered. "Send him up," he said. He held the pistol shakily, hoping he would not drop it. A knock, and he opened the door. His visitor — even to a sick man he did not seem a formidable rival — stared at the unsteady gun. "I'm Frances's husband," Norman Bethune said.

They marched into the living room and Bethune said he was going to kill him. The other man nodded; his apathy was unsettling. Why didn't he struggle, defend himself, instead of slumping with his hands at his sides? "Go ahead, shoot," he said. "I guess I deserve it anyway." Infuriated, Bethune struck him across the face with the pistol. The man staggered, blood coursing down his face, but made no sound. If only he would fight, Bethune could pull the trigger.

He struck him again: nothing; and without warning all hatred evaporated. This was not the face of someone who had perpetrated an injustice, but the damaged face of a victim who deserved the compassion of a doctor. "Here," Bethune said, "let me help you," and threw away the gun.

Once he had treated his visitor, Bethune opened a bottle of whiskey and they shared drinks. Presently it was dark enough to go outside without attracting notice. Bethune turned up the man's coat collar to hide his contusions, assisted him into the elevator, through the lobby, and onto the street, where they found a cab. The would-be murderer shook hands with his intended victim and that night checked out of the hotel and returned by train to Saranac Lake.

The grotesque episode in Pittsburgh marked a turning point. Bethune felt that in an obscure roundabout manner he had somehow conquered his illness. No longer did he sulk over Frances or talk about formulas of suicide; he decided to cure himself. One evening in late summer he came back from the sanatorium's library, dropped an armful of books on his cot, and started reading before he turned out the light. Dr. John Alexander's *The Surgery of Pulmonary Tuberculosis* began:

> Surgery of the twentieth century can boast no more important advance than that now being made in the operative management of pulmonary tuberculosis. [Bethune read the sentence twice. An alternative to bed rest?] . . . It is surprising that the medical profession as a whole knows so little of pulmonary compression [deflation of the lung]. Without doubt it is the most valuable contribution to the therapy of pulmonary tuberculosis that has been made in the present century and, in fact, since Dettweiler advocated sanatorium treatment in the eighteen seventies.

Artificial pneumothorax, the insertion of a hollow needle between the ribs and the pumping of air into the chest cavity so as to collapse one lung, had been practiced infrequently at Saranac. Dr. Trudeau credited collapse therapy with prolonging his own life, Adelaide Crapsey had submitted to it with her customary rueful smile, but, as Bethune soon learned, Alexander had understated the situation. The literature on surgery for pulmonary tuberculosis was sparse. Out of thousands of potential cases only three hundred had received the treatment the previous year. A Canadian, Dr. Edward Archibald, was a leader in this controversial tentative procedure. At once Bethune began begging Trudeau's doctors to let him serve as a guinea pig in a pneumothorax operation. They were reluctant, but he was so persistent they agreed to a staff meeting with him. At the meeting Dr. Lawrason Brown explained in a measured voice why the operation was seldom undertaken. Puncturing the lung was a distinct possibility, he said, and he outlined other dangers. Immediately Bethune bounded from his chair and tore open his shirt. "Gentlemen," he proclaimed, "I welcome the risk!"

Not even Trudeau's medical staff could resist this sensational gesture and voted to operate. Meanwhile Bethune heard that a Michigan court had awarded Frances her divorce decree, and he was obliged to pay her $25,000 at the rate of $100 monthly. He responded by wiring a proposal of matrimony — the first of many he fired off to her during subsequent months. The operation was scheduled for October 27; during the preliminary interval, Bethune bombarded his chosen physician, Dr. Earl Warren, with recommendations, and also covered the walls of the Lea with the colored drawing on paper of "The T.B.'s Progress, a drama in one act and nine painful scenes."

The symbolic narrative, five feet high and sixty feet long, had to accommodate stained yellow pine background panels and the spaces between roof, wainscoting, doors, and windows. Photographs show Bethune's spirited draftsmanship and appropriate if instinctive solutions to the spatial problems involved. (The Lea was torn down in 1931 and the drawings were transferred to the University of Michigan, where Barnwell had become head of University Hospital's TB unit. At length the work left Michigan, was reported in Georgia during the Second World War, and has probably been destroyed. The construction paper used as a ground would require close conservation.) The formal issues, however, are less interesting than the psychology behind the piece, the revelations of a man about to undergo a chancy operation.

Like its probable source, *The Rake's Progress* of Hogarth, the didactic series proceeds through a number of illustrations of moral enlightenment. The rake's downward progress, however, starts in mirth and ends in madness; the T.B.'s ascent starts in illness and ends in exaltation. Hogarth's hero, of course, is individually characterized, and his follies issue from a dissipation for which he alone is responsible; Bethune's alter ego is an allegorical Everyman whose adventures are embellished by doggerel quatrains. In the first scene his prenatal existence is depicted — an unprotected infant lying in a cave. Usually associated with shelter, the cave-womb is a circlet of intimidating darkness invaded by tubercle bacilli represented as pterodactyls or bats. "The theory of intra-uterine infection is highly improbable," remarked Bethune of this scene, yet "for the sake of artistic design it was too good an idea to neglect."

A doctrinaire Freudian interpretation of the narrative evidently never occurred to the artist. "The T.B.'s Progress" is notable for its concern with predestination and its pragmatic account of the conflicts in Norman Bethune's exceedingly complex psyche. His hero is a fatalist, though not a passive fatalist, and the second panel describes him coming into the world in the arms of an angel with iridescent wings. Bethune said, "Facing her, seated on a sort of throne, is a male angel (the Angel of Fate) who unrolls in his hand a scroll on which is inscribed my future. Incidentally, this theory of predestination is probably a relic of my Scotch ancestors. Looking over his shoulder are other angels who, as they read my future, turn away weeping." The third scene depicts childhood as a precarious journey through a thick wood, where creatures from the pages of a medieval bestiary portray disease. In the fourth panel, the hero is out of the woods, setting sail across the Sea of Adolescence, "Youth at the Prow and Pleasure at the Helm," and all seems propitious until he hears the siren songs of Fame, Wealth, Love, and Art. The sirens point the way along rocky cliffs to a distant Castle of Heart's Desire. The hero lands and is assailed and struck down at the castle gates by swarming TB bats. Panel Six, "The Abyss of Despair," traces his fall into the abyss, the bats flocking nearby. "As I fall, I look back and see that the Castle of Heart's Desire, which once looked so magnificently substantial from the front, is actually only a Hollywood set." Lying in the depths, where a dark red river flows, he sees on another high mountain a separate castle flying the Red Cross flag.

> This is Trudeau Sanatorium. Outside the gates is the bronze statue of Trudeau himself. The battlements of the castle are defended by different warriors, the doctors of that place — Dr. Lawrason Brown, Dr. Baldwin, Dr. Heise, Mr. Sampson of the x-ray department, and Miss Amberson. I climb slowly up to this castle where I gain entrance and protection from my enemies. There is a gas filling station (Pneumothorax apparatus) just inside, and music and laughter come through the gates.

The incongruity of gas pumps situated among his *Faerie Queene* imagery didn't bother Bethune; clearly he wanted not only to survive the operation, but to flourish as a result. The seventh drawing returns the hero to the city and more disenchantment; the skyscrapers, seen from above, thrust pile-driver lines toward antlike people while the bats fill the fetid air. Another hallucination beckons the pilgrim in the eighth scene: Health and Happiness, both female, on a bright cloud across a southwestern desert. Finally, after the optimism of the sixth drawing, a luminous Angel of Death appears, holding the hero like the infant of the second scene, "and looking down on me with a kindly and benign expression." Thus the cycle concludes:

> *Sweet Death, thou kindest angel of them all,*
> *In thy soft arms, at last, O let me fall;*
> *Bright stars are out, long gone the burning sun,*
> *My little act is over, and the tiresome play is done.*

As usual, Bethune wanted it both ways — death is terrifying yet also benevolent. The mural delineates a quest. The compassionate Angel of Death is a convenient device for ending the cycle; the hero commands each panel, however, proceeding toward mirages and falling and rising and falling once more, perpetually reincarnated. Might not Death prove as illusory as the sirens of Fame, Wealth, Love, and Art?

On October 27, Dr. Warren completed a successful pneumothorax operation and within an hour Bethune insisted on walking uphill from the x-ray department to his cottage. His recovery was swift, so rapid in fact that his missionary zeal touched new levels: thoracic surgery was the sole answer to the riddle of tuberculosis. Immediately, Bethune sent a letter to Dr. Archibald at the Royal Victoria Hospital in Montreal requesting the opportunity to train under him. Archibald accepted with a proviso that his disciple should improve his biochemistry at nearby Ray Brook.

The first of December 1927, Dr. Norman Bethune, classified Improved, received his discharge from Trudeau. He weighed 176 pounds, nearly ten pounds more than he weighed upon entering; not surprisingly so after the hearty meals associated with the cure. His spirits soared, Saranac had healed him and provided a medical gospel, and for years to come he would sign his Christmas cards, "Yours for a happy pneumothorax." When he dashed off a paraphrase of the Apostles' Creed, he did not intend to ridicule religious doctrine but to express his personal articles of faith:

> I believe in Trudeau, mighty father of the American sanatorium, maker of heaven on earth for the tuberculous; and in Artificial Pneumothorax; which was conceived by Carson, born of the labors of Forlanini; suffered under Pompous Pride and Prejudice; was criticized by the Cranks whose patients are dead and buried; thousands now well, even in their third stage, rose again from their bed; ascending into the Heaven of Medicine's Immortals, they sit on the right hand of Hippocrates our Father; from thence

do they judge those phthisiotherapists quick to collapse cavities or dead on their job. I believe in Bodington, Brehmer, Koch and Brauer, in Murphy, Friedrich, Wilms, Sauerbruch, Stuertz and Jacobaeus, in the unforgiveness of the sins of omission in Collapse Therapy, in the resurrection of a healthy body from a diseased one, and long life for the tuberculous with care everlasting. Amen.

Amid the rocking flakes of a December storm a dim sleigh waited. Bethune shook hands with the Lea's cottagers who had shared his despair and rejuvenation. The sleigh took him, standing up and waving, through the sanatorium gates. In the village he stopped and to Frances, who had gone at last to Edinburgh, he sent another telegram: CURED, LEFT TRUDEAU TODAY. AM FEELING THE SAME ABOUT YOU AS ALWAYS. WILL YOU MARRY ME? Then he continued to Ray Brook where he would remain until April, completing a research project on the study of pseudotuberculosis in rats.

The drama seems over. The curtain is coming down. We ought to fumble for our gloves and programs and leave Bethune waving farewell, shaggy flakes whirling about him, the heroine all but in his arms. The moment, however, is far from climactic, the drama just commencing: Bethune's recovery from TB would not result in a quotidian if productive medical career. He seemed destined for such a role; instead, as Archibald's assistant he developed into a brilliant thoracic surgeon. Moreover, he channeled his creative impulses. Experimenting with the design of surgical instruments, he invented new families of scissors and clamps. These covered a full page of a 1932 catalogue of medical supplies marketed by George P. Pilling & Son of Philadelphia. Bethune's design ideas sprang from diverse sources: his pneumothorax apparatus perfected existing models, while his rib shears were based on a leather cutter he had seen in a shoe-repair shop. Many of the instruments exhibit the peculiar clarity of problems solved under utilitarian conditions, and Bethune recognized how soon these innovations would become obsolete. "The whole backward path of surgery," he warned, "is littered, like the plains of the American desert, with the outworn and clumsy relics of technical advances." Unfortunately, the rebarbative aspects of his personality began to perturb Archibald and several colleagues. Lung surgery requires speed and accuracy in order to reduce loss of blood and time spent under anesthesia; nevertheless, Bethune, his colleagues came to believe, went too fast, accepted too many risks, lost too many patients. His cases recovered more slowly than those of other surgeons. Archibald cautioned him to follow orthodox procedures, they clashed, and Bethune left the hospital. Did he deserve Archibald's condemnation: "He had a superiority complex and he was entirely a-moral"? Other surgeons — a minority — disagreed; they claimed he was audacious, imaginative, and entirely within his rights to race the clock. If he made human and understandable mistakes, he did not treat patients unethically.

While Bethune was at the Royal Victoria Hospital he renewed his epistolary courtship. To Frances he confided his aspirations, his melancholy, and longing. "You wouldn't know me now, I swear," he wrote. Perhaps — since she had so many doubts — they might start again, meeting just as friends? Eventually, acceding to his entreaties (he had never ceased to refer to her as "my wife"), Frances sailed to Montreal, and on Armistice Day 1929 they remarried.

Hardly had the ink dried on the registry than they resumed their pattern of nonstop quarrels. Bethune's grandiloquence oppressed and perplexed Frances. She was not good enough for him, or was he at fault, not good enough for her? They had no children. Instead of children there was a huge doll-child, Alice in Wonderland, whom they treated half-whimsically as theirs. Step by step the marriage crumbled, Frances once more became involved with another man, and Norman agreed to another divorce. An arranged adultery was their sole legal recourse; they planted the evidence and in 1933 the divorce was granted. The trio held a champagne celebration at which, despite his cordial veneer, Norman withheld his blessing. "I don't give away my wife," he said to Frances's future husband, "I only lend her."

Years afterward many women captivated him, but none more than Frances, and they never ceased to correspond. "I left Beth oftener than he left me," she told Roderick Stewart. "The first time I divorced but next time we decided fair play meant him doing it. We meant to have a third time. A third marriage or stay put . . ."

Alice in Wonderland, surrogate child of divorce, six months with Norman, six with Frances, shuttled back and forth until the doll perished one evening during a minor fire in Bethune's room.

On the whole, the early thirties were years in which Bethune consolidated his professional reputation. Archibald somehow overcame his distaste and recommended his protégé to head the new tubercular unit at Sacré-Coeur Hospital, ten miles outside Montreal. Having his own service and issuing guidelines steadied Dr. Bethune; no longer did he resort to such stunts as making his rounds dressed as a lumberjack; through scientific papers and speeches at medical conferences, he began to attract international attention. In Tucson, Arizona, he operated on Renée Adorée, the silent-film actress who achieved stardom for her chewing-gum scene with John Gilbert in *The Big Parade,* and because of their conversations before and after the operation, she said, her life was transformed.

The elite of world surgery applauded Bethune's passionate commitment and the cogency of his arguments, but in Montreal his reputation for flashiness persisted. Rumors surrounded a surgeon who quoted D. H. Lawrence and Katherine Mansfield (consumptives both), who exhibited oil paintings, designed his own furniture, and published poetry and short stories, who earned vast sums and squandered them, and whose crowded parties on Beaver Hall Hill attracted bizarre congeries of artists, doctors, and libertines. Worse still, he had begun proselytizing on behalf of socialized medicine.

Until his arrival in Spain in 1936, Bethune was never a formal Communist. His sympathies were left-wing; he identified with collectivist causes and founded a free clinic for the jobless; nevertheless, when he sold his roadster in the summer of 1935 and journeyed to the Soviet Union to hear Pavlov and attend the sessions of the International Physiological Congress, he was essentially apolitical. "I went to Russia," he explained, "to see what they were doing about eradicating one of the most easily eradicable of all contagious diseases — tuberculosis."

Three weeks in the USSR gave him a favorable impression of socialized medicine. Ever the gadfly, he challenged a Russian official's claim that the regime had eliminated prostitution by offering to escort the flustered official around Moscow after dark; but Bethune came away excited at the inroads made by Soviet medicine against TB. The Soviets had halved the death rate; sanatoriums and dispensaries participated in far-flung rehabilitation programs similar to those he had proposed in Saranac Lake. "Over the portals of Russia should be inscribed, 'Abandon Old Conceptions All Ye Who Enter Here,'" he declared. Because of his appreciative comments he was asked, back in Montreal, to chair the Friends of Soviet Russia. He declined:

> I am not, as yet, perfectly convinced that communism is the solution to the problem [he replied]. If I were, I assure you, I should not only accept your offer but would become a member of the Communist party. What stands in the way of my acceptance? This — my strong feeling of individualism — the right of a man to walk alone, if that's his nature — my dislike of crowds and regimentation.

The Depression's impact on Canadian medical services troubled Bethune, however, and he tenaciously argued the case for socialized medicine as part of a unified assault on disease. Throughout the winter and spring of 1936, doctors, nurses, and social workers — the Montreal Group for the Security of the People's Health — met regularly at his apartment, and when a provincial election was called during the summer of 1936 the group issued a Manifesto calling for overhaul of the Canadian medical structure. Not surprisingly, the Manifesto received abuse from Canadians who considered it Communist propaganda. The hostility of this response coincided with the outbreak of the Spanish Civil War. Bethune resolved to join the Republicans. He would abandon much, for surgeons were flocking from other countries to observe his thoracic procedures, and at forty-six he enjoyed the status of a pacesetter in the struggle against TB. The Canadian Red Cross informed him it had no intention of raising a unit for Spain, but in the magazine of the Social Democratic party he came across an article about the formation of a Toronto-based Spanish Hospital and Medical Aid Committee. He wired that he was volunteering and arrived in Toronto the next day, only to discover the organization didn't exist — it was a figment of the magazine's inventive editor, who hoped to stir up enough interest to make the committee a reality. Undaunted, Bethune launched a campaign that resulted in the Committee to Aid Spanish Democracy, drawing support from all sectors of antifascist opinion, though within the organization Canadian Communists exerted a powerful influence. Toward the end of October, while the Spanish Republicans were in retreat and Franco's armies tightening the noose around Madrid, he boarded the *Empress of Britain*, bound for Spain.

Bethune had no prearranged role. Arriving in besieged Madrid with medical supplies sent by his committee, he was met by the committee's agent, Henning Sorenson, a bilingual Montreal newspaper correspondent. Sorenson as guide and interpreter conducted a hasty tour of the city's military hospitals, the trenches, cellars, and casualty stations of University City. On this tour Bethune perceived Madrid's essential medical problem: the lack of an organized system for the distribution of blood.

He wasn't the first to note the problem, nor was he the first to propose its solution — bring the blood to the wounded rather than bring the wounded to hospitals — but he was the first to put into action the concept of a mobile transfusion service. Unless Bethune had acted it is improbable that anything would have been done at all in Madrid. The Servicio Canadiense de Transfusión de Sangre became the model for similar units in the Second World War. (A more sophisticated mobile transfusion system developed by Dr. Duran Jordan at the same time encountered fewer travails on the relatively placid Aragon front.) An imposing feat of organizational skill, the service grew from idea to round-the-clock shuttles in less than six months. The blood, collected from donors, was refrigerated and stored and then distributed under fire to field stations. Bethune lacked experience in hematology, and blood transfusion was still considered experimental; Canadian officials, wary of the Committee to Aid Spanish Democracy, opposed him, as did conservative Republican higher-ups, but he was in his element, playing a lone hand amid the chaos of war.

In November he flew to Paris and from there to London, where he purchased with the committee's funds a Ford station wagon. (Spaniards dubbed it La Rubia, after its blondish side panels.) Altered for Madrid, it carried four major pieces of equipment — an Electrolux refrigerator, a sterilizing unit, an incubator, and a distilled-water element, each run by gasoline or kerosene — as well as glassware, medical apparatus, hurricane lamps, and gas masks — in all, 1375 separate pieces. The car's shipment to Spain became a headache when the Canadian government refused to endorse the venture as a bona fide humanitarian enterprise, and a fuming Bethune was forced to pay a stiff duty. (The incident would figure in his frequent platform gibes against Canadian Prime Minister Mackenzie King, who had shaken hands with Hitler.) The medical unit was formed quickly — Bethune and his driver, Hazen Sise, a young Canadian who volunteered in London (Sise later became a prominent

architect), liaison officer Sorenson, lab technician Celia Green-
span, two Spanish doctors, four registered nurses, and four office workers. A second vehicle, a Renault truck, was purchased
in Marseilles, and in no time the service was venturing through
shellfire and bombings to supply hundreds of hospitals and casualty stations.

The propaganda value of his work was not lost on Bethune.
At his suggestion the documentary film *Heart of Spain* was shot,
showing the Canadians in action. He took enormous personal
satisfaction in their contribution. "Plans are well underway," he
announced, "to supply the entire Spanish anti-fascist army with
preserved blood." The war's perimeter expanded, and he witnessed the bombing and shelling of thousands of civilian refugees at Málaga, recording in his journal the atrocities he had
seen. The cadences he used would not have sounded inappro-
priate from his father's pulpit: "Where are they tonight, the appointed ministers to the Christian God, bearers on earth of His
love and salvation — where are they, that they hear nothing of
those who cry out to their Lord? Into what dark cave has the
love of *man* been hounded? Where the mercy and the conscience
of a world going its sickly way?" The Battle of Guadalajara was
still in progress when he drove among a barrage of bullets and
delivered blood to a front-line hospital; caught in a lethal cross-
fire during the return trip, the team abandoned their riddled
ambulance and crawled through a field to safety. Bethune relished the stimulus of danger, the panache and improvisations of
guerrilla warfare. In time, however, the Republican army became increasingly disciplined in administrative areas, and Bethune, grown frazzled and irascible through overwork, disdained bureaucratic constraints. He was hostile when drunk and
acerbic when sober. He quarreled with anarchists, Communists,
left-wing splinter factions, and with the Ministry of War. By the
spring of 1937 he had lost his usefulness; the blood-transfusion
program could proceed without him, and Canadian Communists suggested that he would better advance Spain's cause by

returning home on a fund-raising lecture tour. Heavyhearted, Bethune embarked for New York, convinced that through his impulsive conflicts with authority he had disgraced himself once more. He was leaving behind his comrades, Canada's volunteers, the Mackenzie-Papineau Battalion. The good party member must submit to the party. Spain had devoured him in a revolutionary ecstasy; now he was burned out, going home to a country where he had few remaining ties. To save money, he booked his berth in steerage.

Hundreds of shoving, banner-waving supporters met him when he descended from his train in Toronto's Union Station. The Spanish Civil War no longer looked faraway, a fratricidal conflict, but the prelude to a global struggle against fascism. Bethune, who had parted from Canada without fanfare eight months before, returned as a messenger of fate. From the station he rode in an open car preceding two brass bands and a half-mile parade of organizations, and on the lawn of the Ontario Parliament addressed a throng of five thousand and gave the clenched-fist Republican salute.

His greeting in Montreal was rapturous — a crowd of a thousand roared approval as he was borne shoulder-high off the train. "The streets of Montreal were full of cheering people," recalled Bethune's friend Sam Maltin. "Those with no money gave things like streetcar tickets. When I told Bethune this, you could see his face change — 'This is my reward.'" That night he spoke without notes before a capacity audience of eight thousand in Mount Royal Arena.

The Toronto and Montreal speeches were the first in a grueling schedule on behalf of the transfusion service and the Loyalist cause. His tour looped across Canada, into California, and down to Chicago; he spoke and then showed *Heart of Spain* before Rotary gatherings and at lyceums, in prairie grange halls and big-city hotels. The Committee to Aid Spanish Democracy had ordered him to soft-pedal his Communist affiliations, and at first he complied. Asked if he was a Communist, he replied, "Most emphatically, I am not"; but at a July banquet in Winnipeg he announced, "I have the honor to be a Communist." This he amplified: "They call me a Red. Then if Christianity is Red, I am also a Red. They call me a Red because I have saved five hundred lives." Fascism in his view was a political disease, the equivalent of tuberculosis.

It saddened him, however, when he revisited Sacré-Coeur Hospital, that the sisters fled from him and the Mother Superior avoided him as though he served the Prince of Darkness. "If Russia disappeared from the face of the earth tomorrow, do you think that would eliminate communism?" he told hecklers. "I am sure that if Christ walked the earth again, preaching the brotherhood of man, He too would have thrown at Him the label of 'Moscow hireling.'" A professed Communist could never return to Sacré-Coeur, but that summer the Marco Polo Bridge incident ignited the Second Sino-Japanese War, and while Bethune was lecturing in Salmon Arm, British Columbia, Peiping fell to the invaders. At once he resolved to go to China as he had gone to Spain.

The Communist parties of Canada and the United States were committed financially to Spain, but with the support of wealthy New York City liberals, Bethune raised funds and recruited Jean Ewen, a Chinese-speaking nurse and the daughter of a well-known Canadian Communist, and an American surgeon, Dr. Charles H. Parsons. In early January 1938 they left Vancouver for Hong Kong, their only plan, to make themselves available to the authorities of the United Front, the coalition of the Kuomintang and the Chinese Communists that had ended the Ten-Year Civil War and rallied China against Japanese onslaughts. Unfortunately, Bethune and Parsons fell out over the latter's drinking, and when they reached Hong Kong and flew to Hankow a permanent breach occurred. Bethune insisted on joining the Communist Eighth Route Army; Parsons balked and went back to the United States with the China Aid Council's money.

The medical supplies that they stored in Hong Kong were later brought to Yenan by Dr. Richard Brown, a Canadian surgeon from an Anglican mission who joined Bethune's operating team. Meanwhile, Bethune and Ewen had an audience with Chou En-lai, later premier of China, and Chin Po-ku, coordinator of medical supplies for the Eighth Route Army, who made arrangements for the trip north to rugged Shansi province. Even with such high official support, the trip proved harrowing. Japanese troops advanced toward the strategic Hankow–Peiping rail line, on which Bethune and Ewen set forth. At every station they bucked waves of refugees carrying household possessions and animals. Civilians and soldiers swarmed over the locomotive and the flatcars already laden with mules, rice, munitions; soldiers swaddled in dusty, bloodstained bandages filled the platforms; Japanese planes swooped out of the clouds, released clusters of bombs, and strafed the stations and trains. The two Canadians were shunted onto a freight car carrying four hundred bags of rice. The following morning the precious rice, abandoned at a siding, was transferred to a mule train of forty-two carts pulled by three mules apiece, and the doctor and his nurse started westward. Within hours the caravan was attacked by dive-bombers ("the first bomber came back so low I could have hit him with a baseball") and among the casualties was a soldier beside Jean, wounded by a bomb splinter.

Bethune and Jean Ewen were carried piggyback across rivers, slept on the damp sacks of rice, and narrowly missed capture by Japanese cavalry. On the banks of the Yellow River, where the Japanese were shelling Chinese awaiting Eighth Route Army trucks to Sian, the Canadians attended the wounded in caves. Finally the two set out on foot for Sian. Once they reached the city of Han-ch'eng they were informed trucks would arrive. During the interim they volunteered for a hectic week in a hospital

("I treated pulmonary tuberculosis, ovarian cyst, gastric ulcer, everything —") before the trucks, at length, arrived and took them to Sian, where Bethune had "the ineffable bliss" of his first hot bath in a month. Then he pressed on, north to the central base of the Communists in Yenan. A delegation awaited. They informed him that the American news agencies had reported him dead.

Yenan became the site, on the final day of March, of Bethune's meeting with Mao Tse-tung. Summoned at midnight to the Communist leader's cave headquarters, the doctor conversed with Mao for several hours through an interpreter. Their historic encounter by the light of a single flickering candle would enter the mythology of the People's Republic, a scene ultimately reproduced throughout the nation as a patriotic icon. Mao sought to profit from Bethune's Spanish experiences; the Canadian wanted a clearer notion of the fearful conditions he faced under the improvisatory Chinese military-medical system, and presently they agreed Bethune would best serve by working in the Border Region Hospital — fifty caves carved out of the rugged loess hills of Chin-ch'a-chi near Manchuria.

His emotional arrival at the front (Jean remained as head nurse in the Yenan hospital) is described by the Chinese writer Zhou Erfu:

> Lightly falling snow settled on the khaki-colored uniforms of the soldiers, on people's blue or gray cotton padded jackets, on their faces. The rise and fall of laughter with everyone chattering at once could be heard among the ranks of the self-defense militia standing behind the hospital staff as everyone tried to guess what this Dr. Bethune could be like. A few walked forward to try and see further along the road.
>
> Suddenly an excited roar rose up at the front.
>
> "There he is!"
>
> Everyone quickly returned to their ranks, standing in a very orderly and respectful way, but still craning their necks to see along the road. At last, faintly, at the far end of the river bank

could be seen a cavalry brigade of some 20–30 people, moving forward in the foglike whirling snow. The messenger who had been sent off earlier rushed from the woods, waving excitedly. His mouth was wide open as he shouted something, but his words were lost in the howling wind. "They've come! They've all come!"

Out from the dark skeletal woods emerged the small cavalcade. At its head was a large chestnut stallion bravely stepping through the snow, which crunched under its hooves. On its back sat a foreigner wearing a gray uniform with the emblem of the Eighth Route Army on an armband. Round his waist was a broad leather belt and he wore a pair of straw sandals strapped on his shoes just like any ordinary Chinese soldier. When he saw the lines of people awaiting him beyond the woods he dismounted, his right hand raised in a salute in the Spanish Loyalist style.

Bethune's willingness to live "just like any ordinary Chinese soldier" was a valuable asset. Whenever there was dirty work to be done he did not stand aloof, and the Chinese were amazed at his insistence on sharing peasant hardships. He pushed himself unsparingly, impelled by revolutionary ardor and his conviction that at last he was fulfilling his life's mission. The Border Region, an enclave surrounded by Japanese, where the campaigning was fluid and mobility counted, was a theater that might have been designed for his talents. "I am in the center of the center of the war," he wrote. "Now I can truly taste the strange, exalted flavor of this stupendous struggle."

Altogether Bethune would spend nineteen months in China, and during those months he would operate behind enemy lines, train guerrilla fighters to perform surgery, create proper sanitation methods, write three medical textbooks, and set up a medical college, nursing school, and model hospital. Under circumstances where bandages were washed and reused, handmade tongs were employed for forceps and handsaws for amputations, he conscripted blacksmiths to make pails and splints, tailors to make bedding, carpenters to make traction. An incredible achievement, the model hospital had one fatal drawback: it was stationary. It functioned like a western hospital with Bethune's modern medical supplies until the Japanese, launching a fresh offensive, overran and destroyed the facility.

Heading an eighteen-member medical team, Bethune became in effect the ad hoc director of all Chinese Communist medical forces, and he relished this role, though now he was more concerned with improved medical conditions than with himself. He operated ceaselessly, often under fire or incredible pressure. When the Japanese struck in November 1938, he traveled seventy-five miles to establish an operating base in a small temple eight miles from the action. Against subzero weather his sole protection was a blaze near the operating table. A bedsheet served as a roof. Here he operated continuously for forty hours, performing seventy-one operations. While he was operating, Chinese partisans counterattacked, swarming upon Japanese reinforcements and shouting, "Attack! Bethune is with us! Bethune is with us!" and turned the tide of battle. The Eighth Route Army had found a new rallying cry.

Pai-ch'iu-en was the Chinese transliteration of his last name, which, coincidentally, also meant "White-Seek-Grace" and "White-One Sent," and stories of his larger-than-life behavior swept the army. On one occasion he gave his own blood to a wounded guerrilla, and then without pausing completed the operation that saved the man's life; on another, he rode seventeen miles to tend a soldier and returned to base hospital; he would scale precipices and give his clothing to the wounded. His passion frightened more phlegmatic personalities, his medical team urged him to slow down, and General Nieh Jung-chen, the commander of the district, at length ordered him into a room to sleep. Bethune obeyed, but no sooner had he stretched out on the dirt floor than he leaped up, knocked the cigarette from Nieh's lips, and snapped, "In respect to medical matters, I will not take orders, even from you." Instead of sleeping, Bethune stalked back to the operating table.

An air of purgation, as though he had scoured his spirit and reached essentials, now clung to him. Like the classical medical missionaries of the nineteenth century, those forebears who dotted his family tree, he seemed a martyr to his convictions. His supreme effort under fire took place in April 1939 at Chi-hui when he set up his makeshift equipment two miles from the fighting and operated for sixty-nine hours without sleep on one hundred fifteen casualties. A shell demolished a wall thirty feet from the table. Doctors and nurses urged him to rest. He plunged his face into a bucket of cold water and remained operating.

The diet of millet, rice, and eggs, the nights on front-line duty, the vermin-ridden caves, the extremes of cold and heat, exacted a physical toll: Bethune soon looked haggard and ancient, no longer the vigorous middle-aged man who had galloped into the Border Region but a gaunt sage on a silk scroll. Even more than his physical depletion — he was beginning to lose his hearing, his teeth needed attention, he must consult an oculist — he felt oppressed by loneliness. Although he had a smattering of the language and authentic rapport with the Chinese, he was isolated, a stranger. Funds from the China Aid Council were blocked; only three letters had arrived from them in twenty months. His own letters implored friends for books, magazines, newspapers, any reminder, however trifling, of home. He requested officials to forward $100 monthly to Frances ("She is not the sort of person to ask for money"). He was serene, yet his serenity failed to stem a gathering sense of solitude. Riding among gorges and cliffs he remembered North American lakes and trees and skies. How incredible it was that his Saranac Lake experience had terminated in West Hopei. Saranac had been the pivot of his life, and his career had a symmetry to it, the muddled time before his tuberculosis and his apotheosis afterward.

To John Barnwell, his confidant from Saranac days, he wrote:

"I dream of coffee, of rare roast beef, of apple pie and ice cream, Mirages of heavenly food. Books — are books still being written? Is music still being played? Do you dance, drink beer, look at pictures? What do clean white sheets in a soft bed feel like? Do women still love to be loved?"

Late in October, while operating without gloves, his hand slipped and he nicked the middle finger of his left hand. During an operation a few days afterward he plunged his hand into a festering wound, and as a result contracted septicemia. His body could not fend off infection, and on November 12, 1939, surrounded by his colleagues, he died in a peasant hut. The Chinese carried his body four days through snowy mountain passes to a village. Unable to find a Union Jack there, they draped his bier with an American flag, and he lay in state while more than ten thousand people shuffled past.

Mao composed a tribute hailing him as an internationalist, for Mao had promised that international communism would support the Chinese. "Every Communist must learn true communist spirit from Comrade Bethune." Instead of international brigades, however, the China Aid Committee had sent a single contentious and stubborn reformer who might well be deemed ideologically suspect. Four years previously he had written the Friends of Soviet Russia, "To jeopardize the only position — economic and professional — I possess, by even associating with a communistic-leaning Association such as yours would be senseless." But the Chinese would never forget his total identification with them, or his extraordinary feats at operating tables amid rubble, smoke, and the groans of dying soldiers, including Japanese prisoners treated with the same compassion. After the Communists defeated the Kuomintang in 1949, Bethune acquired the status of a national hero; his life story passed into the curricula of elementary schools; and he is commemorated today near the Bethune Hospital in Shichiachuang by an imposing Leninesque statue that stands before his tomb and the Bethune Memorial Hall.

Ironically, although he is perhaps the most highly acclaimed westerner in traditionally xenophobic China, Norman Bethune was unknown to most Canadians until recent years and is still generally unknown in the United States. Ironic too is the reflection that the Walter Pater credo of the hard gemlike flame that shone so brightly for the surgeon shone as bright for a dissimilar and exceptional personality, Oscar Wilde. Bethune considered himself political, yet his views were those of a radical humanitarian rather than a prisoner of ideology: "In this community of pain," he observed in China, "there are no enemies."

Heiress, Scientist, Merchant Prince
1936–1950

OF SARANAC LAKE'S SIX THOUSAND residents in the early thirties, three thousand had TB. Dr. Francis B. Trudeau, grandson of Edward Livingston Trudeau and father of cartoonist Garry, was not as a child permitted to go into the village. The Trudeaus adopted a prudent parental policy, since Saranac was safer than most places if only because the villagers, conscious of tuberculosis, knew how to cope with it. Between 1926 and 1936, in fact, Lawrason Brown initiated a project that x-rayed six thousand village schoolchildren and became a prototype for similar public school health programs. Even so, a mythology of tuberculosis enveloped Saranac like fog off a snowbank — stories about motorists frantically accelerating at the village limits and covering their mouths with handkerchiefs or, in an alternative version, trying not to breathe while passing through.

Coming of age in Saranac Lake during the thirties and forties did mean, however, observing certain communal taboos, such as the ban against spitting on the street. That offense carried a fifty-dollar fine. Youngsters were warned not to make noise between two and four while the patients were resting. The slow siesta of winter afternoons was interrupted only by the drip of icicles. Along Helen Hill (cynically dubbed "Hemorrhage Hill"), a compact concentration of cure cottages displayed an architecture dominated by porch enclosures and influenced by disease. The scores of private cottages constituted a Depression-proof industry, though not quite as Depression-proof as the village fathers might wish. Moribund cases still arrived on the daily trains and Trudeau doctors still visited hotel lobbies where the new arrivals tended to seek refuge. The overcrowded state hospitals required waiting periods, so haggling often took place in the lobbies as doctors wheedled cure-cottage beds for the dying. The indigent were generally accepted out of charity; agencies that might assist them today did not exist. Saranac's cottage TB industry had peaked in 1922, when over sixteen hundred new patients poured into the village. The Veterans Administration then proposed constructing a 500-bed Saranac hospital, but the plan was allegedly scuttled by doctors who considered a public facility competitive with Trudeau. Sunmount Hospital was built eighteen miles away in Tupper Lake, where it still contributes to the local economy.

The opening of Sunmount and the onset of the Great Depression affected Saranac's cure cottages; nevertheless, on a comparative basis they prospered. Consider 110 and 112 Main Street, the Werle Cottages owned by Aletta Werle and Jane Schneiderwind. Miss Werle's forte — and a compelling talent it proved — was cookery; Miss Schneiderwind was her business partner. The cottages fulfilled separate functions: 112 Main, a "nursing" cottage in which patients were confined to their beds or cure chairs (the dumbwaiter survives as testament that many patients were "on trays"); 110 Main, an "ambulatory" or "up" cottage where patients indulged in mild exercise (coping, in the village vernacular, with "dandruff," a mild dusting of TB). Like the aristocracy of the ill, the Trudeau patients, who had a limousine-taxi that brought them six at a time into the village, the boarders at one-ten enjoyed activities like shopping or going to the movies. They ate at one-twelve, however, where Miss Werle produced wondrous picnic baskets for those unable to reach the dining room.

The baskets, famous in the village, were also distributed to "nursing" cottages or establishments without dining facilities.

The Werle Cottages emphasized gregarious proximity to downtown, but each cure cottage had a distinctive character that ranged from stark furnished rooms to commodious apartments in the Santanoni, where Christy Mathewson stayed before buying a house. Helen Hill exhibited all types: cottages for tubercular families, cottages for families with a curing member, cottages for single tuberculars only. The Alta Vista at the crest of Franklin Avenue resembled a hotel, while Mary Prescott's Nursing Hospital catered to a more reclusive clientele. Establishments were often run by ex-patients who shrank from leaving Saranac. Their cases illustrated a poignant phenomenon — the relapse Trudeau patients often suffered when told they could go home. Some patients were institutionalized, others rejected by their families, and some simply dreaded returning to a world that stigmatized them. The sanatorium's medical staff, conscious of the syndrome, found it as difficult to discharge patients as to inform them of their condition. One woman at Trudeau, enduring the cycle of recuperation and relapse seventeen times, ended it by marrying another patient. Settling in Saranac was a popular solution, and many who did felt qualified to open a cure cottage.

Houses built for tuberculars, like the Jennings Cottage on Franklin Avenue, display solid masses, ample porches, wide doorways with no sills, so that beds can roll from porch to bedroom. Apart from these (90 percent of Saranac's housing stock is over fifty years old), already-existing structures were adapted to the purpose and festooned by dormers, annexes, and porches. The hodgepodge façades of redesigned cottages contrast oddly with the proportions of houses designed specifically for TB patients. The architectural abandon has a folksy kitsch-like flavor suggesting that at any moment a gable trapdoor might pop open and release a spring-wound cuckoo.

The clean lines of the indigenous cottage organize the environment, bringing nature and its healing properties inside. To be sure, an Adirondack winter is another matter, but the domestic architecture of a well-designed cure cottage carries an implicit sense of nature as therapeutic energy. Nowhere is this more evident than in the Stonaker House on Glenwood Road, purchased in 1911 by Edwin R. and Jeannie H. Stonaker, parents of a tubercular daughter. The long and low red house, built into a hillside, boasts a massive trapezoidal chimney as well as walls of anorthosite, an iridescent blue-gray rock. From a central octagon stretch wings on either side; the wings contain four octagonal rooms; majestic quartz glass windows surround the central octagon, the largest with three panes nine by six feet. Sunbathing was then in vogue at Davos — later medical research disclosed that exposure to direct sunlight might actually hinder convalescence — and such products as the Alpine Sun Lamp were featured in Saranac drugstores. (TB nostrums appeared in the village with predictable regularity, including, in Dr. Trudeau's day, a turtle serum briefly popular until proven fraudulent.) The Stonakers flooded their interiors with sunlight, a luminous deluge of hope. Twenty years later they sold the house, which passed through subsequent owners of local prominence, including Alice G. Laidlaw, heiress of the Hershey chocolate fortune, and Dr. Harry A. Bray, the director of Ray Brook Hospital, who constructed a nine-hole golf course for his patients, probably the only course devised for tuberculars, with the greens close enough to be played with irons. A passionate player though beset by a heart ailment, the doctor used a golf club for a cane.

The cure cottages and the nearby Adirondack lodges, which Harvey H. Kaiser, their chronicler, calls the Great Camps, occupy opposite ends of the architectural spectrum. Owned by millionaires like the Rockefellers, the Great Camps, splendors of rustic craftsmanship, were lavish wilderness pleasure-domes where guests dressed formally for dinner. The desire to live in accord with nature, however, was no less urgent than in the village.

Ostentatious display influenced the formation of the Great

Camps. So did anti-Semitism. The Jewish tycoons of the mauve decades — Seligmans, Guggenheims, Baches, and Loebs, influential in the Darwinian realm of finance — were excluded from the recreations of the Gentile leisure class. Discrimination was not limited to the Adirondacks, to be sure, but after a nasty and widely publicized 1877 incident involving Joseph Seligman and his family at Saratoga's Grand Union Hotel, Adirondack hotels and resorts became infamous for bigotry. The word *Restricted* appeared in advertising copy, and truculent mottoes sprang up — "Hebrews need not apply" and "Hebrews will knock vainly for admission." The most odious enclave perhaps was the Lake Placid Club, founded by Melvil Dewey. At his death in 1931, few took seriously his lifelong campaign to reform English spelling; he was better known for developing the library classification system that bears his name. Dewey's passion for classification extended to people. The Lake Placid Club, which equated illness with minority status, barred blacks and Jews by fiat and the infirm by a sign near the entrance: NO TUBERCULARS.

When William West Durant, the railway magnate who opened the central Adirondacks to tourism, overextended his empire in the early 1890s, however, becoming embroiled in litigation with his sister and wife, he began to sell his Saranac holdings. "The builders of the Adirondack Railroad were more interested in the ready cash than in the proper parentage of potential buyers," states Kaiser, "and were willing to make their land available to anyone able to pay the asking price." Thus rose the Knollwood Club on Lower Saranac Lake, a 500-acre complex designed by architect William Coulter for Louis Marshall, Daniel Guggenheim, Elias Ashiel, George Blumenthal, Abram N. Stein, and Max Nathan (their descendants still use the club); Otto Kahn's combination Tudor-and-log house on Upper Saranac Lake; Sekon Lodge, Isaac N. Seligman's twenty-building camp; Julius Bache's peninsula compound, Wenonah Lodge, where sharp-edged red-tile roofs define structures from Victorian mansions to a Japanese gazebo; and Adolph Lewisohn's Bavarian retreat, which, for his one-month stay, required a staff of forty, including a chess coach, singing teacher, and two chauffeurs.

Black patients unable to meet Trudeau's qualifications depended on at least two identifiable separate-but-equal cure cottages. John and Hattie Ramsay, brother and sister, opened a Lake Flower Avenue cottage around 1920. Each married and continued the same occupation; Hattie and her husband, John Reid, bought a house on Pine Street to which, in a typical conversion, they added an enclosed verandah, bedrooms, and a kitchen. John Ramsay and his wife, Viola, operated the more stately Lake Flower Avenue establishment. Screened by a honey locust hedge, the private sanatorium acquired a word-of-mouth reputation — the Ramsays never advertised — among West Indians, wealthy New Yorkers, and the domestic staffs of the Great Camps. Bill and Sadie Hall on Margaret Street may or may not have accommodated black patients. Their house with its corner turret and capacious overhanging porch was patently capable of accommodating a tubercular clientele, but Bill, the former personal cook of Cardinal Gibbons of Baltimore, pursued a successful career as a caterer to Park Avenue families. The motif of food was as important in the black cure cottages as it was among Werle patients. The Halls presided over a communal feast on New Year's, while the Ramsays continued to offer a Thursday night buffet long after the curing had ceased and their sanatorium had reverted to a tourist home.

You are, let us assume, a guest of Marjorie Merriweather Post, invited to her 207-acre estate, Topridge, on Upper St. Regis Lake. The time is after the Second World War, although her social pattern, shaped in the twenties and thirties, remains unchanged. Mrs. Post, heiress to the Post Cereal Corporation fortune, has been married four times, most notably to Joseph E. Davies, President Franklin D. Roosevelt's ambassador to the Soviet Union during Stalin's purge trials. Banquets and house parties are her lifework and she maintains a nomadic routine, moving from estate to estate, each a change of backdrop for her performance as hostess. There is Mar-a-Lago, her Palm Beach pleasure-dome designed by Joseph Urban, set designer for the Ziegfeld Follies. There is Hillwood, her Washington residence, surrounded by punctilious formal gardens and stuffed with a medley of Czarist and French bibelots. At various times she has migrated to a 16,000-acre South Carolina plantation, a 70-room Manhattan apartment, and the *Sea Cloud,* a 350-foot yacht with four masts and, as surety, four diesel engines. But yours is a routine invitation to Topridge, proffered on the telephone by Margaret Voigt, Mrs. Post's personal secretary. Subsequently, a letter arrives, specifying the details of your departure aboard the *Merriweather,* based at Paige Airways in Washington's National Airport. The *Merriweather,* the world's largest private plane, was acquired by Mrs. Post from her friend, Dominican dictator Rafael Trujillo, in a swap of the 44-passenger Viscount prop-jet for the heiress's elaborate yacht. She keeps three full-time pilots on her payroll. Captain Hallersmith, her chief pilot, may fly servants and staff on personal errands when she doesn't require the plane; as a rule, however, the *Merriweather* is used to whisk guests between Washington, Mar-a-Lago, and Topridge. "Do whatever you want to do regardless of the planned activities offered," she informs them, "and if there is anything you want and don't ask for, it's your own fault." This, alas, is not precisely correct; Mrs. Post's sincerity is exemplary, but in fact your invitation to Topridge will locate you amid the hedges and blind alleys of ritualized behavior. Your hostess stage-manages the revels by itemized memoranda. No detail is too trivial for her, and you are provided with a return schedule in the event you are inclined to overstay your appointed holiday. Instructions about packing and procedure are included (attention to plan equals contented guests), and if it all smacks of military logistics, why, that too is part of Marjorie Post's rigorous hospitality.

About a dozen of us gather at the airport en route to Topridge. Aside from a General Omar Bradley or an Eleanor Roosevelt, you don't recognize the others. Two or three are celebrities of the Washington social circuit, although they disdain celebrity. Mrs. Post, conscious of what she considers her humbler Midwestern origins, deliberately selects Eastern Establishment guests like yourself, firmly entrenched patricians who sidestep the limelight.

Chauffeurs arrive carrying boxes of orchids and armfuls of fresh flowers, and they distribute the flowers throughout the cabin. The flight to Saranac is uneventful. You swivel on your easy chair and converse while attendants serve drinks and snacks. At New York the plane lands, picks up other guests, then continues to Saranac Lake airport, where chauffeured limousines crawl toward the landing strip. The processional, worthy of a gangster's cortege — the luggage will follow in other limousines — enters Paul Smith's, rolls along Easy Street, and reaches Upper St. Regis Lake. A blue 26-passenger Chris-Craft awaits, its name — *Merriweather* again — fanning across the glossy stern. (A twin Chris-Craft is also available.) The powerful speedboat ruffles the stillness of the lake and the engine drums across the water. Mrs. Post's uniformed boatman skims expertly past islets studded by bent pines. Ahead, beyond the spray, stretch the outlines of a horizontal green-roofed boathouse that shelters a fleet of sailboats, canoes, inboards, and Adirondack guide boats. Tree-trunk pillars buttress the building. The pillars' boughs form traceries, an arbor of interlaced branches embroidering a level series of boat bays. On the dock stand Mrs. Post and her staff framed beneath a sapling proscenium arch.

Disembarking, you greet the hostess. She is the quintessential chatelaine — majestic yet eager, fragrant with welcome. Since she purchased Topridge in 1921 from the Lathrop family, Marjorie Merriweather Post has been expanding it. Like the pyramids or the palace of Versailles, it is an architectural dream without finitude. The dream can end only with the builder's life or a completed cycle of history. Topridge will eventually have sixty-eight buildings and require a staff of eighty-five — a sylvan island ruled by a patroness of masques and tableaux.

Elderly, infirm, and short-of-breath guests board a cable car running between the trees toward the camp's hogback ridge. From the platform at the top of the funicular railway they view pines and cabins, the westward flank of St. Regis Mountain, Upper and Lower Spectacle Ponds lying within the domain. Guests who skip the funicular walk up a paved path to the main lodge. Its 80-by-100-foot living room, illumined by two sizable chandeliers of wreathed antlers, offers a fantastic demonstration of the taxidermist's handicraft. Stuffed owls glide above bearskin rugs; snarling foxes bare needle-sharp fangs; coyotes snuffle the legs of hide-draped sofas. The Eskimo kayaks and Algonquin canoes suspended from the ceiling are destined for the Smithsonian Institution, along with Mrs. Post's American Indian artifacts, pottery, weavings, and Pacific Northwest totem poles. No other site at Topridge so completely expresses her eclectic Victorian taste. Two servants spend their days constantly dusting the collection. The living room also serves as a catchall of Navajo blankets, African tribal shields, carved birds with tassels in their beaks, baskets converted to light fixtures, mooseheads, feathered drums, snowshoes mounted upon the sturdy fieldstones of the fireplace: here is the equivalent of the oppressive excess of a Midwestern drawing room of the Gilded Age, the sort of environment in which Marjorie's father, C. W. Post, the Battle Creek cereal magnate, might feel at home. And yet "oppressive" somehow doesn't fit; the ensemble works *because* of its extravagant romanticism. It is not a curatorial display of primitive art but an extrovert response to native culture, domesticating the Adirondack wilderness as Mrs. Post's version of the Forest of Arden.

First-run movies are screened three evenings a week; above the cavernous space a loft conceals a 35-mm. projection room. The initial social event is a cocktail party in the main lodge while the maid or valet assigned each visitor is unpacking luggage and laying out the evening's costume. You will watch your drinks; Mrs. Post, reared as a Christian Scientist, practices Christian Science. Flexible enough not to impose her views on others, she strongly disapproves of alcoholic ebullience. Only through the influence of Mrs. Post's last husband, convivial Ernest May, are the estate's cabins stocked with fully equipped bars, but covert drinking is watched too.

While you chat amiably with strangers, Frank Moffatt, Topridge's major-domo, hands out cabin assignments. Do you prefer the Ridge Cabin with its color-coordinated fly swatters, the Honeymoon Cottage connected by a footbridge to the putting greens and clay tennis courts, or a Lake Shore Cabin supplied with a wood-burning fireplace, birch logs, and kindling? Mrs. Post's precision is evident in the kindling, planed into artful spirals by a specialist who has no other occupation. Whichever cabin is assigned to you will have a telephone directory of the camp's forty-eight numbers, enabling you to dial a hunting guide, masseur, stenographer, tennis pro, or security guard.

The guards are a prominent and disquieting aspect of the estate. Mrs. Post keeps quantities of jewelry that she enjoys displaying at formal dinners and soirees; but her fears have been aroused following a burglary attempt, and she has had a safe installed in her cedar closet. Furthermore, as a consequence of the Lindbergh baby kidnapping, she is aware she must protect her child Nedenia. Daughter of Mrs. Post's second husband, financier E. F. Hutton, the child, who will grow up to become actress Dina Merrill, has her own cottage for her toys and straight-backed piano.

Adjacent to the main-lodge living room is a huge birch-lined dining room with a seven-foot sailfish over the mantel. The sailfish, caught by Nedenia at the age of seven, casts a cold eye on a table that can seat forty-two guests, an intimate gathering by Mrs. Post's standards. She prefers a grander scale. Early in 1930, for example, when Eleanor Close, her daughter by her first marriage, informed her parents (by then Marjorie was married to

Hutton) of plans to wed playwright Preston Sturges, both Marjorie and E.F. objected. Although Sturges's Broadway hit, *Strictly Dishonorable,* brought in fifteen hundred a week, and he had just sold the Hollywood rights for $125,000, the husband-and-wife master-builders of General Foods judged the boy thriftless, a fortune-hunter, and a mountebank.

"But, Mother," pleaded Eleanor, "he even owns a yacht."

"How large?"

"Fifty-two feet."

"My dear," Marjorie said, "you mean a *yawl.*"

A squat guardhouse protects the entrance to Mrs. Post's cabin. Her own suite, mingling diverse shades of salmon pink and red, includes a massage room and steam bath. The husband's section of the cabin, furnished in a Scandinavian manner, is known as the Norwegian Room, apparently on the principle that Norway suggests Vikings and there are no women in longboats. Here the dominant color accent is blue. The color's association with connubiality is unclear, but Mrs. Post seems to have determined that blue is male. The significant factor, of course, is not the gender of color; it is Marjorie Merriweather Post's autocracy. "If Marjorie were left alone on a desert island," her father once said, "she would organize the grains of sand."

In her extravaganza of hospitality she elected to star and to stage-manage. One day she decided the picture window of the main lodge impeded her view of the summit of St. Regis Mountain. That fall when she had departed for warmer climates, a ten-and-a-half-foot rectangle of plate glass from Utica was floated by barge across the lake. A crew of fifteen carpenters and glaziers inserted the window. Upon her seasonal return to Topridge she could see the mountain entire. She enjoyed the prospect for some time, until in a later year an air force jet's sonic boom cracked the glass. The government paid damages of $3600, but the window was unique and could not be reinstalled.

Having settled into your cabin, you may select from a variety of possible pastimes — always subject to your hostess's zealous ministrations. A warning bell sounds for meals, a quarter hour later tolls the meal bell. You will not arrive late; the meal has been planned by Mrs. Post and Frank Moffat, and the butlers and maids are at parade rest. Topridge's larder consists of three large cold-storage lockers, two rooms filled with dry goods, one cool storage room for fruits and vegetables, plus the deep freezers and stocked shelves of the kitchen pantries. If you are on a "carry" or a similar planned event, however, you are excused. A "carry" is a picnic excursion by Adirondack guide boat, with a portage from one lake to another. To sustain the illusion of "roughing it" while the staff performs the necessary lifting and hauling, you are asked to carry something — a cushion, a frying pan, a butterfly net. At the picnic site butlers set the table and weigh down its plastic tablecloth with sprays of freshly picked fern. Charcoal-broiled steaks, fried potatoes, and peas appear, then Adirondack pie. The dessert, a strenuous gastronomic challenge, is said to have been first improvised by Mrs. Post: flapjacks glued together with maple sugar and syrup and sliced like a cake. Whether or not she was the originator, she will proudly submit the recipe to the 1955 Women's National Press Club in unequivocal Postian tones: "Each cake should be about nine inches in diameter and stacked seven inches high. Each cake should be buttered, maple syrup poured over it, and then sprinkled with crushed maple sugar. This is repeated until pie is complete and the top cake similarly covered." It is not recorded if the Women's National Press Club actually sampled Adirondack pie; the dish customarily accompanied the rigors of a "carry." Less demanding are the meals in the middle of St. Regis Lake, where you dine around a table on a spacious float, the butlers serving the successive courses as these arrive in launches.

The most curious structure at Topridge is the replica of a Russian *dacha* with which Marjorie has commemorated the Moscow tour of duty (1936–1938) of her third husband, Joseph E. Davies. Thus far you have experienced a generalized Topridge weekend after, say, Marjorie's misalliances and her resumption of her maiden name; but the *dacha* magically turns time backward to the thirties, when for a brief interlude she stood near the balefires of terrible historical events, unaware of their terror or their meaning.

Davies's mission to Moscow is still a subject of historical controversy. Tilting toward the Soviet Union as Germany and Japan grew more menacing, Roosevelt wanted Davies to resolve, if possible, the issue of the Russian debt, an obstacle to improved relations, and promote a climate of goodwill. Davies took his assignment seriously — so seriously that he became Stalin's foremost apologist. A preposterous wartime Hollywood version of Davies's memoir, *Mission to Moscow,* depicts Walter Huston as the ambassador who rendered the Russians probably unrecognizable even to themselves. Not only did the film present the most avuncular of Uncle Joes, but it portrayed a Soviet Union in which altruism was a state religion. Like other foreign diplomats, Davies attended the purge trials and as a corporate lawyer had a strong professional interest in them, yet he never seems to have suspected — or else he deliberately overlooked the obvious — these might be show trials with manufactured evidence. Instead of condemning the trials in his dispatches, he resorted to legalistic hair-splitting that legitimized Stalin's regime as a government of laws, and when the entire testimony was published, sent sixty transcripts to eminent Americans as though resting his case. Marjorie supported her husband and his appeal to authority. Were they ingenuous, hoodwinked, or devotedly carrying out FDR's policies? In any event, the purges crimped Marjorie's guest list. How could one be urbane when the evening's guest of honor might depart at any moment under armed escort to a vermin-ridden cell in the Lubianka Prison or a dawn encounter with a firing squad before a blood-spattered wall? Davies felt saddened that men whom he personally liked and had entertained in his own embassy should have betrayed their country. There was no compromise, however, with conspiracy.

The Topridge *dacha,* a log cabin heated by a floor-to-ceiling tiled stove, displays brightly painted, carved window frames. It has a vaulted interior, barge boards, and such adornments as traditional Russian harvest dolls and paintings of buxom peasant maids bringing in the sheaves. The polychrome touches of Slavic folk art evoke a stylized world of domestic animals, huntsmen, and the braided geometries of the ornamental. Each Thursday evening Mrs. Post holds square dances; everyone will participate: professional square-dancers are on hand to assist guests through their paces, and your beaming hostess is in her element. If by chance you feel disinclined to swing your partner and in lieu of that take a stroll in the woods, a guard will halt you before you have gone too far and direct you back to the *dacha*. Then perhaps you might feel that your bucolic holiday, badgered by restrictions and the ubiquitous guards, has many of the aspects of confinement, and then too you might overhear, through the fiddles and clapping, the mournful clang of Russia's prison gates.

Marjorie Merriweather Post properly belongs to the social history of Saranac rather than to American culture seen through the prism of tuberculosis, but she was a fixture of the region until her death in 1973. Topridge, which she left to the state of New York, proved an encumbrance, costing the state about $377,000 annually for maintenance. Public use was minimal under New York's ownership, and the camp was open only for infrequent state conferences and for weekend tours organized by the Saranac Lake Chamber of Commerce. The state tried to give away the property for $1 to the local town of Brighton, but Brighton, which lost a significant portion of its tax base because of Mrs. Post's will, could not afford the gift. After a decade of efforts to take Topridge off the state rolls, New York's Office of General Services sold the estate at public auction during the summer of 1985 to a New Jersey businessman, Roger Jakubowski, forty-two years old and a self-described "hot dog salesman." He also said he owned nine restaurants, two motels, several arcades and amusement centers, a supermarket, and a spring-water bottling plant.

Jakubowski's successful bid of $911,000 (inspired, he revealed, by the emergency telephone number, 911) came after New York divided the property, valued at $2 million, and retained 102 acres, which the state added to the Adirondack Forest Preserve. Calling Topridge the "Hearst Castle of the East," Jakubowski announced he was buying it as a working retreat for himself and his four-year-old daughter, Maria. He saw Topridge for the first time two weeks before his high bid and planned to maintain its tradition by entertaining "acquaintances of national prominence." "I'll be rubbing shoulders with Marjorie Merriweather Post," he said.

If Mrs. Post was migratory yet periodic, Mark Twain, in 1901, and Albert Einstein, throughout the thirties, forties, and early fifties, were Summer Folks, occasional visitors, although Einstein happened to be in Saranac Lake at an especially momentous juncture of his own and the world's history — August 6, 1945.

Mark Twain was returning from his world tour and a period of lionization; his Adirondack summer on Lower Saranac Lake in a rented log cabin, "The Lair" (characteristically, he transposed it to "The Liar"), was idyllic, though marked by concern for the failing health of his wife, Livy. "If we live another year, I hope we shall spend its summer in this house," he vowed. They never came back; still, in 1901, Clemens relaxed and let the world carry on without him. He wrote a spoof of Conan Doyle, "A Double-Barreled Detective Story," read a stuffy biography of Phillips Brooks, and followed events piling on each other after the assassination of President William McKinley. This had an Adirondack link; on the afternoon of September 13, Theodore Roosevelt had climbed Mt. Marcy, and during his descent met a messenger bearing a telegram: THE PRESIDENT APPEARS TO BE DYING AND MEMBERS OF THE CABINET IN BUFFALO THINK YOU SHOULD LOSE NO TIME IN COMING. The nearest railroad station was fifty miles away, and Roosevelt arrived at five-thirty in the morning after a breakneck carriage ride through the mountains. The tidings of McKinley's death greeted the Vice President, who then took the oath of office by the light of a conductor's lantern. For Mark Twain the assassination, as usual, inspired acerbic thoughts about the sanity of the species, but for the most part he simply loafed. Over eighty years afterward Seaver Rice could recall going to the Saranac Lake post office to pick up Mark Twain's mail. Seaver was then working as a caddy, and Mark had materialized on the golf course, looking for boys who would bring his mail out to the lake. He tipped Seaver a dollar, which wasn't bad considering the normal tip for a caddy after a round of golf was twenty-five cents. At lakeside Mark Twain experienced the bliss of doing nothing; surveying Saranac's post-glacial solitudes he felt snug as a Mississippi pilot on course.

> I am on the front porch (lower one — main deck) of our little bijou of a dwelling-house [he wrote his friend Joe Twichell in Hartford]. The lake-edge [Lower Saranac] is so nearly under me that I can't see the shore, but only the water, small-poxed with rain splashes — for there is a heavy downpour. It is charmingly like sitting snuggled up on a ship's deck with the stretching sea all around — but very much more satisfactory, for at sea a rainstorm is depressing while here of course the effect engendered is just a deep sense of comfort and contentment. The heavy forest shuts us solidly in on three sides — there are no neighbors. There are beautiful little tan-colored impudent squirrels about. They take tea, 5 P.M., (not invited) at the table in the woods where Jean does my typewriting, and one of them has been brave enough to sit upon Jean's knee with his tail curved over his back and munch his food. They come to dinner, 7 P.M., on the front porch (not invited). They all have the one name — Blennerhasset, from Burr's friend — and none of them answers to it except when hungry.

Albert Einstein, during the summer of 1936, also came to Saranac Lake in search of serenity. Like Mark Twain, Einstein was an international celebrity of long standing and he was known as the greatest scientist of the century to men and women who had only the vaguest comprehension of his Special Theory of Relativity or his persistent search after unitary field laws for gravitation and electromagnetism. Like Mark Twain, too, Einstein at Saranac felt apprehensive about the condition of his wife's health. Elsa Lowenthal, a widowed cousin with two grown-up daughters, had married him in June 1919 after Einstein's divorce from his first wife, Mileva. That same year the thunderclap of his scientific genius, validated by two British eclipse expeditions, startled humanity. The Einsteins' relationship would have offended contemporary American feminists; nearsighted, dowdy Elsa, with her provincial manners and maternal solicitude, was ridiculed by the envious, but she implemented decisions and made possible the functioning of Einstein's intellect.

"While he devoted himself to discovering how God had made the world, she reduced to an absolute minimum the mundane problems of life," states Einstein's biographer Ronald Clark. Once on a summer night the Einsteins dined outdoors with another couple. As the air cooled, the hostess asked her husband to fetch her coat. Elsa was shocked. "I would never ask the professor to do that," she said.

During a Princeton faculty party a dean's wife observed, "Your wife seems to do absolutely everything for you. Just exactly what do *you* do for her?" Einstein replied: "I give her my understanding."

"They were a happy couple and they laughed a lot," reported the *Adirondack Daily Enterprise* when the Einsteins visited Herbert Leggett's real estate office to sign a summer lease. The newspaper story resuscitated one of the hoariest of Einstein anecdotes, based on his alleged arithmetical woolliness. Perplexed by the small print, the illustrious physicist handed over the documents to Elsa, and she explained, "He isn't any good at figures."

The Einsteins had inspected several places within or near the village and could have taken houses offered free of charge; but, conversant with the wiles of publicity seekers, they evaded such offers and rented architect William Distin's house in Saranac's relatively secluded Glenwood Estates. Leggett served as their volunteer social secretary; requests were channeled through his office and he developed a formula for coping with them: "I'm sorry, but the professor is up the lake."

The happiness remarked by the *Enterprise* was illusory. Elsa, suffering heart and liver complaints, would die before the end of the year. Apart from physical travail, however, she felt the burden of her subordinate marital role. All summer, Einstein, though presumably past his prime as a scientific innovator, sailed his seventeen-foot boat and pondered unified field theory. Einstein's sailing, says Clark, "was not so much a hobby as an extension of himself in which the essentials of his character and temperament were revealed." The professor delighted in the equations of wind, water, and weather, as if the rhythms of his thought had been translated into the swell of a taut sail, the gyrations of a slackening rope. Among his few regrets over leaving Germany was leaving behind his boat on the Havelsee outside Berlin. Slowly tacking across Lake Flower, he would moor the boat and step ashore in a world where Hitler's voice barked on the shortwave from Berlin.

The Distin house was unpretentiously decorated. One could relax, overlooking the lake, and the rooms exhibited a comfortable informality absent from the Einsteins' academic surroundings. The Nazis (incredibly) had released the furnishings of the professor's Berlin home, and after these were shipped to Princeton, New Jersey, Elsa arranged the Biedermeier chairs, the crocheted tablecloths, the busts of Schiller and Goethe, as though duplicating the environment of the early years of her marriage. The décor so appropriate to a bourgeois Germany of the twenties looked ornate in the rooms of a colonial house on an American university campus, and Einstein came to dislike its Teutonic propriety. "When women are in their homes, they are attached to their furniture," he had observed in Berlin. "They run round it all day long and are always fussing over it. But when I am with a woman on a journey, I am the only piece of furniture that she has available, and she cannot refrain from moving round me all day long and improving something about me."

Given Einstein's views on women and furniture, his disparagement of the old Berlin appointments may have reflected a desire for a less prescriptive relationship. He balked at returning to the past. If he was the only piece of furniture available, he would not be an example of Biedermeier. The Nazis had placed blood money upon his head and he had been obliged by Europe's sinister realities to abandon his long-cherished pacifist ideals. Quantum theory was, in his view, advancing fallacious explanations of nature: he would remain forever opposed to the idea of an indeterminate universe. Many younger scientists proclaimed him outdated; physics had developed in different directions. If the new generation thought him obsolete, Einstein knew better. He still had vital work to accomplish, and he would accomplish it, isolated physically and intellectually from the German humanism that had nurtured him and which he never forgave for declining into an ugly travesty of itself.

Elsa's loneliness was emotional. To their mutual friend, the biochemist Leon Watters, she complained of Albert's benign neglect. Watters, a widower about to remarry, would fulfill his marital obligations; forgive her for saying so, aloof and unresponsive Albert should regard him as a model. Elsa was proud of her husband's accomplishments but resented his dismissal of humdrum detail — an indifference she herself made possible.

Often that summer they sailed together, each absorbed by thought, and one evening they disappeared. Early that morning the Einsteins set sail upon the Lower Lake, intending to negotiate the locks to Lake Flower (named for a New York governor, Lake Flower was created by damming the Saranac River). At twilight their boat *Tinef* had not moored and concern spread through the village. Einstein's fatalism included sailing without life belts or preservers, though neither he nor Elsa could swim. The missing-boat bulletin reached the press. Jimmy Munn, a *Daily Enterprise* sportswriter, tapped out the story and wire services relayed it to the nation's front pages. EINSTEIN LOST! State police arrived, search parties formed, and speed-skating champion Ed Lamie jumped into a guide boat and paddled upriver to intercept the couple or bring back evidence of tragedy. Lamie and other convergent rescuers discovered the Einsteins becalmed in Ampersand Bay. No, they did not want a line; Einstein rattled a halyard and looked for a breeze. Why did everyone belabor the obvious? When the wind died out of his sails, he could open his notebook and perform his calculations; there is no record of how Elsa occupied herself.

Eventually the Einsteins finished their sail. A footnote to it occurred, however: Jimmy Munn was hired by the Associated Press.

Until age and infirmity overtook him, Einstein sailed on Princeton's Carnegie Lake and at Saranac in summer. Florida, Long Island, and Watch Hill, Rhode Island, also received a try, but after Elsa's death, Saranac became his favorite seasonal address. During this immediate prewar period the splitting of the uranium atom by Otto Hahn accelerated applied fission research everywhere. Einstein's 1905 paper, which presented the celebrated $E = mc^2$ equation, had predicted the release of energy through a minute amount of mass multiplied by the square of the velocity of light; but the production of a weapon based on Einstein's description of a natural phenomenon would be undertaken by others. "I did not, in fact, foresee that it would be released in my time," he said of nuclear energy. "I only believed that it was theoretically possible." Nevertheless he lent his enormous prestige to the "Roosevelt letter" drafted with Leo Szilard, warning the U.S. government of the doomsday potential of atomic weapons and not, incidentally, inspiring the Manhattan Project. Einstein, however, was considered a security risk. Naturalized only in 1940, he had in the past uttered left-wing com-

ments of a mildly dilute character, so the military-political bu-
reaucracy barred him from any decision making. While he sailed
on Lower Saranac he could only infer from scattered evidence
— the departure from the academic scene, for example, of scientists involved in nuclear research — the true state of affairs.
By late 1944 he had no doubt. Meanwhile, he had accepted a
$25-a-day consultantship with the U.S. Navy Bureau of Ord-
nance, a move he came to regret later when he symbolized the
world's conscience, yet in the context of the times the job allowed
him to take an active part in ending the war.

Stephen Brunauer, a former research chemist in the Department of Agriculture, headed the bureau's high-explosive research. On Einstein's centennial in 1979 he recalled those days:
"I knew the names of two high explosives: TNT and dynamite.
With that knowledge I became head of high explosives research
and development for the world's largest Navy."

Fortunately Brunauer was young and learned fast. At a joint
conference of military and civilian officials Einstein's name was
mentioned. Brunauer inquired if he was working for the armed
services. Einstein is a pacifist, and he is detached from practical
problems, they told him. "He is only interested in working on
his unified field theory." Brunauer reasoned the world's most
renowned scientist, a prominent Zionist, would not espouse pac-
ifism in a war against Hitler. Accordingly, he wrote Einstein, received a reply, and arrived in Princeton on May 16, 1943.

> Einstein was tremendously pleased about the offer, and very hap-
> pily gave his consent. . . . He had not been approached by anyone
> to do any war work since the United States entered the war. He
> said to me, "People think that I am interested only in theory, and
> not in anything practical. This is not true. I was working in the
> Patent Office in Zurich, and I participated in the development of
> many inventions. The gyroscope, too." I said, "That's fine. You
> are hired." We both laughed and agreed that Einstein would talk
> the details over with Dr. Frank Aydelotte, the Director of the In-
> stitute for Advanced Study, where Einstein was employed.

The following day Einstein wrote Brunauer:

> Would it in any way interfere with my usefulness to the Navy if I
> should spend a part of the summer in a cottage at Lake Saranac?
> I do not know whether it would be possible for me to take a hol-
> iday away from Princeton in any case, and certainly if my useful-
> ness to the Navy would be increased by remaining in Princeton I
> should be most happy to do so. If, however, it would be equally
> convenient for you, I think I could probably work to better ad-
> vantage in the more agreeable climate of Lake Saranac during the
> hot months of summer.

As a guest of Louis Marshall, a New York lawyer who was one
of the original six founders, Einstein had begun summering at
the Knollwood Club, and when not sailing took long walks
through the woods and played the violin in his cottage, where
he was often joined by concert violinist Francis Magnus. Here
on August 6, 1945, the physicist heard on the radio the news of
the devastation of Hiroshima.

Assessing his ambiguous position vis-à-vis the bomb, Einstein
refused immediate comment. His secretary, Helen Dukas, issued
a statement: "Although it can be said that the professor thoroughly understands the fundamental science of the atomic
bomb, military expediency demands that he remain un-
communicative on the subject until the authorities release
details."

On August 11 he gave his first post-Hiroshima interview to
Richard Lewis of the *Albany Times-Union*.

> I talked to Prof. Einstein in the home of Joseph Walsh, superin-
> tendent of the Knollwood Club, which is about a half mile from
> the professor's six-room cottage [Lewis wrote]. He walked that
> distance accompanied by his secretary, Miss Helen Dukas, using
> a flashlight to guide his steps in the night.
>
> He wore an old gray slip-on sweater, faded blue denim trou-
> sers, sandals, and no sox. His long white hair was tousled and
> flying in every direction.

Lewis asked about reports of "secondary radiation causing sterilization and a form of leukemia." Einstein shook his head and declared: "I will not discuss that." (The War Department was denying that radioactivity would persist after an atomic explosion.) He went on, "I have done no work on the subject — no work at all. I am interested in the bomb the same as any other person; perhaps a little bit more interested. However, I do not feel justified to say anything about it." Subsequent conversation was, as Einstein put it, "away from the record." Nuclear power was several years removed from commercial harnessing, he speculated, and he confined himself to explaining the principles of nuclear energy. His elucidation was so transparent that Lewis grasped it instantly, though he must have been dashed by the professor's postscript: "Atomic power is no more unnatural than when I sail my boat on Saranac Lake. You will do everyone a favor by not writing any story. I don't believe anyone will be interested." Of course, Lewis was unaware that Einstein's sailboating was a source of anxiety at the Knollwood Club. "He capsized twice and we had to rescue him," said 86-year-old Mrs. Lewis Bloomingdale, president of the club, reminiscing years afterward on the porch of her cottage.

Stephen Brunauer also related memories, particularly of Einstein's amiability. "He laughed heartily at his own jokes and also at mine. His well-known wisecrack, 'I am in the Navy, but I was not required to get a Navy haircut,' was born in one of our conversations." Toward the close of three years as Einstein's putative boss, Brunauer accepted a memento reverberant with overtones.

The great mathematician G. H. Hardy called Einstein "good, gentle, and wise," and it would be difficult to find better adjectives for him than these. . . . In all my visits, I received the impression of a genuinely humble person. On one occasion he gave me one of his books as a present. It was *The Meaning of Relativity*. On the empty page under the cover he wrote in his beautiful, small, clear letters only this much: A. Einstein, and under it the year, 1945.

* * *

Honoria Murphy Donnelly remembers a dark corridor and a closed door at the end — the room belonging to her younger brother Patrick. The memory has the dreamlike power of an abiding childhood image. *Why am I here? What do I dread? A house. A dark passageway. A room. Do I dare knock?*

The door, in fact, opened often, admitting Ernest Hemingway, John Dos Passos, and Archibald MacLeish, among others, who came to Saranac to visit Patrick, the tubercular son of their close friends, Gerald and Sara Murphy. In the fall of 1935, Fernand Léger, visiting the United States, stopped by; the fifty-four-year-old Parisian painter and the sixteen-year-old Patrick had a mutual personal regard (though Léger was apt to bumble the spelling of Patrick's name) and a common interest in the world around them. During Patrick's final weeks, when he lay in bed scratching a portrait of Hemingway on an etching plate, he also kept a diary in which he carefully noted where he was and what he was doing, as if to locate himself in a clean well-lighted place beyond disheveled and encroaching shadows.

Léger brought into the sickroom the sparkle of an effervescent temperament.

> He was especially kind to Patrick during his illness [Honoria records in her poignant memoir, *Sara and Gerald*]. In 1930, after the Murphys had moved to Switzerland, Léger sent Patrick a postcard, which the artist had illustrated with a sketch the boy had done. It was addressed to an *artiste peintre,* and there was a caption, which had been professionally printed: *Un Tableau de Patrick Murphy, Collection de Fernand Léger.*

A Léger pencil drawing of Patrick at Saranac in 1935 was hardly more than a sketch, a keepsake, yet it has elegance. Like the artist's major work of the late twenties and early thirties, it juxtaposes a figurative element, objects, and abstract transitions. Patrick, loosely characterized and recumbent, is quasi-cylindrical; atop a nearby table is an intriguing medley of shapes repeated in the crumpled rhythms of Patrick's pillow, blankets, and scattered papers. Despite the formal disposition of the image, the sketch has a personal touch and the brisk intimacy of a telegram: Enjoyed Seeing You Today. With an economy of means, the artist hints that pencil marks and shadings can transcend physical entrapment. It is no wonder that Léger in his paintings perceived the classic possibilities of machines and people harmonized — an integrated social order where technology is humane and Everyman his own artist. Why Léger, a resolute socialist, should become a devoted friend and admirer of the capitalist Gerald Murphy may seem ironic until one realizes each in his fashion was utopian.

Sara and Gerald did not consider money an end in itself. Conspicuous consumption on the Marjorie Merriweather Post scale appalled them. They sought out Paris in the fall of 1921 partly because they yearned to escape the stultifying protocols of the American upper class. While remaining a director of his family business, the Mark Cross Company, Fifth Avenue purveyors of carriage-trade leather goods, Gerald did not wish to become, in Sara's affectionate and teasing epistolary phrase, her Merchant Prince. Henry James had proclaimed only six years before, in a celebrated riposte to H. G. Wells, "It is art that *makes* life, makes interest, makes importance, for our consideration and application of these things, and I know of no substitute whatever for the force and beauty of its process." Those sentiments might have served as the Murphys' touchstone. Celebrated for their urbane lifestyle, the legendary couple of Calvin Tomkins's *Living Well Is the Best Revenge* and an inspiration for the characters of Dick and Nicole Diver in F. Scott Fitzgerald's *Tender Is the Night* epitomize the mythical epicureanism of the expatriate years. There was, however, another and more obvious reason why they settled in France: the favorable exchange rate. Honoria Donnelly is at pains to indicate that Sara and Gerald lacked infinite resources. True, they were rich and comfortable even during the Depression, when Gerald was bailing furiously to keep the Mark Cross Company afloat. Money, however, mattered to Gerald and

Sara as a vehicle of James's "force and beauty," and their vision of an abundant existence was not so remote from Léger's, although they approached it from a separate direction.

They are misrepresented as "beautiful people," café society types collecting reputations. Gerald as painter was respected by Picasso and Léger, men not inclined to banter about art. "*Sara est très festin,*" Picasso said, fascinated by her habit of wearing her pearls to the beach and tossing them backward to lie on her tanned shoulders. Friendship was her medium and she brought to it a consummate magnanimity; but Picasso's professional gaze assessed the work of Gerald, whom Léger called the only real painter among the Americans in Paris, which is to say, the only one who had thrown off the influence of the School of Paris. A student of Natalia Goncharova, the Russian émigré artist, Gerald had learned the principles of abstraction, and then had developed his own style.

For a brief interval before the war, when he first joined Mark Cross, he was involved in a project to design and develop a cheap safety razor. Gillette brought a similar product onto the market and swept the field; and so it was perhaps fitting that Gerald's first exhibited canvas, *Razor,* should represent the subject in flat, bold, heraldic fashion, crossed with a pen beneath a box of safety matches. In reproductions the picture suggests a giant billboard; one of its subtleties, however, is the actual size, 32 by 36 inches. The subject matter of commerce is absorbed by the traditional easel painting, and the objects occupy a shallow space, pressing against the surface of the picture and achieving an impressive monumental dignity. Gerald's subsequent paintings, all completed during the twenties, address the problem of scale — *Boatdeck, Cunarder,* now missing, was 18 by 12 feet — and of representing objects from multiple simultaneous perspectives while at the same time sustaining a mood, as in *Cocktail,* comprising layers of association with the half-moon of an olive in a glass, the undulations of a corkscrew's metal shaft, the double rectangle of a cigar box and its lid.

Destined to enter museums, notably in Dallas, these paintings have been described as harbingers of Pop Art, yet they lack Pop Art's mockery of consumer objects and the consumer society. Murphy, like Léger, derives pleasure from mechanisms that promise to render drudgery obsolete; with cheerful expectancy they acclaim the modernism of gleaming smokestacks and funnels, and gears and sprockets that mesh efficiently into place. Can one, however, call a dozen or so paintings a true body of work? Yes, if an angle of individual vision incorporates an era.

André LeVot in his biography of Fitzgerald portrays Murphy as a dilettante ("He let himself be consumed by aestheticism, a frivolousness he pretended was serious and that he knew was vulnerable. . . . There was something in him of the impresario and the great clothes designer"), but distorts the case. This may have been a ubiquitous opinion — rich men aren't born to practice art, they are born to support it — and notwithstanding the praise of the two Parisian masters, Gerald more or less humbly accepted his status as a gifted amateur. He maintained high standards, all the same; and perfectionism appeared to be the motive behind his abandonment of art in 1930 with the comment that the world was "full of second-rate painting." Of course, there was more to it than the first or second rate. Gerald Murphy laid down his brush the day he learned his son Patrick had tuberculosis.

Three months before Sara Murphy settled in Saranac Lake with Patrick, she had suffered the loss of her elder son, Baoth. His death at the age of fifteen, on St. Patrick's Day, 1935, was unanticipated. For six years his mother and father arranged their lives around Patrick. He had contracted TB in California from a chauffeur who was bundling him out of the hospital into a waiting car after a routine tonsillectomy, and Gerald received the bad news in France, on the eve of the Wall Street Crash. The Murphys immediately moved Patrick to Montana-Vermala in the Bernese Alps — a move that gave Honoria a lifelong distaste for mountains. She came to identify them with illness and grief, and Patrick agreed: "Melancholy skenery," he said (he liked to coin words), dismissing from his balcony the panorama of alpine splendors. Patrick was coping with pneumothorax treatments; the doctors hoped to save one lung, but the therapy seemed futile. The family closed ranks. To Switzerland flocked friends the Murphys had captivated on the Riviera — Fitzgerald, Hemingway, Donald Ogden Stewart, John and Katy Dos Passos. Dorothy Parker wrote Robert Benchley and described the morale-shattering effects of an illness wearing countless disguises:

> He [Gerald] works every minute — all the energy that used to go into compounding drinks and devising costumes and sweeping out bath-houses and shifting the sand on the *plage* has been put into inventing and running complicated . . . sick-room appliances, and he is simply pouring his vitality into Patrick, in the effort to make him not sick.

The Murphys saw much of Fitzgerald, whose wife, Zelda, was in a psychiatric clinic at Prangins. Having grown up in St. Paul, the city where Dr. Trudeau tried his abortive cure, Fitzgerald feared tuberculosis perhaps beyond anything else, and it is a measure of his feelings for Gerald and Sara that he risked potential infection. The social life of St. Paul, he recollected in 1923, had been much improved by wealthy consumptives. "These Easterners mingled with the rising German and Irish stock whose second generation left the cobbler's last, forgot the steerage, and became passionately 'swell' on its own account. But the pace was set by the tubercular Easterners." Throughout his writing Fitzgerald clung to the standard nineteenth-century view of TB as a "romantic" disease, yet he also acquired enough firsthand experience of it to retain a wary respect. Tuberculosis conditioned his formative years; at the first sign of a cough during his infancy in Buffalo (where his father briefly worked as a salesman for Procter & Gamble) his mother shipped him to the haven of a Washington hotel — a pattern repeated throughout childhood. Mrs. Fitzgerald worried lest the disease ran in the family, for her father and sister Clara were victims. As a Princeton student, Fitzgerald went to the infirmary with a high fever probably caused by TB, and his illness, which was diagnosed as malaria, gave him an opportunity to withdraw gracefully from college, where he might otherwise have flunked out at midyear. In 1919, working and drinking heavily during his courtship of Zelda, he developed a persistent cough and confided to editor Max Perkins an apprehension it might be tuberculosis. Just before Zelda's commitment to a Swiss sanatorium in May 1930, Fitzgerald began spitting blood and consulted a doctor in Cannes. X-rays revealed a slight film along the top of the left lung. Fitzgerald did nothing about it, no doubt hoping it would go away, and miraculously it did: a healed scar turned up on an x-ray of 1932. Even then he was by no means out of danger, and another and more serious flare-up of TB occasioned his relocation in 1935 to the Grove Park Inn in Asheville, North Carolina, where the climate suited him, and once again he got better.

Fitzgerald afterward used his TB as a ruse to conceal his alcoholism. "I think I can honestly say that the 1939 attack of TB was fictional," Frances Kroll Ring told Arthur Mizener. "He was drinking heavily at the time and preferred to have as few people as possible know about it. Specifically, he tried to spare Scottie [his daughter] or rather to conceal from her the fact that he drank so much, so he referred to his confinement as TB."

In 1930, however, Fitzgerald had tangible reason for misgivings about his health. The elegiac dedication of *Tender Is the Night* would read "To Gerald and Sara, Many Fêtes," an evocation of happier times. Long vanished was the aureate mood of Antibes in the twenties when Rudolph Valentino drove an open Voisin automobile down the beach at La Garoupe; now there was a dejection that found its way into Fitzgerald's short story *Babylon Revisited,* where the young daughter of the protagonist is named Honoria and the emptiness of post-Panic Paris expresses a spiritual void: *Nada*. Gerald and Sara realized they must not submit, despair was out of the question, and for the next six years they hovered, solicitous and uneasy, around Patrick. It was Patrick who endured the painful operations and probing needles; Patrick who accompanied his mother to Key West to visit his idol, Ernest Hemingway; Patrick who had trouble breathing and whose face was flushed by persistent fever; Patrick to whom Baoth mailed his schoolboy puns in an effort at cheer — but it was robust Baoth who died.

An uncomplicated case of measles at prep school had worsened into a desperately complicated case of meningitis. Baoth, rushed by ambulance to Massachusetts General, the great Boston hospital, lingered nearly a fortnight. Toward the end Sara tried to keep him alive through sheer force of will. Archibald MacLeish wrote: "Poor kid — tortured with knives, wracked with agony. Sara kept him alive for four hours sitting beside him saying 'Breathe Baoth! Breathe Baoth!' He didn't hear her but the will came through and he went on."

Sara, inconsolable, could scarcely believe Baoth was dead, and resolved against all logic to save her surviving son. Only the year before she had written Hemingway:

> We needed some cheering, I can tell you, as we are in bad luck again about Patrick. (God, how I hate to write bad news in letters.) He seemed well all summer and is discovered to have a patch on his other lung. Patrick, as normal, has been very brave, braver than any of us by a good deal — although his plans, school, fishing and shooting have all been broken up for months to come. Isn't it horrid? And what a fool's paradise it is to *ever* think you have won a victory over the White Plague!! — Well, he *is* going to be all right ultimately and all our fighting blood is up again — and perhaps this is that setback that is so common when children go into puberty — but at times it *does* seem too much — especially as he himself is so decent about it all.

Saranac Lake was recommended. Living in Saranac meant separation from Gerald, who was struggling with his New York business obligations, so he visited every fifteen days, first at Steel Camp, a lakeside clump of cottages, then at fall and winter quarters, 29 Church Street, a large, rambling, gabled house near the foot of Helen Hill. Honoria, meantime, was attending Spence School in New York. During the summer the literary expatriates who had rallied around the Murphys in Switzerland — notably MacLeish, Dos Passos, and Hemingway (Fitzgerald was recuperating in North Carolina) — again rallied around the Murphys in Saranac.

Just spent a couple of days at Saranac with the Murphys [noted Dos Passos]. Patrick, after having been very bad indeed since he got up there, seems to have taken a turn for the better, but he looks terribly small and thin. They are on Middle Saranac Lake, a handsome northwoods lake somewhat trampled by Guggenheims and Untermeyers and speedboats, but it has the advantage of being in the State Park so that it has less camps and possibly more bass and whitefish than most such places. [Gerald's exertions at Mark Cross and with the Fifth Avenue Association warranted Dos Passos's approval.] He has something to use his brains on — he's like he was years ago when he was painting.

Sara's correspondence of this period, though illumined by her charm, indicates a palpable loneliness. The "Sarapauline" letters to Pauline, Hemingway's second wife, are punctuated with wistful pleas for the Hemingways to visit 29 Church Street. The distance between Key West and Saranac, though, was not as easily traversed as the distance between Paris and the Bernese Alps.

"I've taken a house up here for the winter — big enough, good lord, for lots of guests who want to help me out. Wine cellar, cook, music." Would Pauline and Ernest be tempted by a three-day canoe trip? Why not bring their boys? They could live apart, in a guest house, without danger of contagion. "Patrick's dishes, silver, laundry, etc. are separate . . . Dos has been up with the MacLeishes, but Katy hasn't been yet."

Another glimpse of Sara that fall:

"Here Patrick and his nurse and I live in a solitary state and he is off in isolated quarters so I roam the place in desolate grandeur. I can't go away to New York to live for Patrick counts on me to be here and tell him jokes and bully him. It is awfully cold, you need sweaters, but lovely and hot in the middle of the day." With the settling of her mother's estate, which had been tied up for over fifteen years, Sara sent Dos Passos and the Hemingways, who were financially straitened, an undisclosed amount of cash. "Listen, we have plenty — no boy to put through school," she wrote Hemingway. "It is cheaper than New York to live at Saranac. Our friends are the dearest things we have. Please don't say that again about being bad luck."

Winter drew on, the snow slanting across the high windows while she disposed bright bursts of blossoms throughout the house. Sara's temperament did not favor hibernation, and she even tried out bobsledding and allowed Gerald to whisk her by train to Boston for the flower show. Hemingway, as soon as he could arrange matters, made at least three trips to Saranac — which brings up the issue of his somewhat problematic relations with the Murphys. His posthumously published memoir, *A Moveable Feast*, berates Dos Passos as "the pilot fish" who precedes the rich, "sometimes a little deaf, sometimes a little blind," but moving "one dollar's width to the right with every dollar that he made." And who are these rich idlers? — "the good, the attractive, the charming, the soon-beloved, the generous, the understanding rich who have no bad qualities and who give each day the quality of a festival and who, when they have passed and taken the nourishment they needed, leave everything deader than the roots of any grass Attila's horses' hooves have ever scoured."

Hemingway's disparagement of Dos Passos is at least consistent with his contentious attitudes toward other writers; but his unwarranted savaging of the Murphys can only be explained by his need to shift the burden of guilt for the failure of his first marriage, and by the progressive physical deterioration that clouded his judgment at the close of his life. His scorn is especially saddening because of his behavior in Saranac, where he was a responsive, devoted, and kind friend. Gerald and Sara had seen Ernest through earlier crises, particularly the collapse of his first marriage to Hadley Richardson Hemingway in the summer of 1926, when Ernest read proof on *The Sun Also Rises* in Gerald's studio and was again bolstered financially by him. Ernest's concern for Patrick derived too from a strong paternal instinct. The man who would call himself Papa, whose preferred relationship to anyone else was that of teacher to novice, had a true fondness for children. When Patrick's TB was diagnosed, Ernest and Pauline invited Baoth to stay with them in Paris. (He politely declined.) Letters to Patrick were couched in man-to-man rather than man-to-boy diction, and in Patrick's room hung a mounted impala head and hunting trophies that the author had given him. Why should the dying boy not hero-worship the writer? "They talked about fishing," Honoria records, but Ernest found his voice starting to break, and he stalked into the hall on the verge of tears and exclaimed, "Goddamn it, why does that boy have to be so sick?" Like any other middle-class Midwesterner born around the century's turn, he immediately apologized in mixed company for his language.

"Patrick loved seeing you so," Alice Lee Myers, Sara's close friend, wrote Hemingway after Patrick's death in January 1937, when Sara was too stricken for correspondence. "The last work he did were a few little scratches that he made on his etching of you. When he was so weak that no one else could have lifted a finger, he insisted on doing everything for himself."

On Ernest's final trip to Saranac Lake two weeks earlier he had promised Patrick a bear-cub's pelt as an eventual present. Patrick's situation by then was desperate; Gerald had joined the others in the house at Glenwood Estates where they had gone after spending the summer of 1936 at Camp Adeline (named for Sara's mother), near Paul Smith's. "Am here indefinitely," he informed Hemingway, sending a postcard of Mt. Baker. Apparently Hemingway was contemplating his visit, for Gerald gave the out-of-towner explicit and detailed tourist tips — the Hotel New Weston served Brevoort's old cuisine; Gray and Lampel, tailors, were "a very good reliable old New York house, no chi-chi, sensible cut, best materials." Then, anxiously, "Do you know New York?" Hemingway, his sister-in-law Virginia, and Sidney Franklin, the American matador, drove from Manhattan in the latter's car. "There was, it seems, a certain amount of conversational sniping going on between Ernest and Ginnie," Gerald wrote Pauline. He tried to maintain gregarious appearances: "Both were in the pink of condition. Someone won on points, I suppose."

Dos Passos and Katy visited Camp Adeline over July Fourth, and Patrick's bed was rolled to the dock and he fished for perch. Circumstances no doubt altered Dos's opinion of mountain scenery: "God, but it's gloomy on those Adirondack lakes," he observed in accents no less desolate than Honoria's. At nineteen her life might otherwise have centered around boys and parties and the rituals of the debutante; instead, she was traveling intermittently with her father to Saranac and the bedside of her younger brother.

> Patrick had an extraordinary maturity — more and more every time I saw him, he seemed a little wise old man [Honoria recalled forty-six years later]. Helen Trudeau [the wife of Dr. Francis] was very kind to mother and was always organizing social situations in which I could fit with other young people, sleigh-rides, square-dances and picnics; but I was very shy. A young person living with illness feels under a sentence. First Baoth died; now Patrick; I was frightened and I thought, *Maybe I'll be next.*

Honoria was present when her mother and father, each holding one of Patrick's hands, spoke to him for the last time: "You're just fine, Patrick. We're right here with you." She would not only survive, but in the passage of the generations have children of her own. Eventually, as well, the playground of St. Bernard's parochial school would border the sizable house at 29 Church Street and the shouts of children would drift from slides and sandboxes.

The day after Patrick died, Dos Passos, who had been traveling, appeared, incredibly, at Glenwood Estates. "Sara wished me to ask you if you would like the mounted heads," Alice Myers inquired of Hemingway. The Murphys were leaving Saranac and thought it better for Ernest to have the trophies than to store them. "In going over Patrick's possessions, they asked me to send you his gun racks and for your boys, two engines that he loved. He had not played with them so they are quite safe."

CHAPTER NINE

Quartet
1941–1945

THE PARALLELS BETWEEN Dr. Edward Trudeau and Walker Percy are perhaps more striking than their disparities of personality and period. Ancestors of both rose to prominence in the South under Spanish rule. Charles Percy, an Englishman called Don Carlos and the American dynastic sire, was a mayor and judge, or *alcalde,* and landowner in the buffalo country south of Natchez. Exhibiting traits of vagabondage, individualism, and a chivalric sense of probity, his descendants became highly regarded professional men. William Alexander Percy, the second cousin who adopted Walker, successfully fought the Ku Klux Klan throughout its twenties heyday, just as an earlier William Alexander Percy, "the Gray Eagle of the Delta," cast his unpopular lot against secession.

Like Trudeau, Walker Percy was a boy left fatherless. Then, two years after the 1929 suicide of LeRoy Percy, a Birmingham, Alabama, lawyer, Walker's mother died in an automobile accident, and he and his brothers LeRoy and Phinizy were adopted by their bachelor "Uncle Will." The cosmopolitan belletristic milieu of Uncle Will — lawyer, poet, essayist (*Lanterns on the Levee*), friend and confidant of William Faulkner, Carl Sandburg, Dorothy Thompson, Stark Young, and Langston Hughes — must have seemed immensely glamorous to an adolescent orphan. Walker began submitting poetry to magazines; but at the University of North Carolina a growing interest in the physical sciences displaced the poetic impulse, and he went on to and graduated from Columbia's College of Physicians and Surgeons, Dr. Trudeau's old school.

A residency in pathology at Bellevue Hospital gave Percy, positive as Trudeau that science held the key of truth, an opportunity to acquire experience. It was September 1941: the wards teemed with the diseases of poverty and squalor, and, repeating Trudeau's pattern, the new resident pushed himself beyond exhaustion. Immediately before the war's outbreak he was hospitalized and diagnosed as tubercular. Saranac was recommended and Percy arrived there early in 1942, just before Uncle Will died — a personal blow that seemed part of a darkness flowing over the world. For the fledgling M.D., Saranac signified banishment from the experience of his generation. His brothers and contemporaries were marching to war while he lay coughing on an Adirondack porch, far from the vortex of history and the menacing reality implied by Hitler's Third Reich.

Science hadn't done much to alleviate tuberculosis [Walker Percy said in Covington, Louisiana, recently]. In those days a rest cure literally meant doing nothing. I was young and lonely and very depressed. When I arrived at Saranac I wasn't admitted to Trudeau right away. The sanatorium was crowded so I stayed in a boarding house, Mrs. Ledbetter's, and it was the eeriest time of my life. A woman came in to give me a bath; otherwise I saw no one.

The Moviegoer, the novel Percy would publish nineteen years later, derives its epigraph from Kierkegaard's *The Sickness Unto Death:* ". . . the specific character of despair is precisely this: it is unaware of being despair." By that standard neither Trudeau nor the young Southerner had reached the ultimate limit; their despair occurred daily and recognizably.

"Total bed rest meant not getting up. I went through highly structured events, although later I could take a fifteen-minute walk a day. Like most medical students, I had a one-sided education. In short, I was a professional skeptic."

The blankness of an invalid's existence possibly harrows the skeptic more than the optimist. Forever recumbent on a porch cot beneath an electric blanket, the patient watches the upright crimson groove of a thermometer rise and fall, fall and rise, the indifference of nature heightening the folly of getting well. Norman Bethune, motionless in the same mortal hush, seethed with gadfly schemes to outwit administrators and cry havoc through the corridors of convention. Adelaide Crapsey counted syllables, Robert Louis Stevenson envisaged palm-girdled coral reefs, and the muses smiled upon their illusions. Dr. Trudeau hoarded his strength and inhaled the balsamic air that, he believed, held mysterious healing properties. Even Jeffries Wyman, facing the determinism of his Darwinian principles, had the consolation of truth however dismal, an explanation of existence pegged like a safety net over a prodigious void. Percy's problem was the problem of Binx Bolling, the twenty-nine-year-old New Orleans stockbroker-hero of *The Moviegoer:* the affliction Binx calls the "malaise." "What is the malaise? you ask. The malaise is the pain of loss. The world is lost to you, the world and the people in it, and there remains only you and the world and you are no more able to be in the world than Banquo's ghost."

In *Walker Percy: An American Search,* the psychiatrist and author Robert Coles conveys a graphic picture of Percy, the medical man trained to observe, transformed into an object of observation evaluated by others. The staccato bulletins of war saturate the radio; brother Phinizy is serving with John F. Kennedy aboard PT boat 109, and brother LeRoy flying missions over Germany. Few civilian Americans are aware of the death camps, but many believe the traditional forms of western civilization will radically change, either change or crumble into barbarism.

Shivering through a Saranac rest cure, Percy attempted the

first experimental step away from preoccupation with his own illness.

> I was in bed so much, alone so much, that I had nothing to do but read or think [he told Coles]. I began to question everything I had once believed. I began to ask why Europe, why the world had come to such a sorry state. I never turned my back on science. It would be a mistake to do so — throw out the baby with the bath water. I had wanted to find answers through an application of the scientific method. I had found that method a rather impressive and beautiful thing: the logic and precision of systematic inquiry; the mind's impressive ability to be clear-headed, to reason. But I gradually began to realize that as a scientist — a doctor, a pathologist — I knew so very much *about* man, but had little idea what man *is*.

Thus began the process that Binx in *The Moviegoer* terms "the search," disentangling oneself from absorption in daily routine in order to achieve a state close to the Henry Jamesian conception of the ideal novelist (a participant in life as well as an observer), a man on whom nothing is lost. The search begins when one "comes to, suddenly looks closely around, and notices just about everything." An invalid can do this as proficiently as a person in robust health, so Percy started seeking out books not associated with his medical education, the authors he never had a chance to open at Columbia — Mann, Kafka, Tolstoy, Dostoyevski. The fervor with which he consumed their work transformed a routine passive act: he might have been reading for his life.

Week after week he saw only an occasional doctor or attendant. Isolated, a Crusoe among the cure cottages, he felt the absence of external voices. Sometimes he listened to radio programs from Montreal; nevertheless, he was learning to exist within himself. Shelby Foote, a close high school friend who would also become a distinguished novelist, visited and found Walker "living the life of a hermit." A distressed Foote suggested

Walker needed more company, but this was not unlike trying to
coax a Hindu mystic out of meditation: Percy seemed happy
with his books. As it happened, he would soon enter a more
sociable sphere when a place opened for him at Trudeau. There,
like Bethune, he was assigned a doctor's cottage, sharing quarters with two other doctors, and again like Bethune, finding
himself reminded of a college fraternity. Larry Doyle, the jovial
second baseman of the old Giants, Christy Mathewson's teammate, had also entered Trudeau in 1942. He and Percy would
talk baseball for hours, but the statistical improbability of two
players on the same championship roster sharing a common fate
in the same remote Adirondack village may have occurred more
readily to the doctor than to his new acquaintance.

Mann's *Magic Mountain,* of course, afforded a fictional coun-
terpart of Percy's experiences. The silver cigar (or temperature
stick), the x-ray, and weight chart defined him clinically. "When
you went to the Director's waiting room to find out what they
were going to say about your x-ray or your weight chart — that
was the moment of truth," Percy says. "A bad x-ray meant you'd
have to go back to the beginning. In the waiting room, you knew
what anxiety was." Percy had not at this time read the European
philosophers Marcel, Heidegger, Sartre, Mounier, and Jaspers,
vital influences on his postwar thinking, and Camus was on the
threshold of international recognition; but some of Kierkegaard
was available, and Dostoyevski, in particular, stirred Percy. The
modes of fiction constituted a method of moral inquiry not foreign to science or psychology or other descriptions of the nature
of humankind.

"Had I not gone to Saranac I should have practiced medicine,
probably psychiatry," he concludes. "Saranac was the critical
turning-point."

Apparently he was almost well. Two years later he was allowed
to return to New York City and assume duties as an instructor
in pathology at Columbia medical school. It was a brief tenure;
his tuberculosis, unshakable and duplicitous, returned, and he

was forced again to abandon medicine. This time he entered the Gaylord Sanatorium in Connecticut, and presently recovered.

Not until 1954 did Percy publish his first article, "Symbol as Need," a response to Suzanne Langer's *Feeling and Form*. During that decade he had married, reared a family on a modest independent income, and had become a Roman Catholic. Instead of practicing medicine he pursued a contemplative life. *Who hears modern man's haunting cry for redemption?* The discipline of his Saranac experience, nothing less than a fresh apprehension of the world, would continually affect his subsequent outlook. Scientific learning would play a large role in it, and philosophy, theology, and linguistics — he is a novelist of ideas, and his own search for grace exemplifies the meaning of "the search."

"Writing is very seductive, once you realize you can do it," he says. As a patient he had two ironic historical encounters with authors. The second was at Gaylord, where he brought the necessary books and submitted to the familiar schedules: "'Well, here you are again,' I thought. They noted that I was interested in literature so they assigned me the same bed Eugene O'Neill had occupied in 1912 — a strange, strange feeling."

The other junction had occurred on Helen Hill during Shelby Foote's visit. Percy was taking his quarter-hour constitutional, and on the opposite side of the street approached the short yet unmistakable figure of W. Somerset Maugham, then at the zenith of his fame. Foote, aspiring young novelist, hesitated, caught between the shock of recognition and the awkwardness of intruding on the great man. Maugham drew abreast, and the moment passed, Foote en route to the war and the two medically trained writers proceeding in opposite directions.

Seventy-year-old Somerset Maugham considered Saranac "a hell of a place, nothing but nursing homes and hospitals and a very indifferent hotel." Staying at that hotel he may have derived sardonic satisfaction from its letterhead, still displaying in July 1944 the motto reiterated since the twenties: Hotel Saranac — Modern — Fireproof — European Plan — Tuberculous Patients Not Received. Maugham, an erstwhile consumptive, did not attempt to conceal it. Out of his 1917 experiences at Banchory, a Scottish sanatorium twenty miles outside Aberdeen, had sprung one of his finest short stories, "The Sanatorium," in which a couple decide to wed although marriage will truncate their life spans. (*Trio*, the second film anthology made from the short stories, used "Sanatorium" as its final segment.)

Maugham at Saranac had more to hide than an ancient bout with TB — his American-born secretary-companion Gerald Haxton was in the last stages of the disease, and while their homosexual relationship was an open secret in literary circles and had been for a quarter century, Maugham never publicly alluded to their attachment. An Edwardian gentleman whose initial successes in the theater had taken place in the shadow of the Oscar Wilde trials, he concealed his sexual identity, and not without reason, for the decriminalization of homosexuality in England seemed a remote prospect. (The Sexual Offences Act, which legalized homosexuality between consenting adults, was passed only in 1967, two years after Maugham's death.) Despite changing social mores, the author maintained his façade to the end, at the age of ninety-one, and whenever asked to petition on behalf of other homosexuals, indignantly refused. Which did not prevent him from confiding to his nephew Robin that "I tried to persuade myself that I was three quarters normal and that only a quarter of me was queer — whereas really it was the other way around." Since Maugham frowned on the subject, however, certain close friends like Emerald Cunard, who scorned homosexuals and referred to them as "popinjays," were unaware of his duality.

Haxton played Hyde to Maugham's Jekyll. Mercurial, jocular, and reckless, Gerald could have been typecast as a charming scoundrel in one of his employer's stories. Britain had deported him as an undesirable alien in 1919 for reasons still under official seal. The charge apparently was more serious than gross indecency — espionage or some form of intelligence-gathering may have gotten mixed up with it — and Haxton's persona non grata status prompted Maugham's shift of residence to the Riviera. They had met on the Flanders front in 1915; the forty-year-old Maugham was serving with the Red Cross ambulance corps and Haxton, aged twenty-two, joined the unit. Half-a-head taller, he had a brusque mustache and a faintly pockmarked complexion, wore his brown hair brushed straight back, and his features were affable though undistinguished. He was outgoing (Maugham was introverted), spendthrift (Maugham was penny-wise), alcoholic (Maugham was temperate), violent (Maugham was conciliatory), devious (Maugham was principled), disorderly (Maugham was methodical), and fickle (Maugham was — comparatively — constant). Rumor alleged that Gerald's hold over Willie was blackmail: underlying sadomasochism whetted a relationship in which their roles were reversed, the secretary became the master, the famous writer his minion. They tormented each other without respite, but leaving aside the pathological, Haxton was an alter ego useful to Maugham. The secretary's bonhomie compensated for the author's stutter and shyness. "He had an amiability of disposition that enabled him in very short time to make friends with people in ships, clubs, barrooms and hotels," Maugham recalled in *The Summing Up*, "so that through him I was able to get into easy contact with an immense number of persons whom otherwise I should have known only from a distance."

Maugham during most of a quarter century idolized Haxton and tolerated his transgressions. Excepting *Of Human Bondage* and the Edwardian plays, the writer's best work appeared during these years when Maugham's marriage of convenience with Syrie Barnardo Maugham had collapsed because of her unwillingness to permit him protracted trips in Gerald's company. By 1944 the fires of passion were long since banked, indeed Maugham announced he was fed up with Gerald's antics and had located a replacement in Alan Searle, a docile and sweet-tempered English YMCA worker. On his part, Gerald was beginning to evince belated maturity and, having forsworn alcohol, wished to escape Willie's shadow. The Villa Mauresque, setting of their Riviera idyll, now accommodated German and Italian occupation forces: Maugham, serving as goodwill ambassador for the British Ministry of Information, had flown to the United States. No doubt he was instrumental in securing Gerald an independent job supervising the commissary of the Garden City, Long Island, quarters of the Doubleday publishing firm, but, to everyone's surprise, Haxton administered a staff of forty-seven with crisp efficiency and later landed a clerical job with the O.S.S. in Washington. Maugham approved. "I am hoping he will stick to it not only for the duration, but for long after. One of the troubles with him was that he thought himself too good for the work he had to do with me, and did it grudgingly and badly, and he had too much time on his hands without resources in himself to occupy his leisure."

While Haxton settled into a Washington apartment, Maugham prepared to see through the press the book destined to become his greatest commercial success, *The Razor's Edge*. The instincts of a best-selling author had not deserted him; religious novels were enormously successful in wartime, and Maugham's story of a western pilgrim's search for serenity among the teachings of Asia was an immediate triumph. No sooner did the book appear, however, than Gerald, suffering from what he believed to be an attack of pleurisy, entered a hospital where doctors diagnosed a severe case of tuberculosis. One lung was doomed, the other affected. In June 1944 a pneumothorax operation failed in New York and Haxton was plainly deteriorating. Maugham reflected upon their years of happiness together; he could not bear the image of an emaciated Gerald dying alone and friendless, and in desperation and the hope that mountain air might have a therapeutic effect, Maugham decided to move him to Saranac.

The differences of the recent past evaporated, and Willie now felt only tenderness and resignation before the inevitable. All the same, he and Gerald faced a peculiar emotional plight, since Maugham could not express his feelings and, circumspect as always, maintained the mask of a smiling public man. Initially, Gerald appeared to improve somewhat. Maugham awaited the daily medical reports from the Alta Vista Lodge on Franklin Avenue, and took his solitary meals at the coffee shop and restaurant of the Hotel Saranac. His novelist's eye and ear, conditioned by a lifetime of observation, remained vigilant. He noticed the waitresses duplicating a verbal oddity widespread throughout the Adirondacks — they appeared to have lost the use of the word "yes." Unlike the waitresses of Manhattan or Washington, they did not respond "Yup" or "Ya," or even with "the word spelt 'yeah,'" which Maugham was unable to pronounce. Instead of "yes" they said, "H'm H'm."

"I daresay it's OK when my waitress's boy friend asks her to go to the movies and she says 'H'm H'm,' but when, after holding hands with her all the evening, he asks her to be his wedded wife does she just say 'H'm H'm'?" Maugham wondered. "It sounds a little indifferent to me, but it may be of course that she puts more expression into it than when I ask her for a cup of coffee. I wouldn't know."

The author of *The Razor's Edge* was not long permitted to remain a detached observer, and the village fathers, cognizant of the celebrated man of letters in their midst, asked him to judge a short story contest. Many writers might have begged off or treated the Blanchet Memorial Contest as a task better left to high school English teachers, but Maugham acceded. Perhaps he was bored by the perpetual Sunday afternoon vacuum of small-town America, or then again he may have sought distraction from the memento mori of Gerald's condition. In any event, Maugham judged the contest and, always a thoroughgoing professional craftsman, scrupulously inspected each apprentice manuscript before setting down his conclusions.

The piece which is titled "No Title" seems to me the best, neatest and most original bit of writing; but I don't see how it could possibly be described as a short story. [The tale opens with a formula ominous to every teacher of creative writing, "This is the story of a person trying to write a short story."] If you don't think this matters, I would certainly give it first place.

The best of the others in my opinion are "Eyes So Blue" and "The Silent Fisherman of Lost Crick."

There is nothing to choose between them. The author of "Eyes So Blue" has had a good idea but has spoiled it (to my mind) by laying on the deaths too thick. Otherwise the story has a nice feel to it.

The trimmings of "The Silent Fisherman," by which I mean the local color and the dialogue, are well-done, but the author through want of experience has missed the thrill of surprise and the shock that he should have got . . .

If you decide to givve three prizes I will contribute $5 so that numbers II and III may have the sum they would have had if only two prizes had been awarded.

The Blanchet Memorial Contest interrupted the arid hours at the Alta Vista. Specialists recommended another operation for Gerald and suggested Boston's Leahy Clinic. Accordingly, Maugham decided to take him there in August. With luck, they might spend the winter in Arizona; Gerald's downward spiral continued, however, and at Saranac he had less than four months to live.

Before their departure, Maugham delivered a radio address from his hotel room on July 30. The talk was aimed at the patients of the Saranac Lake Study and Craft Guild, the organization that had developed out of Norman Bethune's proposals for a Trudeau University. A year later Maugham's words would appear, drastically edited, in *Life Story Magazine* under the title "What Reading Can Do for You," but the original version is of interest for its varied autobiographical elements. Once more he prepared the script meticulously, writing with blue ink on a pad of lined paper and making corrections in pink pencil. Because of his stutter he left nothing to chance: there were no impromptu passages, no unconsidered pauses. Called upon to utter public sentiments, Maugham declined unless these were committed to memory. In front of the microphone he repeated his waitress anecdote, and next addressed the patients directly:

> I am talking about something I know, because I suffered from TB myself. I contracted it during the last war and when the symptoms showed themselves I happened to be in New York. I had just been asked to go on a mission to Russia and I went to see a specialist and asked him what he thought about my going. He examined me and said: "Well, if there weren't a war on I'd advise you to go to a sanatorium, but as there is and your mission looks important, I don't see why you shouldn't risk it." The Bolshevik revolution broke out and I was hustled home on a destroyer. I was then quite sick and was sent to a sanatorium in the north of Scotland. I spent the best part of two years there.

Maugham outlined the potential benefits of sanatoriums. Time ceases to matter. One may lie in bed with an easy conscience. While curing he had written *The Moon and Sixpence,* and he supplied his literary recipes, familiar to devotees but new to a majority of his Saranac listeners. Write about the places you know, the people you know, and your own experiences. "That is the only way you can write anything worthwhile." Read for pleasure. "The doctors can do a great deal for you, and so can the air of the Adirondacks, but you can also do a great deal for yourselves." The advice was sensible and edifying. The postwar world would be enormously different from the world of the past; "believe me, you will cope with it more competently if you have used this period of illness to acquire a wider vision, greater knowledge, more culture and a keener sympathy with your fellow man."

To this he appended a slight but startling sign-off joke which his audience must have regarded as British and inscrutable. A pair of English soldiers meet in Normandy. "'I see a sissy's (Assisi) been captured,' one says. 'What,' replies his friend, 'another of them German generals? You can 'ave him.' That's all, ladies and gentlemen. Thank you." Given the patent sincerity of Maugham's maxims, an air of uneasy contrivance marks the joke. Did it appeal to Maugham because of the captured sissy, his opposing self at last confessed? Or does "You can 'ave him" indicate defensive hostility? Is Maugham, no friend of sissies, telling the world that never would he, under any circumstance, admit his ambivalence? The Saranac audience may have received more than it bargained for. Maugham's radio chat, however, was a triumphant occasion and officials of the Study and Craft Guild had the text duplicated and sent to TB sanatoriums nationwide for the columns of patient magazines.

In the days when the movies were the movies, Taking the Collection was an event comparable to passing the plate in church. It usually happened between the halves of a double bill, after a flounced curtain rippled shut over the screen and parted again in a gauzy cascade to reveal, say, Tyrone Power, star of *The Razor's Edge*, introducing himself. Since the audience was about to see the film — a bona fide masterpiece taken down from Hollywood's Five-Foot Shelf of masterpieces, for Maugham's story did not occupy the lesser half of the program — Mr. Power's introduction may have seemed superfluous. But he was not appearing as Larry Darrell in search of the eternal wisdom of the Himalayas; no, he was stepping from the fantasy realm to which he belonged, shreds of that realm still coruscating around him, and addressing us. The sudden shock of reality often proved so overpowering that audience murmurs inflected the performance. It was like meeting a film star on the street, as, in *The Moviegoer*, Binx sees William Holden passing through the French Quarter of New Orleans, his "resplendent reality" making people aware of their own "shadowy and precarious" existence. Then, as the close-up of Tyrone Power lingered, scalloped curtain flowing over it, the houselights came up and revealed ushers or usherettes in obligatory tuxedos, which exhibited a slightly waxen sheen, and the ushers passed celluloid milkshake containers from aisle to aisle. The coins dropped into the containers, pocketbooks snapped, somebody grumbled about coming to the movies and paying extra, and then, just as the ushers reached the middle aisle, the lights blinked out, the second feature appeared, and the weighted containers rattled from hand to hand like the batons of a relay race.

Few moviegoers understood the precise goal of their contributions. "It's for old actors," was commonly advanced, but some may have known that money gathered in this fashion went toward the maintenance of the Will Rogers Sanatorium for theater and film people in Saranac Lake. The relations of Saranac, the entertainment business, and the performing arts began in 1905 when the showman William Morris arrived as a patient and recovered his health. Captivated by the Saranac region, he built, in 1915, Camp Intermission on Lake Colby, where his friend Sir Harry Lauder was a semipermanent house guest. The stars of the Morris agency — Sir Harry, Eddie Cantor, Leon Errol, Blanche Ring, Sophie Tucker, Lou Holtz, and scores of others — each Fourth of July gave performances to aid a day nursery, churches, and local charities. Al Jolson, of whom it was said he would not perform in the Adirondacks unless the theater was a hundred miles away from Saranac, obviously changed his mind, for he delivered an astonishing 1927 benefit at the Pontiac Theater, during which he held the stage alone for more than three kinetic hours.

William Morris, with Sime Silverman, the founder of *Variety* and also a former patient, and Pat Casey of the Keith Albee–Orpheum Circuit, were instrumental in proposing a sanatorium for theatrical people. Who needed a sanatorium more than the smalltime vaudevillians, with their lopsided unhealthy lives of split weeks in one-horse towns, their damp dressing rooms, shabby hotels, and all-night train rides to make the jump between engagements? Milton Berle, trained from childhood in the disciplines of the road, said, "The only thing I know for certain is that, great as working in vaudeville was, it was also exhausting. Even kids came home worn out, sick of living out of trunks, sick of meals in diners and hash houses. Maybe there was big money to be made by some in vaudeville, but everybody earned every backbreaking cent." A letter from Fred Allen, who was performing on the Western Vaudeville Time, declared, "I had to rise at 3:45 to leave Cedar Rapids. I have to rise again to leave here [Mason City, Iowa] for Clinton. Rip Van Winkle must have played a season out here, and took the twenty years' rest to get acquainted with a mattress."

The National Variety Artists Lodge, constructed in 1928, was a large compound of half-timbered Tudor buildings that resembled a resort more than a hospital. The collective entertainment background of the patients helped foster that illusion, and the main dining room like Topridge's was equipped with a projection booth. At the NVA Lodge every service was free to members of the American Guild of Variety Artists or their families, except transportation to Saranac; and the patients over the years included Conrad Nagel; Arthur Tracy, the Street Singer; Belle Baker, Lila Lee, Veronica Lake, and Bert Wheeler. Their proximity attracted other show folk. Ernie Burnett, the composer of the song "Melancholy Baby," came to cure his TB in Saranac, settled down on Franklin Avenue, and for years afterward could be counted upon to reprise his lyrics over Tri-Lakes radio. In 1935 cowboy actor and folk philosopher Will Rogers perished with Wylie Post in an Alaskan plane crash, and a subsequent memorial fund, it was decided, should support the Variety Artists Lodge. Renamed for Rogers, the sanatorium assumed its new name the day before Christmas, 1936.

As an institution, the Will Rogers Hospital reflected the decline and fall of vaudeville and the rise of the movies. Ex–vaudeville performers became a decreasing constituency while mounting numbers of projectionists and technicians applied for admission. The sanatorium remained full until the advent of drug therapy during the 1950s. The patient population gradually dwindled, the Tudor doors closed in 1975, and Will Rogers Hospital moved to White Plains, New York.

Associated today with Burke Veterans Hospital, the Will Rogers carries on pulmonary research as well as research on Alzheimer's disease and other forms of dementia, and, most recently, a long-range nutritional study. There is limited patient care, but the center is best known for preventive medicine and health-education programs: Will Rogers Hospital is the foremost supplier of American medicine's public service spot announcements, among which the famous two-minute trailer is still important. Every year a major entertainment company sponsors the drive and raises research funds with the assistance of a Frank Sinatra, a Lily Tomlin, or a Dudley Moore.

Reminders of Saranac, however, multiply along the corridors in White Plains — a rotunda's life-sized, aw-shucks bronze statue of Will Rogers, sepia banquet photographs of powerful long-forgotten showmen, citations from *Variety* Club meetings, plaques galore: Mr. and Mrs. Conrad Nagel, Belle Baker, In Memory of Bert from The Lambs. The building rises amid satiny lawns and in summer presents a pastoral aspect; squirrels scurry across the shadows of breeze-ruffled foliage, and choirs of crickets drone in counterpoint to the tremors of distant traffic. It is a bucolic vista, but pastoral, alas, does not suit the memory of performers spellbound by the brash delights of applause. One imagines a noisier Elysium where they compare clippings and speak in *Variety* lingo of "bowing off to heavy mitts." The old sanatorium in Saranac, meanwhile, has experienced several transformations and is presently a cluster of apartments, having at one time been proposed as a gambling casino, Saranac Lake's retort to Atlantic City and Las Vegas. Undeniably, a nip of show business lingers in the air.

* * *

From the summer of 1943 until the following August, Saranac was intermittently the seat of the Philippine government-in-exile. The man who headed that regime would never again set foot in his homeland.

Manuel Luis Quezon Antonia y Molina, the sixty-five-year-old president and first democratically elected head of state of an Asian nation, had been voted into office by a landslide on November 13, 1935. Six years later he was re-elected leader of an interim Philippine Commonwealth government until the islands achieved full independence in 1946. He sought office on the issue of independence and stressed independence as a political theme; unlike many Filipino nationalists, however, he was not inclined to appease Japan in the rapidly approaching Pacific conflict. Quezon sided with the United States. This had not always been his position; during the insurrection of 1899 he had fought the Americans and afterward was jailed for six months. Once he said that he preferred "a self-governing Philippines, be it so troublesome and destitute as hell, to the enjoyment of heavenly comfort and happiness under American rule." Nevertheless, he had come to believe American withdrawal would wreck the islands' economy and open the Philippines to Japanese domination, and with the outbreak of war he joined the Allied cause.

General Douglas MacArthur, who had known Quezon since 1904, feared his capture by the Japanese and convinced President Franklin D. Roosevelt to request him to establish a government-in-exile. From beleaguered Corregidor the Commonwealth president was evacuated by submarine, and ultimately, in Mindanao, boarded a B-17 bomber to Port Darwin, Australia, the first leg of a journey toward America. There were factors other than political behind the flight: Quezon, tubercular for some fifteen years, was desperately ill. The trip, nine hours nonstop to Bachelor Field, sixty miles from Port Darwin, bombed daily by enemy planes stationed in Timor, presented unforeseen dangers. President Quezon had never flown in a plane and was susceptible to heights; indeed, he found the less-than-a-mile-high altitude at Baguio, his summer retreat, overly taxing. An oxygen tank, therefore, was held in readiness by his personal physicians, but the flight took place without incident. It did not take place, however, without criticism. Shortly after Quezon's arrival in the United States, congressmen debating legislation that placed him in office until the restoration of Philippine constitutional processes carped about the escape: Congressman Walter H. Judd (R.-Minn.), who wanted to shunt the resolution to committee, read out a list of the passengers on the B-17 and pointedly observed that with space at a premium, Quezon's Chinese valet Ah Dong might have been dispensable.

This notion Quezon would have rejected out of hand. His wardrobe was the wonder of the islands. In his vigorous youth he had been dapper and gregarious, and even in his midsixties, ill and wan, he retained a peacock's strut of pride. Short, slim, and swarthy, with graying hair and thick black eyebrows, he looked younger than his years, and behind a pince-nez his eyes glittered, often wary, sometimes magistral, always alert. From 1909 to 1916, when he had himself appointed resident commissioner of the Philippines in Washington, D.C., he had earned a reputation not only as an effective lobbyist but as the capital's best ballroom dancer. Quezon on a dance floor moved with a suave grace that gave his foxtrots the polish of a pas de deux. Dance instructor Arthur Murray considered him unarguably — *pas de question* — the best pupil he ever had, and Quezon one night demonstrated his mastery of the terpsichorean arts by taking out sixteen Murray instructresses — all at once.

The expansive gaiety of such gestures, a candid pleasure in the ornaments of office, did not diminish his single-mindedness. If there was a touch of the playboy in Quezon, he frolicked for a purpose. As one commentator put it: "He still has the knack of charming, cajoling, trading or bullying his way to victory." The friends he made in Washington also became partisans of his cause. His charismatic personality combined Spanish courtesy and American dynamism, and in Manila he seemed to draw on the best of both cultures. What if the Malacañan Palace was more imposing than the White House and he took frequent trips through the islands aboard his sparkling white yacht, the *Casiana*? Talking to presidential-palace visitors in his large baroque private office, he rocked back and forth and spoke elatedly from a brocaded swivel chair. Elements a westerner might interpret as pomp acquired a different meaning in the Latinate culture of the Philippines; the trappings attested to and reinforced Quezon's authority. On any issue he could count on 75 to 80 percent of the vote; he absolutely controlled patronage, even appointing village schoolteachers; and he maintained power by giving something to the masses who previously had had nothing, while convincing the Spanish millionaires of Manila he represented stability. Along with his élan and penchant for seizing the limelight, his political machine was as potent as that of any of the city bosses of America. Rumors that he planned to rename the islands for himself he denounced as preposterous, but students at the University of the Philippines were said to be organizing an informal "Quezon for King" society.

Quezon's family had a history of tuberculosis. Born to schoolteacher parents in a provincial village on the east coast of Luzon, he gloried in his humble origins and the role of self-made man. At school in Manila he was nicknamed *gulerato*, or "bluffer," by his classmates, but if his predisposition to pounce on the winning side of any issue proved the schoolboy's drawback, a foolish consistency is the bane of the politician, and when Quezon went into public service in 1906 after practicing law, he prospered. His early coup, the Jones Act of 1916, abolished the Philippine Commission and allowed Filipinos to legislate for themselves subject to a veto of the American governor general. The Jones Act was popular when the governor general was the pro-Filipino Francis Burton Harrison; when General Leonard Wood received the appointment, however, his policies initiated a protracted struggle with Quezon. Constantly seeking to checkmate the power of the governor general, Quezon shuttled back and forth between

Washington and the provinces; and it was in the period of tension with Wood that Quezon came to suspect that he had inherited his family's debility.

In 1924 a New York physician found him "in good physical condition" and pronounced his lungs "normal and healthy." Then, late in 1927, Senate President Quezon and Senator Sergio Osmena, the key figures of the majority Nacionalista party, went to Washington on a successful mission to influence the choice of a governor general following the death of Wood. They persuaded Chief Justice William Howard Taft to intercede with President Calvin Coolidge on behalf of their candidate, Colonel Henry L. Stimson. During this mission, Quezon, who had been bothered by a wracking cough, again saw New York specialists, but this time received unwelcome news: the stresses of the past six years had finally undermined his constitution; both lungs were infected, and he must rest for at least a year if he expected to regain his health.

The Pottenger sanatorium in Monrovia, California, where he would spend the ensuing months, depressed Quezon. Spending Christmas alone in an aseptically bare white room, he read away the weeks, longing to return to his wife, Aurora, and their three children. Unlike Walker Percy, he did not read in order to discover himself, but simply to pass time, skipping from detective stories of all sorts to history, biography, economics, and politics. He felt that he "was going to die — just like an animal, without any spiritual consolation or hope." Not surprisingly, perhaps, he received such consolation — Quezon had strayed from his cradle Catholicism — though from an improbable source, a tract by an American mystic, Annie Fellows Johnston. After his discharge from Pottenger, he thought seriously about returning to the Church (in his student period he had aspired to the priesthood), but the process of reconversion remained incomplete until another critical bout with TB five years later.

If pulmonary tuberculosis influenced Quezon's spiritual endeavors, characteristically, he also turned his illness to political account. Rather than accompany Secretary of War Patrick J. Hurley, an outspoken opponent of independence, to Manila in 1931, Quezon again entered Pottenger for several weeks, and when he finally returned to the Philippines, submitted his resignation as Senate president. "Under the circumstances, when the solution of the Filipino problem is so near at hand, a man of greater physical energies than I should direct it," he declared. Doctors Homer B. Whitney, an American who had accompanied him across the Pacific, Andreas B. Trepp, a Swiss TB specialist, and a personal physician, Antonio G. Sison, issued a statement affirming the frailty of Quezon's condition. The Senate granted him an eight-month leave of absence. Quezon's maneuvering on this occasion was a resourceful effort to avoid losing ground, but with the 1934 passage of the Tydings-McDuffie Bill, promising complete independence in 1946, his leadership was assured. Forming a Coalition party, he reunited dissident followers and, with Osmena as running mate, defeated his old foe, Emilio Aguinaldo, the leader of the Philippine insurrection.

Aguinaldo, rankling still from the American suppression of his short-lived Philippine Republic and from the political setbacks inflicted upon him by Quezon, a mere major in the army that Aguinaldo had directed, surfaced again after Pearl Harbor. He threw in his lot with the Japanese as Quezon had thrown in his with the Americans, and, during the siege of Corregidor, broadcast a surrender plea to Filipinos fighting with MacArthur. For Quezon, confined to a field hospital inside the Rock's damp Malinta Tunnel, it must have seemed the wheel had come full circle; Aguinaldo was in the ascendant while he, Quezon, torn by spasmodic coughing, lay helpless. As Japanese bombs whistled down, the efforts of Dr. Andreas Trepp to relieve Quezon's condition proved futile. Amid the smoke and confusion he was moved by ambulance to a cottage near MacArthur's quarters, and a tent was erected for the president outside the tunnel. Here he slept nearly a month except for the intervals of air raids when his aide-de-camp, Colonel Manuel Nieto, picked him up in his arms and carried him to safety.

"I want you to understand," Quezon said, when he reached Washington several weeks later, "that my present sojourn in the United States was not planned or contemplated by me." Determined to return, he had no choice save biding his time and observing the phantom protocols of an exiled head of state. Summer in Washington, even for someone no stranger to the climate, compares unfavorably with summer in Manila; Washington jeopardizes the consumptive; winter and summer, dampness prevails. The Quezon family endured the kiln-like temperatures of the capital in 1942 since affairs of the government-in-exile required Washington residence at the Shoreham Hotel, but the next summer they left for Saranac Lake, where they stayed at a former hunting lodge, Camp McMartin. (They also lived in winter near Miami in a large house with ample gardens on an islet offered them by Henry Stimson.)

Much of Quezon's time was spent in bed, following the progress of the Pacific campaign. He still remained a pragmatic politician, however, a wily *gulerato*. In November 1943 at the Shoreham, when it became apparent that in less than a fortnight he would cease to remain constitutionally the president of the Philippines, his staff started to temporize. Quezon's reaction threw them into a panic. Wheezing, his face twisted in paroxysms of pain, he thrashed about on his mattress so alarmingly that everyone hurried out of the room except Vice President Osmena. "If you want the government you can have it!" Quezon blurted. Osmena hesitated. Naturally, he wanted to be president, but he heard himself saying, "No, it isn't that." What if the disappointment killed Quezon? "Leave the question of your continuance in office entirely in my hands," Osmena said, and Quezon replied, "It's up to you, it's up to you." Quezon, of course, remained in office. The next morning his physician, a Dr. Rotor, called upon the patient. Rotor was surprised to find Quezon looking hale and cheerful. Had yesterday been a *palabas,* a show?

The doctor thought he heard the president exclaim, "Rotor, how was my performance yesterday?" A decade later, recalling the event, Rotor said, "Ah, what a great dramatic actor the Philippines lost when Manuel L. Quezon took up the law instead of the stage!"

The first summer at Saranac, Quezon was preoccupied by the exile government and the progress of the war; a year later, once again at Camp McMartin, only his desire to see the Philippines once more sustained him. Occasional flashes of his former vitality impressed others, but his reflexes were slower and he seemed almost incorporeal. His will was strengthened by the war news. Emissaries reported that between 95 and 98 percent of the Filipino people remained loyal to the United States; MacArthur's troops were leapfrogging along the coast of New Guinea. "This is the beginning of the end," Quezon exclaimed after a particularly encouraging broadcast. No one could understand him, his voice was a husk, and he was forced to scribble the words on a scrap of paper.

The Quezon family arrived in Saranac for the summer early in June 1944. So rapidly, though, did the president's condition deteriorate that by the end of the month uniformed Filipino doctors alternated shifts at his bedside. He read, or had read to him, Fritz Marquardt's *Before and After Bataan*, Clark Lee's *They Call It Pacific*, Gandhi's *An Appeal to the British*. One of the doctors played solitaire for the president, and if the cards fell wrong, was ordered to cheat, which amused Quezon enormously. He wrote testy directives — illness had made him petulant — but for the most part he sat silent, occasionally mustering strength to speak of the men with whom he had fought for an independent republic at the turn of the century. On the last evening of July, while reciting the rosary, he tried to raise himself on his elbows, fell back, and whispered to Dr. Dino, the attending physician, "Dino, pray for me — pray for me so that God will allow me to return to the Philippines. I feel so weak that I am afraid I may not make it."

The following morning at eight Quezon snapped his fingers and pointed at the back of his left wrist — a sign he wanted Dr. Cruz to dial the morning news. Americans, they heard, had landed on Noemfoor in Dutch New Guinea, six hundred miles from the Philippines. "It won't be long now," gasped Quezon, and motioned for an attendant. The doctor stepped outside the room, then, startled by a loud noise, rushed back and found his patient, supported by the attendant, laboring for breath, coughing violently, and hemorrhaging. "Trepp," Quezon pleaded.

Cruz ran downstairs and phoned Andreas Trepp, who was breakfasting at the Hotel Saranac. Although he arrived within minutes, his emergency efforts proved unavailing. Aurora Quezon and the children were summoned to the bedside, and shortly before ten the president's pulse stopped.

Quezon, born in an isolated village, had died in an isolated village on the other side of the world. Saranac was for him an illusion, the two-dimensional landscape of exile in a Nabokov novel, a scenic curtain on which painted evergreens, lakes, and mountains scroll upward and reveal the spaces of reality created by other and familiar voices.

When Béla Bartók composed the Concerto for Orchestra in a bungalow tucked in a rear corner of the lot on which stood Margaret Sageman's cure cottage at 32 Park Avenue, he broke a four-year silence. His previous score was the Sixth String Quartet dedicated to the Kolisch Quartet and written during the late summer and early fall of 1939 — his final European composition. The subsequent years held a surfeit of vicissitudes. The death of Bartók's mother, to whom he had been devoted since childhood — the composer was only seven at his father's untimely death — occurred a month after he completed the Sixth String Quartet, and he felt his final bond with Hungary severed. The spreading Nazification of the country's cultural and social life had disturbed him throughout the thirties; in 1937 he refused to let the radio networks of Italy and Germany perform

his works, and after Hitler's occupation of Austria Bartók began
to make arrangements to safeguard his music by sending the
scores to Switzerland and England. Protesting the racist regulations of the German Copyright Association, along with his fellow
composer Zoltán Kodály, Bartók transferred to the British Performing Rights Society. The move produced positive consequences later on, since it permitted ASCAP, the equivalent U.S.
organization, affiliated with the British society, to assist Bartók;
but at the time it only served to bring him into further disfavor
with Hungarian officialdom. His career in any event had not
been comfortable; contending with public apathy, he had long
endured the gibes, lampoons, and cabals of the Budapest concert scene, and so, after a brief concert tour of America in the
spring of 1940, Bartók and his wife, Ditta, immigrated that autumn to New York City. Before leaving, he signed a will stipu-
lating that as long as Hitler and Mussolini streets and squares
existed in Hungary, "then neither square nor street nor public
building in Hungary is to be named for me, and no memorial
tablet is to be erected in a public place."

They arrived with the clothes on their backs — their luggage
had been detained at the Spanish border and would not arrive
for several weeks — but they were stimulated by the prospect of
Bartók's honorary Doctor of Music degree from Columbia University and, even more, by his appointment to carry out research
on Serbo-Croatian folk music there. The appointment, however,
was dependent on a grant that expired at the close of 1942, leaving the sixty-one-year-old Bartók groping among the farcical
cross-purposes and tragic misunderstandings of emigrés in
Manhattan. He then tried to find a job. Protracted negotiations
came to nothing with the University of Washington, interested
in offering him a post. Throughout this period at Columbia he
had continued to give piano recitals, often in company with
Ditta, herself a professional musician who had been his pupil;
they remained strangers to American ways, however, and adjusted with difficulty.

The first of their American addresses was a large apartment house in Forest Hills, where the constant shudder of subway trains shook the ceilings. The pelt of wayward horns and sirens from the traffic below exacerbated Bartók's nerves. So refined was his legendary aural acuity it was said he could hear a whisper through closed doors, and even at home in Buda he used earplugs while composing. Agatha Fassett, a friend who called on them, was struck by "the raw smell of plaster and paint not yet dried into the flimsy walls," but an evening with Béla lent hearing precedence over the other senses, and soon she was conscious of radios on all sides, "some soft, some loud, seeping through the walls that might have been made of cheesecloth for all the protection they gave. Overhead, heavy footsteps sounded. Bartók followed them with his eyes as they passed from one end of the room to the other."

Once Béla and Ditta spent three hours on the subway, "traveling hither and thither in the earth; finally, our time waning and our mission incomplete, we shamefacedly slunk home — of course, entirely underground." They struggled with New Yorkese and can openers and the intricacies of electrical appliances, and watched, awestruck, "human beings ruminating like cows," since every other person seemed to chew gum; more discouragingly, the musical world of the United States seemed oblivious to Bartók's musical significance, and his sixtieth birthday transpired without commemoration. "Apart from five people who cabled greetings, nobody cared a red cent about March 25," he wrote his son, Peter. The "red cent" showed Bartók was acquiring a few Americanisms, though he still could not find enough concert work for an income, and just before his birthday he received a letter from the Baldwin Company, which until then had placed two pianos at his disposal, that one of the pianos must be returned. The Bartóks, furthermore, were in a precarious bureaucratic limbo, classified as "visitors" rather than as immigrants. "My career as a composer is as much as finished; the quasi boycott of my works by the leading orchestras continues,

no performances either of old works," he wrote his pupil Wil-
helmine Creel. "It is a shame — not for me, of course."

Bartók's health had begun to deteriorate markedly, too. During his student days at the Budapest Academy of Music he may
have been tubercular, for TB was suspected as the cause of his
respiratory disorders in 1899. The summer of 1900 he fell seriously ill with pneumonia and pleurisy; one of his doctors abandoned hope and it appeared for a time Bartók might have to
give up music, but after several months of rest at a Carinthian
mountain resort he returned to the keyboard with renewed energy. His latest symptoms seemed to indicate a recurrence. He
could scarcely walk between rooms and his temperature often
soared. Harvard University, fortunately, invited him to lecture
just as the Columbia appointment expired, but, exhausted and
faint after his third lecture, he could not fulfill the contract. His
Harvard sponsors persuaded him to have a thorough physical
checkup at their expense, and the examining doctor relievedly
announced the composer had TB. "I was less joyful at hearing
the news," was Bartók's wry comment. New x-rays revealed a
lesser degree of lung trouble, however, and doctors confessed
bafflement. In fact, Bartók suffered from leukemia, which rapidly manifested unmistakable symptoms.

While he lay despondent and feverish in Doctors' Hospital, in
the spring of 1943, his weight fallen to eighty-seven pounds,
there took place an event which, had it been a scene in a Hollywood film biography, would have been dismissed as preposterous dramatic license. Serge Koussevitzky, the conductor of the
Boston Symphony Orchestra, arrived at Bartók's bedside to offer him a thousand-dollar commission from the Koussevitzky
Foundation to compose an orchestral work in memory of the
conductor's late wife. Koussevitzky's arrival was not as fortuitous
as it seemed; the violinist Joseph Szigeti and the conductor Fritz
Reiner had interceded on behalf of Bartók and the circumstances of the commission were concealed lest the composer, as sensitive to honor as an impetuous hussar, interpret it as charity.

Even so, he assented reluctantly for he was afraid he would not be able to complete the commission, but Koussevitzky, pressing a check on him for half the amount, won the day. Once Bartók made his decision, the depression of his early years in America evaporated somewhat. Ditta wrote Szigeti, "I am so glad that plans, musical ambitions, compositions are stirring in Béla's mind — a new hope discovered in this way quite by chance, as it were incidentally. One thing is sure: Béla's 'under no circumstances will I ever write any new work' — attitude has gone. It's more than three years now . . ."

Upon diagnosing leukemia, doctors simply told Bartók it was "a baffling case." He managed to put on weight, and at the beginning of July the Bartóks left for Saranac Lake on the recommendation of doctors Edgar Mayer and Israel Rappaport, who became Bartók's attending physician. Dr. Mayer was director of Will Rogers and, since ASCAP had volunteered to pay medical expenses (a different matter for Bartók from accepting the creative responsibilities of a commission), it seems probable this connection accounted for the selection of Saranac.

Margaret Sageman, the nurse and school board member who rented her corner-lot bungalow to the Bartóks, had a reputation as an astute businesswoman; her rates were double or triple those of Trudeau and she catered to an elite clientele. An advertisement for the cottage in the May 1931 *Journal of Outdoor Life* emphasizes her home cooking, but the Bartóks were not encouraged to dine in the bungalow. They liked Mrs. Sageman and, Ditta said, "I wish you could see her with the patients, so you could understand her great kindness mixed with that overwhelming authority," yet, "I am somehow just a little bit afraid of her." Mrs. M. A. Levy, a neighbor, came to give English lessons: Bartók had progressed to the point where he could borrow the Motteux translation of *Don Quixote* from the Saranac Lake Free Library and derive pleasure from his mastery of the seventeenth-century cadences of the prose, but Ditta's English remained rudimentary. Noting the Bartóks had been refused kitchen privileges and were not permitted to store their food in Mrs. Sageman's refrigerator, Mrs. Levy invited them to her home. When Ditta saw the piano in the living room, she uttered a single word, "Please," and sat down. Mrs. Levy, who had at that point never heard of Bartók or his music, instantly realized Ditta was no amateur player.

"From the moment we arrived," Ditta informed Agatha Fassett, "Béla began to get better, waving away his sickness by his own strong will as if it had never been. For in order to do his work of composing, he knows that the first step is to feel completely free, and guarded from all disturbances, and remain for a while calm and restored in his own world." His fever abated. Every day he followed the war news in the *New York Times,* carefully stacking the copies for reference. Ditta also practiced on the high school piano, and a Saranac historian, Esther Myrick, recalls entering one evening while Ditta was playing in the darkened auditorium.

The Bartóks in wartime Saranac Lake were outsiders indeed — the gaunt, pallid composer, his flowing white hair worn long, Lisztian fashion, and the much younger second wife who might have been his daughter. In her Hungarian peasant skirts and blouses, Ditta not only acted like a child, she looked like one. Slight of build, she braided her long blond hair, but unbound it on occasion and let the sun stream through it while she played ball on the lawn with Mrs. Levy's boys. Ditta loved the relief of these coltish interludes: when her son Peter Bartók visited, prior to enlisting in the navy, he too joined the ball game. Béla, unmindful of the provincialism around him, felt hale enough to take walks. Hatless, he strode along in a costume appropriate for hiking in rural Hungary — old-fashioned knickerbockers, woollen socks, heavy shoes, and a long cape — and carried an Alpine staff. Uncritical eyes might view him as picturesque, a magus-like figure set down in the Adirondacks, but attire appropriate to Transylvania only identified him to Saranac know-nothings as a distant relative of Count Dracula. Bartók, however,

was conditioned to provincial suspicion. Traveling in the Trans-
danubia and Transylvania in 1906–7, collecting folk songs on
Edison wax cylinders, he had endured repeated snubs. A letter
to Stefi Geyer describes his banal and circuitous conversation
with a peasant woman from whom he was trying to extract a
ballad. "Endurance, perseverance, patience . . . to hell with you
all . . ." he fumed. "I'm going home. I can't do with this farce for
more than six weeks at a stretch." Magyar peasants distrusted
anyone wearing city clothes, and only by exercising extreme tact
had Bartók induced them to sing. Certain Saranac natives, Mrs.
Levy recalled, had an equivalent mistrust. They claimed Bartók
looked "like that nut Einstein," although Einstein favored tat-
tered pants or shorts and a T-shirt and always seemed rumpled,
whereas Béla was scrupulously neat.

Worse than hinterland pettiness, philistinism, and backbiting
were the merchants who actively exploited Ditta. Sometimes she
was an involuntary collaborator. The intricacies of food-ration-
ing stamps eluded her: "When she got food stamps she spent
them all in one swoop," Mrs. Levy said. A baffled Ditta more
often than not helplessly handed over her entire book of ration
stamps, which would be accepted without demur. Béla in his del-
icately accented Oxonian English tried to explain how the system worked and Ditta would nod yes, but she never understood
the process.

> She seemed very helpless [Mrs. Levy continued]. I took her to the
> bank to teach her about a checking account and how to wait in
> line. Her response was, "But in Hungary I never waited on line."
> I tried to help by inviting them to dinner, but I, also, had to be
> careful. I could get neck bones without stamps, so we made thick
> soups out of them. We ate in restaurants at times to save stamps,
> but the Bartóks couldn't afford this: it was really pitiful.

Dr. Mayer and his colleague Dr. Rappaport, like Mrs. Levy,
represented a more enlightened Saranac. Though not musical,
Mayer was aware of Bartók's reputation, and the physician came

to admire his patient unreservedly. They seldom discussed music; Bartók, however, did venture the opinion that violinist Yehudi Menuhin was the greatest living musician and one of the few who truly understood Bartók's music. Curiously, Dr. Rappaport at length found an opportunity to make a direct medical contribution toward Bartók's commission.

> To compose, he [Bartók] needed great silence, [but] one of his ebony earpieces got lost and he was in distress. I had the fortunate idea of trying an earpiece from my stethoscope. This he could not forget, it was the greatest good deed I did for him. It helped him more than any medical service I gave him.

With the aid of Dr. Rappaport's improvised ear-stopple, Bartók was prepared to embark on one of the most remarkable musical compositions of the twentieth century, the Concerto for Orchestra. The score was composed in Mrs. Sageman's bungalow between the fifteenth of August and the eighth of October, when the Bartóks, in advance of the cold weather — he had found the summer excessively chilly — returned to New York. Fecund in invention, complex and substantial as any symphony, the Concerto released a flood of ideas; in its five movements Bartók, momentarily reprieved from death, could voice everything stifled, everything apprehended, everything accumulated in the years of silence. Within its measures, states Halsey Stevens,

> may be discovered procedures that owe their presence to his early acquaintance with Brahms, Liszt, and Strauss; others that to the discerning eye and ear indicate relationships, however remote, with Debussy, Stravinsky, Schoenberg, with Bach and his predecessors; and, inextricably interwoven, the essence of Magyar peasant music which colors all the melodies, the harmonies, the rhythms.

The Concerto is eclectic, but the eclecticism works — the folk art song given a fresh context, a thesaurus of popular musical styles integrated into the fabric. Moreover, the music is blithe as no other Bartók score is — particularly in the second movement, where pairs of instruments frolic through stylized patterns, bassoons in sixths, oboes in thirds, clarinets in sevenths, flutes in fifths, muted trumpets in seconds. During the first rehearsals in Boston, Bartók disclosed that he had pictured the instruments as animals making their way two-by-two into Noah's Ark. The score contains a reverberation from the internal monologues of the composer's opera, *Bluebeard's Castle,* a frivolous couplet from Lehár's *Merry Widow,* an interrupted serenade that may have its origins in the first book of Debussy's Preludes. Clothed in shimmering harmonic colors, the work's bold handling of quotation looks back on the vast dramatic structures of Beethoven and ahead, toward constructions yet undreamed. Bartók himself supplied the program notes for the first performance, which, unfortunately, did not occur until a year and a half later, at Symphony Hall, Boston:

"The general mood of the work represents, apart from the jesting second movement, a gradual transition from the sternness of the first movement and the lugubrious death-song of the third, to the life-assertion of the last one . . ."

There is scarcely any other opus by Bartók that is so openly programmatic and that might almost be said to have a plot worked out from its inception to the final conclusion, declares the composer's biographer Josef Ujfallusy.

When we hear the choral trio of the second movement and the American dance-music tone of the last movement we are stirred by a faint memory of Mozart's *Magic Flute* in which the master made use of the most popular street songs together with the rich traditions of baroque genres, in order to people a world in which all humanity had its rightful place.

That fall Béla and Ditta moved into the Hotel Woodrow at Eighty-fifth Street on the West Side. Agatha Fassett was amazed by Bartók's high spirits and physical improvement. Teasingly he showed her the score of the Concerto. "Even if you are too lazy to follow a score, and are interested only in books besides, at least you may well see for yourself how many notes I wrote!" he exclaimed. She returned the pages and he added in a lively confiding manner, "What nobody could possibly see in this score is that through working on this concerto, I have discovered the wonder drug I needed to bring about my own cure." Further elation came from a first hearing of his 1938 Violin Concerto, for he had been unable to attend the Amsterdam premiere. Tossy Spivakovsky's Carnegie Hall performance Bartók thought excellent. The well-received Violin Concerto would soon be scheduled by major orchestras, and meanwhile in November Yehudi Menuhin played the First Violin Sonata on a New York recital program. Menuhin, furthermore, commissioned Bartók to write a solo violin sonata, so Bartók — once more under the medical auspices of ASCAP — went to Asheville, North Carolina, where he spent the winter of 1943–44, Ditta and Peter remaining in New York. Completing the Menuhin commission the following March, Bartók still demonstrated continued physical improvement. His temperature was gone and at 105 pounds he considered himself robust. He felt too ill to work regularly, but his music was achieving recognition; Menuhin, his steadfast champion, was touring with the Violin Concerto, and though the most powerful among journalistic reviewers, Olin Downes of the *New York Times,* routinely berated Bartók, other and influential critics were sympathetic. The composer sensed a new phase dawning in his art, developments that would reshape his musical imagination, liberate his energies. His domestic circumstances had altered somewhat — Peter joined the navy and Ditta had leased a tiny apartment on Fifty-seventh Street. Despite constant anxiety over the war and the fates of his elder son, Béla, and colleagues like Kodály, still in Hungary, Bartók could anticipate an artistic rebirth. What he did not know, of course, was that he was living on charity, that his Columbia University grant was exhausted, and that funds collected for the most part by Szigeti from various musical groups, recording companies, and individuals permitted the university to renew Bartók's contract.

ASCAP again agreed to send them to Saranac Lake.

> The early summer was already spreading a heavy breathless haze over the city, flooding the Bartóks' Fifty-seventh Street apartment with motionless liquid heat [Fassett recalls]. The thought alone that the transparently fresh atmosphere of Lake Saranac was only a few short weeks away was in itself an escape.

They did not escape; the heat lingered. "Last year I almost froze here," Bartók complained from Saranac; "this year we have had day after day when the temperature has been above 90 degrees. The peak was reached some 8 or 10 days ago, with 96 degrees. Even the nights were so hot that one could not bear to have more than a sheet on the bed." He spent his days correcting the proofs of the Serbo-Croatian folk songs to which he had devoted so much of his time. Columbia University Press sent him a revised and typed preface, and he wearily objected to "colons and semi-colons" and editorial quibbles. "The whole thing is very interesting and, above all, most instructive, but sometimes tiresome and annoying just because of this over-fussiness."

The nights were exceptionally clear and star-filled, and Béla, with the aid of a star map, pointed out the constellations. His relations with Ditta, occasionally stormy, were aggravated by the heat and his health. According to Mrs. Levy, he would succumb on occasion to an invalid's self-pity: "In the presence of other people, Béla seemed cold and distant. He encouraged her to go out with others, including men, since he realized the great difference in their ages." Responding to such accusatory and essentially masochistic melancholy, Ditta was protective in the classic manner of the wife of a genius, a keeper of the flame. "Ditta spoke to me about this," Mrs. Levy declared, "and said, 'He is not only my husband — he is my god.'" Florid enough for the curtain speech of a Bernhardt, the sentiment left no question where she stood.

There were noted visitors that summer, however — Koussevitzky, Menuhin, and Dr. Wilhelm Reich, former director of Sigmund Freud's Seminar for Psychoanalytic Therapy. A controversial psychoanalyst who had tried to merge Freud and Marx in Weimar Germany (running afoul of both camps), and whose theories of psychic energy eventually resulted in his arrest (on charges of violating the Food and Drug Act) and sentencing, to Pennsylvania's Lewisburg federal penitentiary, Dr. Reich at that point was neither social martyr — thirteen years later he would die in prison — nor tribal shaman, but a scientist with radical therapeutic views. Psychic energy, he contended, was an area little understood, although he concluded he had tapped a source that he named "the orgone." Through the orgone box, an accumulator that looked like an upended telephone booth, he maintained he could gather "orgone energy" from the air. Bartók agreed. Separate fragments of his music crackled each into its own incandescent climax before merging with the next fragment — a process that bore comparison, however remote, to the pulsations of a galvanic current. Nevertheless, while endorsing Reich's experiments, Bartók did not undertake a Reichian cure. His health remained precarious, and when he went to the hospital for tests he insisted on following his own unorthodox procedures. He reminded Dr. Mayer of a Gandhi-like figure,

> sitting in bed with legs drawn under him, naked upper body — a small emaciated man with a big head and huge dark eyes, very soft-spoken and talking very little. He never complained. With a 102-degree fever, he sat up writing music from his head, composing from memory. He hated to be disturbed even by his doctor; he did not believe we knew what was wrong with him anyhow; he would not take any medicines and injections horrified him.

Hospital food was another taboo. Ditta brought "crusts of bread, and nuts and grapes, which he would chew when hungry, irregularly during the day."

Ironically, the composer's greatest popular acceptance, following the premiere of the Concerto for Orchestra, would occur as his health declined. Within three years American symphony orchestras would perform the work of Bartók more frequently than that of any other composer of the twentieth century except Richard Strauss and Prokofiev. The advent of the long-playing record would give Bartók further impetus. The Concerto, showing off the integral strengths of the orchestra section by section and then ensemble, fitted the acoustical requirements of LPs and yet, despite its virtuosity, the music was indicative of masterful compositional methods rather than surface brilliance. Against doctor's orders, Bartók went to Boston for the Concerto's premiere, which Koussevitzky would conduct. Advance excitement mounted; at the rehearsal Koussevitzky proclaimed the score the best of the last twenty years (after the performance he more than doubled the figure to the last half century); and the Symphony Hall performance on December first constituted for Bartók an apotheosis. "The Bartok Concerto for Orchestra was an absolute spellbinder," the *Boston Globe* reported, "a genuine, full-scale musical experience which closed the program with a storm of bravos." It was the last time Bartók would hear his music performed.

That same December, Ralph Hawkes, head of the music publishing firm of Boosey and Hawkes, commissioned a seventh string quartet, and the following February William Primrose asked for a viola concerto. Had Bartók not contracted pneumonia, he might have completed these; thanks to recently developed antibiotics he recovered, but canceled a projected visit to Menuhin in California. Instead the Bartóks returned for a third summer in Saranac.

Their quarters on this visit, a cottage in the backyard of Max Haar at 89 Riverside Drive, were even more unprepossessing, a makeshift shell containing low-ceilinged rooms and a kitchen. The bathroom boasted a tub but no washbasin. Although the cottage was equipped with electricity, Béla and Ditta warmed their bathwater on the stove. While he liked the icebox — "it

works with natural, god-created ice (delivered every other day)"
— he was under no illusions about the accommodations, which
he described as "a hovel or hut."

Mrs. Levy, on coming to call, found her visit a trying experience; Ditta "just stared into space," obviously coping with accelerating emotional depression. On the other hand, Bartók's letters and Ditta's to Agatha Fassett suggest a summer of relative
tranquility. At the beginning of July he had to enact a charade
of emigration and re-entry into the United States, and visited
Montreal for the necessary papers. Otherwise there were few
interruptions: Bach's organ preludes and Beethoven's string
quartets in hand, Bartók rested and watched frisking chipmunks
or busied himself with the composition of the Primrose concerto
and a new but uncommissioned Piano Concerto, No. 3, intended
as a surprise present for Ditta. The war reached its traumatic
abrupt close; Peter Bartók, stationed in Panama, was mustered
out and rejoined his mother and father. On family picnics Bartók seemed rejuvenated, even scaling hills. A cable from friends
in Budapest requested him to return and take his place in the
reorganized parliament. Other news from Hungary offered a
dismaying picture of war damage, but owing to the efforts of
Béla, his son by his first marriage, Bartók's manuscripts, folk-
song archives, and household goods had survived intact. Showing Mrs. Levy his cable, he said, "They still remember me."

During the final days of August, however, Bartók's abnormal
temperatures revived and doctors advised treatment in New
York. Bartók wondered whether it would be possible to continue
the work there. The family left Saranac by train on a muggy
Labor Day weekend and endured a wretched journey that
ended amid the maelstrom of Grand Central Station. Béla vainly
sought a porter; at length he picked up the luggage and reeled
across the terminal before Peter could prevail upon him to surrender his bags.

Though failing rapidly, Bartók continued work on the Piano
Concerto. Tibor Serly visited on the evening of September 21

and found him lying in bed, the pages of the orchestral score scattered across the blankets. They discussed the Viola Concerto, which was half-hidden by a clutter of medicine bottles. Peter had drawn the bar-lines on the manuscript and Bartók was struggling to fill in the last measures. It was only, he told Serly, a matter of necessary detail. The following day Dr. Rappaport ordered his patient moved to the West Side Hospital, but Bartók pleaded for time; he had important work to complete. Dr. Rappaport was adamant, so Bartók marked on the score the number of bars still to follow and awaited the ambulance.

On September 26, he died, having made a remark to a doctor, variously reported as "I am only sad that I have to leave with a full trunk," or, "The trouble is that I have to go with so much still to say." The urgency of his words in any case was undeniable, and his last musical utterance should have crowned his career; but the Viola Concerto, sketchy in outline, and the attenuated Third Piano Concerto lack distinction. Bartók's Concerto for Orchestra remains the supreme composition of his American years, in the words of the critic Halsey Stevens, "a great work, one of the greatest produced in this century." The music succeeds through "the complete appropriateness of the language to the vitality of the idea," rather than through novelty, and in this sense it exhibits qualities characteristic of such otherwise unlike works as the Brandenburg Concertos, the St. Matthew Passion, the Jupiter Symphony, and the late Beethoven quartets. "They are inevitable works — works which convey such impact that it is impossible to think of their having been written in any other way."

Mrs. Sageman's bungalow, perching on the slope behind the erstwhile cure cottage — now an apartment house — seems apologetic at occupying space dominated by the more imposing building. Small, brown, and as functional as a bird's nest, there is nothing to indicate anything out of the ordinary ever took place inside.

CHAPTER TEN

Last Out
1944–1954

SYLVIA PLATH BROKE A LEG on her only recorded visit to Saranac. The skiing accident, significant in terms of her emotional life, comprises a pivotal episode in the autobiographical novel, *The Bell Jar*, when Esther Greenwood, a novice skier, rebels on a rope tow against the devouring expectations of her boyfriend Buddy Willard. Poised upon the crest of Mt. Pisgah, where "the cold air punished my lungs and sinuses to a visionary clearness," Esther digs the spikes of her poles into the snow; she has been transported to a place separate and remote from other people, and "the thought that I might kill myself formed in my mind coolly as a tree or a flower."

Had she been born in the nineteenth century like Adelaide Crapsey, Plath too might have evolved as a bluestocking marooned in a genteel enclave of female academics. Smith College served as a crucible for both of them — white, middle-class, overachieving women apparently conforming to male-defined roles as daughters, teachers, and poets. Crapsey's revolt, however, bursting forth as she lay dying, denounced the classic inequities of fate; Plath's involved a different reflex in contention against stereotypical female identities that she must reject in order to discover her persona as a creative artist. Superficially, both poets were All-Round Students, outwardly gregarious, well organized, and correct, but the contrasts are obvious: Adelaide Crapsey belonged to and accepted a pre–World War era of sunlit rationality in which problems had solutions and science (including research into a more precise prosody) promised abundance; Sylvia Plath was dissociated from what she saw as the unreality of the catatonic postwar America. Once more, chance had brought to Saranac a culturally expressive figure — an archetype of the early fifties female college student.

The historical circumstances of her suicidal descent of Pisgah originated in Plath's ties with Dick Norton, the Buddy Willard of *The Bell Jar*. Over Christmas vacation, 1952, when she was a junior at Smith, she visited Norton in the Adirondacks. He had contracted tuberculosis and, as a Harvard Medical School student on scholarship, was sent expense-free to Ray Brook. Norton had been her "steady" during her initial years at Smith, but their relationship was deteriorating. The unflattering picture of Buddy in *The Bell Jar*, Edward Butscher, Plath's biographer, points out, overemphasizes the faults of a man who eventually became known as a proficient and compassionate doctor. In any event, Norton exemplified the well-scrubbed boy next door, thoughtful, sweet, sincere, and so blandly eligible that Plath's closest friend at Smith compared him to vanilla ice cream. Notwithstanding his naïveté, Plath at first idealized him. A college senior, he invited her to the Yale Junior Prom, and her status changed among her classmates from grind and outsider to Ivy League sylph. Dick became "the foremost-doctor-to-be-in-the-next-decades." He knew everything. He was not an ardent lover to be sure, which may have comforted Plath since the evidence of her poetry and short stories indicates that physicality disturbed her. Nevertheless, she submitted with relief to the complaisant role of hero-worshiper: Dick would guide an insecure and vulnerable college student into confident maturity.

Instead of guiding Esther, however, *The Bell Jar*'s Buddy demonstrates a brutal competitiveness. Scientific dogmas, he asserts, are superior to her humanism.

> "Do you know what a poem is, Esther?"
> "No, what?" I said.
> "A piece of dust."

Buddy, the polymath, instructs Esther in the disciplines he feels will make her a better mate. A doctor's prospective wife must understand the demands of medicine, so Buddy supplies her with data, anatomy lessons, and diagrams and escorts her to the dissecting amphitheater and the maternity ward. And in the same experimental spirit he takes her to his clinical bedroom where he removes his clothing. "I think you ought to get used to me like this," he says. Esther, for whom they might be playing the childish voyeuristic game of "doctor," transforms him into viscera in the manner of a Picasso drawing: "The only thing I could think of was turkey neck and turkey gizzards and I was depressed." Buddy urges her to undress, but undressing appeals to Esther "about as much as having my Posture Picture taken at college." From the absurdity she perceives in nakedness it is only a matter of minutes to the disillusioning revelation that Buddy, whom she associates with decorum and a formidable domestic tyrant of a mother, has been sleeping with a Cape Cod waitress.

The double standard of the fifties earmarks the scene; so does Esther's pent-up hostility. Her detached language takes on angry colloquial cadences, the waitress is "slutty," and Esther tells herself that it isn't Buddy's infidelity that matters but his unforgivable humbug, so like the sham of his mother's suburban lifestyle. Esther determines "to ditch Buddy Willard once and for all," but then he phones and in a toneless voice informs her that he has TB.

After Dick Norton's departure for Ray Brook, his mother, having picked out Plath as her son's future wife, pursued matchmaking plans. Couldn't Sylvia find a summer job in Saranac near the sanatorium? The romance sputtered on remorselessly through the mails; and meanwhile Plath attracted other young men. To disentangle herself from Dick, whose family was on cordial terms with Sylvia's mother, entailed conflicting feelings as guilt over his illness mingled with rage over his duplicity. Such was the situation when Plath, driven to the Adirondacks by Dick's father, visited the younger Norton for the last time.

She had expected a Swiss chalet of a sanatorium, "with rosy-cheeked young men and women, all very attractive but with hectic glittering eyes, lying covered with thick blankets on outdoor balconies." The environment — Ray Brook in its current incarnation of federal prison looks virtually the same as it did in 1952 — provided a somber contrast. The liver-colored institutional walls, dark woodwork, and shoddy furnishings had a funereal air. Dick, a flaccid stranger grown plump on the sanatorium regimen of continuous meals and lack of exercise, greeted her. Plath felt revulsion. "Though still a great lover of food," declares Butscher, "she could not abide obesity in herself or others and viewed it as a sign of inner deterioration."

As the boorish Buddy of *The Bell Jar* and the coarse Austin of Plath's *New Yorker*–like story "In the Mountains," Dick Norton has few redeeming features. Actually, he made fumbling attempts to prove he had changed. From the sanatorium he mailed Plath a William Carlos Williams poem; a scene from the novel has Buddy showing Esther a lyric he has published in a literary backwater "somewhere in Maine." Esther scorns the poem: it is too late for Buddy to retrieve lost emotional ground. Plath did find a congenial auditor, however, in her Adirondack landlord, a Dr. Lynn, who does not appear in *The Bell Jar*. He and his family lived near Ray Brook and she boarded with them on her extended visit. After the accident, the cultivated and intelligent Dr. Lynn supervised Plath's recovery while she read the bulky manuscript of his unpublished novel, which she later described as "a passionate James Joyce-ian study of introspection involving every controversial subject from sex to God to modern

art." Buddy's blundering efforts to regain Esther bracket —
along with the skiing smashup — his proposal of marriage. The
proposal is couched insensitively, "How would you like to be
Mrs. Buddy Willard?" and Esther responds by accompanying
him to the mountain, leaving him, and flying down the slope
toward destruction.

David Holbrook interprets this forecast of suicide in *The Bell
Jar* as explicit vengeance for Buddy's disloyalty and a reaction
against parental pressures — an interpretation borne out by the
text. Esther, standing atop Pisgah, measures the distance to
Buddy with her eye, aims her trajectory, and rushes at him like
a projectile. "But at a deeper level, the skiing accident," Holbrook continues, "is a suicidal manifestation of her desperation
over *being a woman, unable to respond to a man*," which is also ver-
ified by Esther's recollection of the incident.

> Every time it rained the old leg-break seemed to remember itself,
> and what it remembered was a dull hurt.
> Then I thought, "Buddy Willard made me break that leg."
> Then I thought, "No, I broke it myself. I broke it on purpose
> to pay myself back for being such a heel."

Plummeting "past the zigzaggers, the students, the experts,
through year after year of doubleness and smiles and compromise, into my own past," Plath moves with schizoid detachment
through symbolic manifestations of her life, a spectator of her
otherness. People and trees recede; she hurtles toward the nucleus of being, "the pebble at the bottom of the well, the white
sweet baby cradled in its mother's belly."

Before reaching the bottom, she executed a windmilling cart-
wheel, lost her poles, and vanished in a smother of snow. Then
she attempted to clamber to her feet and collapsed. Her left leg
was fractured twice.

Plath's Saranac mishap would seem a fugitive painful incident
in most lives, but given her autobiographical affinities and what

John Simon calls the blowing up of "the tiniest personal experience into an event of vast, universal, and, preferably, mythic importance," the Mt. Pisgah episode acquires unusual resonance. The undergraduate poet sought to treat it lightly: BREAK BREAK BREAK ON THE COLD WHITE SLOPES OH KNEE, she wired her mother. ARRIVING FRAMINGHAM TUESDAY NIGHT 7:41. BRINGING FABULOUS FRACTURED FIBULA NO PAIN JUST TRICKY TO MANIPULATE WHILE CHARLESTONING. ANYTHING TO PROLONG VACATION. The humor, rarely associated with Plath, concealed a terrifying awareness: the destruction of the male figures blocking her path required the destruction of herself.

On the sunny morning of June 1, 1943, a small group of men met in a room at the Pennsylvania Hotel in New York and discussed hypothetical approaches to the chemotherapy of tuberculosis. The conversation, which had a pessimistic undertone, seemed pointless. Recently developed sulfa drugs and penicillin had proven ineffectual against the disease. Leroy U. Gardner, the bacteriologist of the Saranac Laboratory, Dr. William C. White, director of research of the National Tuberculosis Association, representatives from pharmaceutical companies, and a group of university researchers presented their views. White suggested the possible isolation of digestive enzymes from earthworms. Selman A. Waksman of Rutgers objected, maintaining that any enzyme system powerful enough to destroy the bacteria of tuberculosis would inevitably ravage human organisms. Somewhat grumpily, White asked Waksman how he intended to address the problem, and Waksman replied, "The antibiotics will do it. Just give us time. Sooner or later we are bound to find one or more chemical agents that will be able to bring this about. They will kill the bacterium not by digesting it, but by interfering with its metabolism and growth without injuring the host." The argument failed to sway anyone, however, and was dismissed as speculative.

Waksman had neither suffered from tuberculosis nor developed a particular interest in it; his specialty was the study of microbes inhabiting the soil and their production of chemical compounds called antibiotics. In 1932 he had been requested by White to undertake a survey of the fate of the tuberculosis bacillus in soils and water basins, and after three years of research carried on with a graduate student, demonstrated that the bacillus gradually disappears in such habitats and that other microbes saprophytic in nature seemed responsible. Unprepared to pursue the implications of this finding, Waksman did not attempt to determine the precise mechanisms involved. He continued to search for new antibiotics and, in 1940, succeeded in isolating actinomycin and, two years later, a compound designated as streptothricin, a water-soluble white powder active against a variety of bacteria though toxic to lab animals. As a result of the development of streptothricin, techniques for screening and testing microbes grew more sophisticated. Less than three months after the debate in the Hotel Pennsylvania, a breakthrough led to streptomycin — a breakthrough that did not originate in a laboratory but on a New Jersey chicken farm.

The farmer noticed that one of his chickens appeared to have an ailment affecting its breathing. The chicken was immediately dispatched for examination at an Agricultural Experiment station, where the poultry pathologist routinely swabbed the bird's throat and transferred the result to several culture plates. A few days later three colonies of actinomycetes were observed on a plate, and, since one of Waksman's assistants happened to be studying viruses at the laboratory, the pathologist gave the plate to her. The culture arrived at Waksman's laboratory as a graduate student was working on the actinomycetes, so Waksman told him to apply the innovative testing methods for isolating and investigating microbe cultures. The antibiotic activity of the sample seemed similar to streptothricin, but with a significant

difference: it was less toxic. The new substance was named streptomycin, and in January 1944 its discovery was announced.

Who was the discoverer of streptomycin? Waksman enjoyed
arguing from the chain of causality like a Thomistic philosopher.
He had first recognized the physiology of the organism in 1915,
and through his work on actinomycin discovered the requisite
lab techniques. But did the accolade belong to the chicken who
picked up the culture from the soil? The poultry pathologist
who recognized the actinomycete colonies on the plate? The students who tested the colonies and experimented with the lab
animals? Or to William H. Feldman and H. Corwin Hinshaw,
who first tested streptomycin in the control of tuberculosis?
Waksman likened the discovery to the creation of a mosaic. "Did
it begin with the central figure, or with the signature of the artist
after the work was completed?"

November 20, 1944, was the day on which streptomycin was
first administered to a human being. The patient, a twenty-one-
year-old white female, had advanced pulmonary TB, and her
condition was deteriorating so swiftly that material then being
used in guinea pig experiments was appropriated for the clinical
trial. Until April 7, 1945, she received five courses of streptomycin, each extending from ten to eighteen days. On July 13,
1947, she was discharged from the Mayo Clinic with a diagnosis
of apparently arrested pulmonary tuberculosis. Subsequently,
she experienced no relapses, married, and became the mother
of three children.

The rapidity with which streptomycin, isoniazid (developed in
Saranac), and PAS powder — the so-called wonder drugs — rendered previous treatment obsolete stands in marked contrast to
the millennia in which TB reigned as a prime scourge of humanity. Tuberculosis may have comprised the first pestilence; it
is present among the exhumed skeletons of prehistoric epochs;
in ancient India no Brahmin was allowed to marry into a family
where it existed; and Hippocrates considered it the most deadly

of all the diseases. Within a decade, tuberculosis, the second-ranking cause of death in the United States, fell to seventh place and took only 6 percent as many lives as it did in 1900.

Margaret Sageman, the first of Saranac Lake's cure-cottage proprietors to acknowledge the trend, had by 1948 converted her Park Avenue facility. That same year the Annual Report of Trudeau Sanatorium noted "a sharp drop in the number of patients from January to April, the lowest for many years."

As a sanatorium, Trudeau was the victim of its own success. When Dr. Gordon M. Meade announced its closing shortly after Thanksgiving Day, 1954, the record spoke for itself — of 12,500 patients cared for since 1885, more than 5000 were still alive. Trudeau would henceforth devote its three-million-dollar endowment to basic research; the fifty-two buildings and the land valued at $1.8 million were on the market.

For Trudeau's staff of 144 and for Saranac the closing of the sanatorium signified the end of a way of life — a happy ending despite the economic consequences. Like the passing of chattel slavery, the transition would leave some people impoverished and others nostalgic, but it was necessary, inevitable, and just. Only 60 patients were treated in the closing year, when Trudeau ran a deficit of $90,000.

Among them, destined to be the last patient discharged, was Larry Doyle, the buoyant second baseman of the 1912 Giants. *Life* magazine photographers were present to record the event. Larry had found a room in the village where he would board until his death in his mid-eighties. Preserving his zest and waving from his porch at passers-by, he would become a Saranac landmark. Year after year villagers would lobby for his election to baseball's Hall of Fame at Cooperstown, where Matty had been enshrined from the start. Larry was never selected, but he was never embittered either. It was great to be old and a Giant.

The photographers snapped him eating the last meal at a long and empty table. The clink of utensils and drone of voices drifted into silence. Then he put on his hat and coat and walked into the gray winter afternoon. A shroud of snow covered Dr. Trudeau's statue. Larry Doyle continued past the statue and out the gates. The previous night's fall of snow burdened branches and bushes and gables, and a haze of cold flakes flew in the direction of the pine-sheltered cemetery. He did not look back, going home through the snow.

TB REMAINS an obdurate public health problem; the International Union Against Tuberculosis in Paris estimates there are eight to ten million new cases each year. Underdeveloped countries have not made significant inroads, and throughout South America tuberculosis is actually on the increase. The United States in 1984 reported 22,255 cases, including a virulent outbreak that swept the shelters for the homeless in Boston. The Boston epidemic illustrates the complexities of the disease; although TB is no longer ubiquitous, it is flexible and specialized. Increasingly, it is a disease of the elderly, the foreign-born, and the statistical group identified as "lower socioeconomic level." Treatment programs, spasmodic in Asia and Africa because of difficulties of transportation and of obtaining drugs, have left global pockets of drug resistance. A dying patient might begin a program, get his TB arrested, but not finish the treatment, and thus build drug immunity. New diagnostic techniques in the United States have reduced the recommended therapeutic regimen from twenty-four to nine months; even so, TB may erupt as it did in 1984 in New York, Mississippi, Maryland, and Montana among indigenous populations of drug-resistant subcultures — prostitutes, drug-takers, and others. Tuberculosis, having adapted to the marginal and disenfranchised elements of western societies and losing scant ground elsewhere, is not extinct. What is extinct, of course, is the former style of treatment: the sanatoria; the full six-course Berghof dinner; the tyranny of the weight chart and temperature graph; the palm-court orchestras playing while coffin-stacked freights chug through the evergreens: Saranac before closing time.

Gutzon Borglum's bronze statue of a seated Dr. Trudeau and Little Red have been moved outside the Trudeau Institute Research Laboratories beside Lower Saranac Lake. The statue and the cottage have lost context. Dr. Trudeau, looking toward the hills from the site of his fox-run, once reclined on a patio symbolically located between sanatorium cottages, fieldstone-studded Baker Chapel, and all outdoors — the triangulation of his principles. The new surroundings diminish him, oddly minimalistic near Little Red, which seems foreshortened too, like scenery en route to the warehouse from a dimly remembered pageant. Yet who would want it otherwise? Only these icons once exerted magic against a plague uncontrollable and omnipresent as the Black Death or the epidemics of the Florentine Renaissance and Defoe's London.

The same dislocation affects the whole village. For generations the world pressed in upon it; today it seems as distant from the world as a flyspeck oasis in the Sahara, although the *Daily Enterprise* and television bring in the rest of the planet. No community exists apart from the web of electronic circuitry defining the late twentieth century; but the factors that made a spa, boom town, and ultimately a form of sensibility are missing. The American Management Association, which purchased Trudeau Sanatorium, uses it for occasional meetings and the distribution of computerized mail. Snap-chains hang across each exit and stone pillars display NO TRESPASSING signs. Empty paths, gently turning and dipping, glide out of sight among empty buildings. Literary pilgrims still visit the off-the-beaten-path Stevenson Cottage, a memorial sustained by the devotion of its caretakers,

the Delehant family. The lapel-sprig of heather on the glass-en-
cased coat (incredibly small) of RLS is sere and brown. An off-
track betting office occupies the premises of the once-elegant
Santanoni Apartment House for Health Seekers; Governor
Mario Cuomo is trying to remove the grandeur and upkeep of
Topridge from the state rolls; the Alta Vista is a vacant lot; and
North Country Community College inherited the dilapidated
Bartók cottage of 1945. (The structure was donated, not the land
on which it stood, and college officialdom appears nonplused
over the gift.) Pine Ridge Cemetery, however, has not changed
materially since Adelaide Crapsey watched the diggers in the
frozen earth.

Saranac still gropes for an identity while neighboring Lake
Placid, with its Olympic speed-skating rink, huge arena, and
crowds sauntering along Main Street, exudes confident afflu-
ence. Lake Placid is spruce and synthetic and grand as the cur-
vature of the mammoth ski jump over its horizon; Saranac, idyllic but comatose, has been declared by Albany a depressed area.
Going from Lake Placid to Saranac means going from boutiques
and souvenir shops to a locale where deer carcasses sprawl in the
wells of pick-up trucks, NRA bumper stickers abound, and un-
shaven young woodsmen subsist on smallmouth bass and un-
employment checks. Yet things are never as trite and transparent as that: Saranac failed as a glossy resort because Saranac was
in the business of negotiating with death. Only superficially does
the village resemble the deserted mill towns of northern New
England. Saranac's past is not rooted in the mill, although the
sanatorium fulfilled the role of the mill, but in a profounder
knowledge of the elementals of human experience. As time
flows, it was a twinkling of six decades from Trudeau's vision to
the doors closing behind Larry Doyle; but all the same, Saranac's
rejection of centuries of suffering constitutes one of humanity's
memorable denials, Emersonian in its defiance of limits. After
all, what did Edward Livingston Trudeau bring to the conquest
of TB? An eccentric theory about resins and ozone, an incalcu-

lable will, and the conviction he could prevail over the disease that claimed his brother. Trudeau's battle against tuberculosis coincided with the publication (1894) of Frederick Jackson Turner's theory of the closing of the American frontier; Trudeau opened that frontier into the domain of illness as American astronauts opened it into space. Sentenced to die, he felt resurrected for a purpose. From Pisgah, Trudeau, like Moses, gazed upon illimitable possibility, the Promised Land where others would emerge from bondage. Saranac, in the phrase of Emerson's essays, became "the all in *each* of human nature," and if the cult of Trudeau's personality eventually overwhelmed his achievement, that achievement was nevertheless authentic. Patients were cured. Tuberculosis, though not checked, was stalemated. Hope endured.

> I have lived through many of the long and dark years of ignorance, hopelessness and apathy, when tuberculosis levied its pitiless toll on human life unheeded and unhindered; when, as Jaccoud has tersely put it: "The treatment of tuberculosis was but a meditation on death" [as Trudeau said in greeting delegates to the 1903 International Congress on Tuberculosis]. But I have lived also to see the dawn of the new knowledge, to see the fall of the death-rate of tuberculosis, to see hundreds who have been rescued, to see whole communities growing up of men and women whose lives have been saved, and who are engaged in saving the lives of others.

Air is to Saranac what water is to Venice, the element of the spirit of place. Like Venice, too, Saranac can seem secretive and inward-looking, conscious of history to a degree unique even among older American settlements, for Saranac incorporates in its past a European comprehension of death. It is not morbid; it is merely interwoven with time. Ascend Helen Hill and consider its congeries of cross-linked destinies, the combinational possibilities of, say, a single summer's month in 1944: Einstein sailing over the lakes, Bartók transcribing musical ideas, Quezon dreaming of exile's return, Percy reading Kafka, Maugham, distraught and pale, following this same steep sidewalk. Eminent men, but what of those others, Dr. Trudeau's anonymous allies in his great enterprise? The donors of sealskin robes and electric blankets; the nurses who fell in love with patients and the nurses fearful of infection who changed the sweat-soaked sheets and took the sputum samples; the dietitians and librarians and occupational therapists; the lab workers who stained the slides and dusted the microscopes; the secretaries and radiologists, the pharmacists and telephone operators and groundskeepers and busy post office clerks? On the other side of the hill, the peak of Stevenson's cottage signals the Saranac of Pliny Miller and the early guides and loggers. Beyond lie the woods that Adirondack Murray celebrated, the woods that seduced and frightened Stillman, where Emerson chased after deer, and where the original owners of the land, the Indians, built their bark long houses. Further in time the panorama stretches — trees, streams, and mountains merging into geologic eras before the advent of man. Further still, at the edge of time, trees and mountains dissolve into air, the clear air of Saranac dispensing mysterious life.

Acknowledgments

Notes

Index

✒ ACKNOWLEDGMENTS ✒

This account is neither regional history nor a systematic study of tuberculosis in America from 1859, though obviously it involves elements of both. Saranac Lake has excellent regional historians such as Maitland DeSormo, whose books extend the tradition of the great pioneer of Adirondack history, Alfred Donaldson; and oral chroniclers such as Seaver Rice on tape in the Saranac Lake Free Library. The civic annals of Saranac, however, are not cardinal here. Instead, this is the story of the world coming into Saranac, a story of crossed destinies in a unique American community at once a sanctuary and the site of a decisive struggle against an epidemic as malignant as the plagues of the Middle Ages.

Without Mrs. Janet Decker of Saranac and Tupper Lake I should never have been able to complete these pages. I owe a profound debt to her, to Joyce Meagher and the staff of the Saranac Lake Free Library, and to Charles Liftman, systems editor of the *Boston Globe*. Others instrumental in the making of this book have been James Bell, Lisa Browar and the staff of the Special Collections of Vassar College, Edwin Briggs, Charles Claffey, Charles Decker, John Deedy, William Delehant, Honoria Murphy Donnelly, William Doolittle, Dr. Laurence Farrar, Mark Feeney, James Halsema, Arthur Hepner, Mary B. Hotaling, Amy Jones, Don Lessem, Lois J. Lewis, Robie Macauley, Margaret Manning, Timothy Malakie, Dr. Edgar Mayer, M. R. Montgomery, William Morris Jr., Esther Myrick, Martin Newman, Joan O'Connor, curator of the Hemingway Collection at the John F. Kennedy Library, Richard Pennington, Walker Percy, Martin Quigley, Lois M. Randall, Katherine Slattery, Dr. Dixie Snider of the Center for Disease Control in Atlanta, and Anne Wyman, who also supplied the rare photograph of Jeffries Wyman taken by Oliver Wendell Holmes.

The Saranac Lake of these pages, called Saranac by its inhabitants, is, of course, not the village of the same name near Plattsburgh, a nomenclature resulting in perennial confusion of mail.

Chapter One

W. J. Stillman's *Autobiography of a Journalist* (2 vols., Boston: Houghton Mifflin, 1901) and the *Journals* of Ralph Waldo Emerson (10 vols., ed. with annotations by Edward Waldo Emerson and Waldo Emerson Forbes, Boston: Houghton Mifflin, 1909–14) for August 1859 remain essential portrayals of the Philosophers' Camp. In 1898, Stillman wrote a preliminary account, the last essay of *The Old Rome and New, and Other Studies* (London: Grant Richards). Valuable sidelights on members of the expedition are provided by *The Early Years of the Saturday Club* (Boston: Houghton Mifflin, 1918); and Alfred Lee Donaldson, the great pioneer historian of the Adirondacks, includes a vivid description in Chapter 16 of his 2-volume *A History of the Adirondacks* (New York: The Century Company, 1921).

The accomplishments of Jeffries Wyman appear in the chapter titled "Zoology" in *The Development of Harvard University, 1869–1929,* ed. by Samuel Eliot Morison (Cambridge: Harvard University Press, 1930), but a more intimate perspective animates *Dear Jeffie,* ed. by George E. Gifford Jr. (Cambridge: Peabody Museum Press, 1978).

For an overview of Emerson's life, Gay Wilson Allen's *Waldo Emerson* (New York: Viking, 1981) provides an excellent vantage point. John McAleer's sound *Ralph Waldo Emerson: Days of Encounter* (Boston: Little, Brown, 1984) discloses from an Adirondack standpoint a more extensive treatment of the Philosophers' Camp. The clinical history of the Emerson family and tuberculosis is given by René and Jean Dubos in

The White Plague: Tuberculosis, Man and Society (Boston: Little, Brown, 1952), and in connection with this, Joel Porte's study of Emerson's ideas, *Representative Man, Ralph Waldo Emerson in His Time* (New York: Oxford University Press, 1979), is also pertinent.

Chapter Two

Jay Monaghan's *The Great Rascal: The Life and Adventures of Ned Buntline* (Boston: Little, Brown, 1952) chronicles the adventures of the sodden and bumptious dime novelist. *Adventures in the Wilderness* (Boston: Fields, Osgood and Company, 1869) has been republished in a replica of the first edition, William K. Verner, ed. (Syracuse: Adirondack Museum, 1970), preceded by a sympathetic, generously illustrated introduction by Warder H. Cadbury. A large periodical literature surrounds the Murray Rush, of which "Mr. Murray's Mistakes" in *American Sportsman*, Oct. 25, 1873, 3:57, is a good example. The Rev. Dr. Lundy's *The Saranac Exiles: A Winter's Tale of the Adirondacks, Not by W. Shakespeare* (Philadelphia: privately printed, 1880) is quoted by Donaldson, but the only copy I have been able to find is in the Saranac Lake Free Library.

Chapter Three

Edward Livingston Trudeau's *Autobiography* (Philadelphia: Lea & Febiger, 1916), which he managed to complete just before his death, is the basic source of this chapter. New editions were published for the National Tuberculosis Association (New York: Doubleday, Doran) in 1928 and 1936. The Duboses' *White Plague* and Selman A. Waksman's *The Conquest of Tuberculosis* (Berkeley: University of California Press, 1964) are useful on early suppositions about TB, while Susan Sontag's *Illness as Metaphor* (New York: Farrar, Straus & Giroux, 1978) is indispensable on the mythology of the disease.

Chapter Four

Among Stevenson biographers, Margaret Mackay in *The Violent Friend: The Story of Mrs. Robert Louis Stevenson* (New York: Doubleday, 1968) presents the most detailed treatment of the family's domestic arrangements at Saranac. But the diversity of the household is also seen in Mrs. Margaret Isabella Balfour Stevenson's *From Saranac to the Marquesas and Beyond* (New York: Scribner, 1903), which suggests interesting psychological overtones among the relationships of a Victorian mother and her son's wife. The same resonances exist in Stevenson's *Letters*, 2 vol., selected and edited with notes and introduction by Sidney Colvin (New York: Scribner, 1900), and in "An Intimate Portrait of R.L.S.," by his stepson, Lloyd Osbourne, *Scribner's Magazine*, Nov. 1923–Feb. 1924.

J. C. Furnas's *Voyage to Windward: The Life of Robert Louis Stevenson* (New York: William Sloane Associates, 1951) examines the author's physical health more closely than other biographies. Sir Graham Balfour's *The Life of Robert Louis Stevenson* (New York: Scribner, 1901) is the "official" biography; but among more recent titles, *Robert Louis Stevenson: A Life Study* by Jenni Calder (New York and Toronto: Oxford University Press, 1980) is preeminent, and James Pope Hennessy in *Robert Louis Stevenson* (New York: Simon and Schuster, 1974) fashions a fluent narrative-biography. Of special interest is *Stevenson and Saranac*, a pamphlet that the Stevensonian physician Lawrason Brown wrote for the Grolier Club in 1914, and Stephen Chalmers's *The Penny Piper of Saranac* (Boston: Houghton Mifflin, 1916), which, as the title suggests, is not unmarred by period diction, but which also sets forth Stevensoniana otherwise unpublished. Dr. Edward Trudeau served as the pamphlet's editor, the work is still sold as a "souvenir" for the upkeep of the Stevenson Cottage in Saranac, and the sketch helped prompt the founding of the international Stevenson Society.

"Stevenson and Saranac, Reminiscences of the Celebrated Author's Stay in the Adirondacks," *Journal of Outdoor Life*, Feb. 1905, and the well-organized *Robert Louis Stevenson* of Irving Saposnik, from the University of Beirut (Boston: Twayne, 1974), have also been helpful.

Chapter Five

H. T. Lowe-Porter's translation of *The Magic Mountain* (New York: Knopf, 1927, 1955) is the standard English text. The early history of Saranac receives ample justice from Donaldson. In *The Life of Thomas Bailey Aldrich* (Boston: Houghton Mifflin, 1908), Ferris Greenslet traces a poignant picture of the family's ordeal in its "pocket Switzerland." *D. W. Griffith: An American Life* by Richard Schickel (New York: Simon and Schuster, 1984) tells the story of *Judith of Bethulia*.

The "Adelaide Crapsey, 1901 file," in the Alumnae Collection of Vassar College, contains much relevant material, including her senior thesis. Central to all comment upon the poet, however, is Susan Sutton Smith's imposing *The Complete Poems and Collected Letters of Adelaide Crapsey* (Albany: State University of New York, 1977), the definitive volume. Both students and general readers ought to appreciate *Verse* (Rochester: Manas Press, 1915, foreword by Claude Bragdon; reprinted New York:

Knopf, 1922, 1926, 1934, 1938), but *A Study in English Metrics*, introductory note by Esther Lowenthal (New York: Knopf, 1918), has, aside from its foreword, limited appeal. Edward Butscher's comments provide a judicious introduction to the poet in *Adelaide Crapsey*, ed. by David J. Nordloh (Boston: Twayne, 1979), while Sister Mary Edwardine O'Connor's unpublished master's thesis, "Adelaide Crapsey: A Biographical Study," University of Notre Dame, 1931, and Mary Elizabeth Osborn's unreliable yet often insightful *Adelaide Crapsey* (Boston: Bruce Humphries, 1933) pave the way for Susan Smith. *Vassarion, 1901* documents the undergraduate Adelaide; and critical responses from Llewellyn Jones, *First Impressions* (New York: Knopf, 1925), and Yvor Winters, *In Defense of Reason* (Denver: Swallow, 1947), represent male responses at first encountering *Verse*. In particular, Winters's partisanship of Adelaide has been considered evidence of critical eccentricity, although it is clear that he read her, whereas other partisans such as Carl Sandburg never did; indeed, the orotund remarks of Louis Untermeyer, who included her in his anthologies, have doubtless harmed her reputation. Sidney Algernon Crapsey's *The Last of the Heretics* (New York: Knopf, 1922) adds necessary background.

Chapter Six

The last years of Dr. Trudeau are covered by the *Autobiography* and in contemporary articles like Hamilton Wright Mabie's "Dr. Edward Trudeau," *American*, June 1910. The *Adirondack Daily Enterprise* gave his death in November 1915 larger headlines than any other event in the newspaper's existence. Donaldson writes a graceful summary of the career in "Trudeau's Life, a Rare Romance in Medicine," *New York Times Magazine*, Nov. 1921.

For Christy Mathewson's baseball years I have relied upon contemporary newspaper accounts, Lawrence Ritter's *The Glory of Their Times* (New York: Morrow, 1984), Frank Graham's *McGraw of the Giants* (New York: Putnam, 1944), *The Ultimate Baseball Book*, ed. by Daniel Okrent and Harris Lewine (Boston: Houghton Mifflin, 1979), which includes a valuable Mathewson essay by Jonathan Yardley, Arthur Marin's *William Branch Rickey: American in Action* (Boston: Houghton Mifflin, 1957), the ghost-written *Pitching in a Pinch; or Baseball from the Inside* by Christy Mathewson, foreword by John N. Wheeler, recently reissued, ed. by Ziegel and Neil Offen (New York: Stein and Day, 1977), and Ken Smith's *Baseball's Hall of Fame* (New York: Barnes, 1947). Harold Kaese's

The Boston Braves (New York: Putnam, 1948) is highly informative about Matty's front-office period.

Meet the Town, Saranac Lake, N.Y. (Saranac Lake: Sheridan Advertising Service, 1927) has been published annually to the present, and village publications such as "A Past to Remember" contain relevant passages. In the *Adirondack Daily Enterprise*, stories by William McLaughlin evoke Saranac's early film history, and Maitland DeSormo touches upon it and the visits of Legs Diamond in *The Heyday of the Adirondacks* (Saranac: Adirondack Yesteryears, 1975). Prohibition in general is addressed by a legion of scholars; I have consulted Andrew Sinclair, *Prohibition, the Era of Excess* (Boston: Little, Brown, 1969), Sean Dennis Cashman, *Prohibition, the Lie of the Land* (New York: The Free Press, 1967), Kenneth Allsopp, *The Bootleggers and Their Era* (New York: Doubleday, 1961), John Kobler, *The Rise and Fall of Prohibition* (New York: Putnam, 1973), James A. Inciardi, *Careers in Crime* (Chicago: Rand, McNally, 1975), and *The American Way of Crime* (New York: Praeger, 1976), ed. by Wayne Moquin with Charles Van Doren.

A lively regional account of bootlegging centered about the Plattsburgh area and Clinton County, *Rum Across the Border* by Allan S. Everest (Syracuse: Syracuse University Press, 1978), concerns customs officers, bootleggers, and their customers. From a Saranac Lake perspective, however, the most important study of the era of excess is Elizabeth Mooney's *In the Shadow of the White Plague* (New York: Thomas Y. Crowell, 1979), which combines a moving memoir of the author's terminally ill mother with a specific picture of boomtown Saranac. For Jack Diamond, the principal sources are the Albany author William Kennedy, whose novel *Legs* (New York: Coward, McCann & Geoghegan, 1975) captures the insouciant violence of the gangster's myth, the factual *Bloodletters and Badmen: A Narrative Encyclopedia of American Criminals from the Pilgrims to the Present* by Robert J. Nash (New York: M. Evans, 1973), and contemporary press accounts. Kennedy, who has interviewed Diamond's contemporaries, doubtless knows the subject better than anyone today, and in *O Albany! An Urban Tapestry* (New York: Viking, 1983) his treatment of Diamond's death must be considered definitive. The story of Eddie Diamond's bodyguard is in both Kennedy and Mooney; and *Legs*, furthermore, adds that at Saranac Eddie "got religion," much to his brother's dismay.

Allen Seager's debonair patient reminiscence, *A Frieze of Girls: Memoirs as Fiction* (New York: McGraw-Hill, 1964), contrasts markedly in tone with other patient-and-staff narratives, which were mostly inspirational: Francis Dewitt's *The How to Get Well Book*, by a former patient of the Adirondack Cottage Sanitarium (Saranac Lake: Riverside Publishing Company, 1906); John E. Lathrop's "Back to Life," *Collier's*, May 24, 1913; Fred Rice's *Fifty Years in a Health Resort* (Saranac Lake: n.p., 1937); Isabel Smith's *Wish I Might* (New York: Harper's, 1955); and Marian Spitzer's *I Took It Lying Down* (New York: Random House, 1961), among others.

Chapter Seven

The Ted Allan and Sydney Gordon *The Scalpel, the Sword: The Story of Norman Bethune* (Boston: Little, Brown, 1952) should be regarded with extreme caution. Although it was the first study of Bethune to appear in America, and although it has been a perennial best-seller in many countries, especially in the developing nations, much of the text falls under the heading of hagiography. Nevertheless, Allan and Gordon make an interesting contrast to the work of Roderick Stewart, on which this chapter is largely based. Stewart's carefully researched *Bethune* (Toronto: New Press, 1973) is the standard volume, and while the same author's *The Mind of Norman Bethune* (Markham, Ontario: Fitzhenry & Whiteside, 1977) presents some of the same material, the pictorial element (for example, photographs of the missing Saranac murals) establishes additional understanding of Bethune. Zhou Erfu's *Doctor Norman Bethune* (Beijing: Foreign Languages Press, 1982) concentrates on the Chinese experience, but through the thickets of Marxist prose a man may be glimpsed. *Bethune: The Montreal Years* by Wendell MacLeod (Toronto: James Lorimer and Company, 1978) is a good specialized study, and "Norman Bethune: The Rebel China Reveres," by Harold Horwood, *Canadian Reader's Digest*, Jan. 1975, contains a deft summary of Bethune's posthumous reputation.

Chapter Eight

The cure cottages were the subject of a five-part series by Phil Gallos in the *Adirondack Daily Enterprise* in 1982. For the Great Camps the basic source is Harvey H. Kaiser, *Great Camps of the Adirondacks* (Boston: David R. Godine, 1982), while William Wright, *Heiress: The Rich Life of Marjorie Merriweather Post* (Washington: New Republic Books, 1978), remains the primary source of information on Mrs. Post's lifestyle. I have benefited from visits to Topridge during the stewardship of Gov. Mario

Cuomo. Cleveland Amory's *The Last Resorts* (New York: Harper and Brothers, 1948) also concerns the recreations of Mrs. Post's social class.

"Mark Twain on the Adirondacks, an extract from a letter to a personal friend in New York," appeared in *Four-track news,* Sept. 1902. See also *Mark Twain's Letters,* 2 vols., ed. by Albert Bigelow Paine (New York: Harper and Brothers, 1917).

For Einstein in Saranac, the *Adirondack Daily Enterprise* is the main source; useful too have been Ronald W. Clark's *Einstein: The Life and Times* (London: Hodder and Stoughton, 1973), Jamie Sayen's *Einstein in America* (New York: Crown, 1985), and "Einstein in the U.S. Navy," a talk delivered by Dr. Stephen Brunauer on the Einstein centenary, subsequently reprinted in the *Journal of the Washington Academy of Sciences* and *The Clarkson,* the alumni magazine of Clarkson College, Potsdam, New York, Jan. 1981.

The dark corridor and the closed door come from an interview with Honoria Murphy Donnelly, as do other details of her visits in Saranac to her mother and brother. Her *Sara and Gerald: Villa America and After* (New York: Times Books, 1982), with Richard Billings, along with Calvin Tomkins's *Living Well Is the Best Revenge* (New York: Viking, 1971), provide the fullest portraits of Gerald and Sara Murphy. Other apposite works are Werner Schmalenbach's *Léger* (New York: Doubleday, 1983), André LeVot's *F. Scott Fitzgerald* (New York: Doubleday, 1983), Arthur Mizener's *The Far Side of Paradise* (Boston: Houghton Mifflin, 1949). The "Sarapauline" correspondence, the letters of Alice Myers, and Gerald and Sara's correspondence with Hemingway in the John F. Kennedy Library have been necessary documents.

Chapter Nine

Walker Percy's recollections of Saranac are based on a personal interview but also appear briefly in Robert Coles's *Walker Percy: An American Search* (Boston: Atlantic–Little, Brown, 1978). While this is the main biographical source, critical works such as Jac Tharp's *Walker Percy* (Boston: Twayne, 1983) and Patricia Lewis Poteat's *Walker Percy and the Modern Age: Reflections on Language, Argument, and the Telling of Stories* (Baton Rouge: Louisiana State University Press, 1985) also shed light on Percy's writings.

Somerset Maugham's views on Saranac are expressed in Ted Morgan's *Maugham* (New York: Simon and Schuster, 1980), but the radio speeches and essays composed during Maugham's stay are in the Adirondack Collection of the Saranac Free Library. For his relations with Haxton, see Morgan, though others have detoured around the subject or, like Robin Maugham, focused upon it to the exclusion of everything else.

Visits to the old Will Rogers Hospital and the new make up the background of the Will Rogers passages. The Milton Berle and Fred Allen quotes come from *American Vaudeville as Seen by Its Contemporaries*, ed. by Charles W. Stein (New York: Knopf, 1984). William Chapman White, son-in-law of William Morris, was one of the most gifted writers of the region, and his *Adirondack Country* (New York and Boston: Duell, Sloane & Pearce; Little, Brown, 1954) is still as fresh and trenchant as it was three decades ago. White's "Saranac Lake, New York," *Saturday Evening Post*, Aug. 25, 1951, 224:no.8, conveys the ambience of the sanatorium on the eve of drug therapy.

For the section about Manuel Quezon I have relied on contemporary press accounts and on conversations with and material supplied by James Halsema, son of the former mayor of Baguio.

The memories of Dr. Edgar Mayer and Mrs. M. A. Levy are fundamental to the account of Bartók's Saranac summers. Agatha Fassett's *The Naked Face of Genius: Béla Bartók's American Years* (Boston: Houghton Mifflin, 1958; reprinted as *Béla Bartók's American Years*, New York: Dover, 1970) presents a close friend's view of the composer's travail. Other accounts include the *Letters* of Béla Bartók, selected and edited by Janos Demeny, with a preface by Sir Michael Tippett (New York: St. Martin's Press, 1971); *Béla Bartók*, by Josef Ujfallusy, tr. by Ruth Pataki (Boston: Crescendo Publishing Company, 1972); Halsey Stevens's *The Life and Music of Béla Bartók* (New York: Oxford University Press, 1953 and 1964); and the delightful Bence Szabolcsi and Ferenc Bonis, *Béla Bartók, His Life in Pictures* (London and Budapest: Boosey & Hawkes, Corvina Press, 1964).

Sylvia Plath's broken leg on Pisgah is interpreted from her point of view in *The Bell Jar* (New York: Harper and Row, 1971), from her mother's in *Letters Home*, selected and edited by Mrs. Aurelia Schober Plath (New York: Harper and Row, 1975), and by diverse critics: Charles Newman, ed., *The Art of Sylvia Plath* (Bloomington: Indiana University Press, 1970); Lynda K. Bundtzen, *Plath's Incarnations: Woman and the Creative Process* (Ann Arbor: University of Michigan Press, 1983); Edward Butscher, *Sylvia Plath: Method and Madness* (New York: Seabury Press, 1976), and *Sylvia Plath: The Woman and the Work* (New York: Dodd, Mead, 1977); and in *Ariel Ascending: Writings About Sylvia Plath*, Paul Alexander, ed. (New York: Harper and Row, 1985). In *A Closer Look at*

Ariel (New York: Harper's Magazine Press, 1973), Nancy Hunter Steiner proffers a college roommate's comments.

Waksman gives a vital depiction of the Hotel Pennsylvania treatments with streptomycin. "A Victim of Progress / Sanatorium Closes on Optimistic Note," *Life,* Dec. 27, 1954, describes Larry Doyle's walk and the last hours of Dr. Trudeau's sanatorium.